The Political Bible

of

Humorous Quotations
from
American Politics

Politicians Unplugged

What they Said – When they Said it – And Why

* **Outrageous Political Insults**
* **Hilarious Comments**
* **Off-the–Wall Responses**
* **Political Blunders**
* **Bizarre Misstatements**
* **Speeches Gone Wrong**

By
Rich Rubino

Flag Border on Cover: Photograph by Allen Matheson/Photohome.com

Dedication

I dedicate this book to the politicians who say what they say and do what they do, and to the political junkies like myself who live to analyze, characterize and chronicle virtually everything related to American politics and the political process.

Table of Contents

Introduction   **vii**

Chapter I: **Presidents**   **1**

Chapter II: **Vice Presidents**   **43**

Chapter III: **Cabinet Members**   **55**

Chapter IV: **Presidential Campaigns**   **67**

Chapter V: **U.S. House of Representatives**   **141**

Chapter VI: **Speakers of the U.S. House of Representatives**   **167**

Chapter VII: **U.S. House of Representatives Campaigns**   **175**

Chapter VIII: **U.S. Senate**   **181**

Chapter IX: **U.S. Senate Campaigns**   **209**

Chapter X: **U.S. Supreme Court Justices**   **225**

Chapter XI: **Governors**   **231**

Chapter XII: **Gubernatorial Campaigns**   **245**

Chapter XIII: **Mayors**   **255**

Chapter XIV: **Celebrities Commenting on Politics**   **263**

Chapter XV: **Miscellaneous Quotations**   **271**

Glossary of Political Terminology   **285**

Appendix   **299**

Index   **304**

Introduction

While shamelessly promoting my first book, *The Political Bible of Little Known Facts in American Politics,* I did a number of television and radio interviews. The interviews usually turned to the funny, unusual, bizarre political quotes in the book and the circumstances surrounding them. The interviewers couldn't get enough of the humorous and off-the-wall quotations. Radio producers made it clear that I should keep the chat light, funny, and entertaining. They highlighted the fact that most of their listeners were stressed-out while engaging in the horrors of their morning or evening commutes, and needed some humor to lighten their life.

Accordingly, I became obsessed with finding and researching the most hilarious, weird, and off-the-wall political quotes that I could find. To my amazement, there was ample material for a new book. I also decided that rather than just present a series of hilarious and unusual political quotes, that I would also include the context in which the words were said. This would provide the reader not only with a laugh, but also with an historical understanding regarding what prompted the particular comment. Finally, I researched the on-line archives of the Library of Congress and Presidential Museums to locate pictures to go along with "each" political quote.

It is now about two years later and my book has finally gone to print. I hope you enjoy the read and get a laugh while doing so. In the pages that follow, you will find the answers to burning questions such as:

➢ Which President, after losing renomination from his own party, deadpanned: "There is nothing left to do but get drunk."

➢ Which U.S. Representative called his redheaded colleague: "A Howdy Doody looking nimrod."

➢ Which U.S. Senator characterized luncheons attended by U.S. Congressmen and lobbyists as including: "anything you can eat, drink, or fornicate in one afternoon."

➢ Which political candidate after losing an election complained: "The people have spoken. The bastards."

➢ Which Governor, noting the corruption of his state's electoral process, quipped: "When I die, I want to be buried in St. Martin's Parish so I can remain politically active."

➢ Which Governor vetoed a piece of legislation because of: "bad spelling, improper punctuation and erasures."

- ➤ Which U.S. House Speaker chided his House colleagues by exclaiming: "They never open their mouths without subtracting from the sum of human knowledge."

- ➤ Which U.S. Senator (running for re-election), when asked by an opponent to take a drug test, retorted: "I'll take a drug test if you take an IQ test."

- ➤ Which President appointed future President James Buchanan to the post of Minister to Russia, exclaiming to friends: "It was as far as I could send him to get him out of my sight, and where he could do the least harm. I would have sent him to the North Pole if we kept a Minister there."

- ➤ Which President defended his drunk Vice President following the Vice President's "slurred" Inauguration Speech by exclaiming: "He made a slip the other day, but you need not be scared; Andy ain't a drunkard."

- ➤ Which California Gubernatorial candidate said: "Unemployment insurance is a pre-paid vacation for freeloaders."

- ➤ Which New York Political Boss and State Senator was enraged by a newspaper political cartoon depicting him as corrupt and told a News Reporter from that Paper: "I don't care a straw for your newspaper articles, my constituents don't know how to read, but they can't help seeing them damned pictures."

- ➤ Which U.S. Representative issued the following press release: "Americans For Tax Reform are lying sacks of scum, and anyone who knowingly repeats this information is a liar."

- ➤ Which Republican Governor of a Democratic state joked: "Being a conservative in Massachusetts is like being a cattle rancher at a vegetarian convention."

- ➤ Which U.S. Representative called a former Presidential nominee of his own party: "A Bellowing - - Blatant - - Bellicose - - Belligerent - - Blowhard."

- ➤ Which Presidential candidate observed: "War has rules. Mud wrestling has rules. Politics has no rules."

- ➢ Which U.S. Representative never lived down the true story of shooting 14 escaped burros (small donkeys) allegedly in self-defense, claiming 20 years later: "I could find a cure for cancer and they'd remember me as the guy who shot the burros."

- ➢ Which U.S. House Speaker advised his House colleagues that: "A closed mouth gathers no feet."

- ➢ Which President said: In my many years I have come to a conclusion that one useless man is a shame, two is a law firm, and three or more is a Congress."

- ➢ Which U.S. Supreme Court Justice said: "I have a lifetime appointment and I intend to serve it. I expect to die at 110, shot by a jealous husband."

- ➢ Which Gubernatorial candidate was so confident of victory that he said: "The only way I can lose this election is if I'm caught in bed with either a dead girl or a live boy."

- ➢ Which Presidential candidate publicly asked the question: "Why does the Air Force need expensive new bombers? Have the people we've been bombing over the years been complaining?"

- ➢ Which big city mayor who was dealing with a city crisis informed the media: "Gentleman – get this thing straight once and for all – the policeman is not there to create disorder, the policeman is there to preserve disorder."

- ➢ Which Presidential candidate said of an opponent: "When his library burned down, it destroyed both books. He hadn't finished coloring in the second."

All of the information in this book was collected from various sources. As I discover these interesting quotations and related stories, I verify them as much as reasonably possible. If an information item doesn't seem probable, I discard it.

In the pages that follow, quotations are in bold font to help the reader differentiate the quotation from the context.

I hope you enjoy this book.

Chapter I

Presidents

Presidents

Master of the Obvious: During the Great Depression, former President Calvin Coolidge noted the dire circumstances of the American economy. In a 1930 Newspaper column, he stated: **"The final solution for unemployment is work."**

Calvin Coolidge
Library of Congress

No Love for James Buchanan: Andrew Jackson, in explaining why he appointed James Buchanan to he post of Minister to Russia, said: **"It was as far as I could send him to get him out of my sight, and where he could do the least harm. I would have sent him to the North Pole if we kept a Minister there."**

Andrew Jackson
Library of Congress

Take This Job and Shove It, I Ain't Working Here No More! Martin Van Buren was President during the Panic of 1837. He was blamed for the Depression and was chided as: "Martin Van Ruin." Van Buren was an unpopular President who lost re-election in 1840. Although he had yearned for the Presidency for much of his life, Van Buren came to despise his job. He later said of his Presidency: **"As to the Presidency, the two happiest days of my life were those of my entrance upon the office and my surrender of it."**

Martin Van Buren
Library of Congress

First Lady Jailed? While First Lady Eleanor Roosevelt was visiting a penitentiary, her husband, President Franklin D. Roosevelt, asked an aide where Eleanor was. The aide told him: **"She's in prison."** The President responded: **"I'm not surprised, but what for?"**

Franklin D. and Eleanor Roosevelt
Franklin D. Roosevelt Presidential
Library and Museum

Presidents

Play it Again, Harry: Harry S. Truman, in reflecting on his choice to become a politician (after failing as a haberdasher), deadpanned: **"My choice early in life was either to be a piano-player in a whorehouse or a politician. And to tell the truth, there's hardly any difference."**

Harry S. Truman With Actress Lauren Bacall
Harry S. Truman Library and Museum

Not A Resounding Display of Confidence: Warren G. Harding felt overwhelmed in the Presidency. In a conversation with his Liaison Officer and Presidential Speech Writer, Judson Welliver, the President said: **"Jud, you have a college education, haven't you. I don't know what to do or where to turn in this taxation matter. Somewhere there must be a book that tells all about it, where I could go to straighten it out in my mind. But I don't know where the book is, and maybe I couldn't read it if I found it."**

Judson Welliver
The Judson Welliver Project

FORE! Gerald R. Ford was arguably the most athletic President in American history. His athletic prowess was exhibited on the football field. He was a star football player at the University of Michigan. Ford was offered contracts by both the Detroit Lions and the Green Bay Packers. He turned them down to attend Yale Law School instead. Ford was also a good golfer, having played the sport for most of his life. He sported a handicap of 12. However, while President, Ford took a shot that went off course and hit a spectator on the head. The press had a field-day with this, characterizing Ford as a klutz. Comedian Bob Hope quipped: **"It's not hard to find Jerry Ford on the Golf course – You follow the wounded."** Ford in his self-deprecating humor deadpanned: **"I know I am getting better at golf because I am hitting fewer spectators."**

Gerald R. Ford
Gerald R. Ford Library and Museum

What Did Nixon Mean? At the funeral for French President Charles de Gaulle, Richard M. Nixon inexplicably called the event: **"A great day for France."**

Richard M. Nixon (L), Charles de Gaulle (R)
U.S. Government Photograph

Presidents

The Weight of the Press: Lyndon B. Johnson often mused: "**If one morning I walked on top of the water across the Potomac River, the headline that afternoon would read 'President Can't Swim.'**"

Lyndon B. Johnson
Lyndon Baines Johnson Library and Museum

Wilson Slips Out of Mental Assessment Trap: In 1919, U.S. Senator Albert Fall (R-MT) came to the White House to visit President Woodrow Wilson, who had recently suffered a stroke. The official reason for Fall's requesting the meeting was to discuss U.S.-Mexican relations. However, the real reason for calling the meeting was so that Fall could determine if Wilson was too impaired to discharge the duties of his office. Senator Fall, who was one of Wilson's harshest critics, began the meeting by stating to the President: **"We have been praying for you Mr. President."** In a flash, Wilson proved his mental dexterity with the following clever retort: **"Which way, Senator?"** Fall later reported that the President was not too impaired to serve.

Woodrow Wilson
Library of Congress

John Adams Uncensored: John Adams had many quarrels with the U.S. Congress. Adams complained: **"In my many years I have come to a conclusion that one useless man is a shame, two is a law firm, and three or more is a Congress."**

John Adams
Library of Congress

Newspaper Pollution: In an 1807 letter to Newspaper Editor John Norvell, Thomas Jefferson wrote: **"Nothing can now be believed which is seen in a newspaper. Truth itself becomes suspicious by being put into that polluted vehicle."**

Thomas Jefferson
Library of Congress

Presidents

Family Members Need No Senate Conformation: When Herbert Hoover found out his new granddaughter was born, he said: **"Thank God she doesn't have to be confirmed by the Senate."**

Herbert Hoover
Library of Congress

The Silent Man Dies: When the news was reported that former President Calvin Coolidge ("Silent Cal") had died, satirist Dorothy Parker, noting Coolidge's silent nature, quipped: **"How do they know?"**

Dorothy Parker
Library of Congress

Grammar Ain't Everything: After the 1923 death of Warren G. Harding, the esteemed poet Edward Estlin Cummings commented: **"The only man, woman, or child who ever wrote a simple declarative sentence with seven grammatical errors is dead."**

Edward Estlin Cummings
Library of Congress

The Slugger and the President: In 1930, New York Yankees Right Fielder Babe Ruth's salary increased from $70,000 to $75,000. This was during the Great Depression. Ruth now made more money than President Herbert Hoover. Many Americans were blaming the President for the Depression. When asked about the situation, Ruth deadpanned: **"What the hell has Hoover got to do with it. Besides, I had a better year than he did."**

Babe Ruth (L), Herbert Hoover (R)
Herbert Hoover Presidential
Library and Museum

Presidents

The Barbarian President: In 1833, Harvard University awarded an honorary degree to President Andrew Jackson. John Quincy Adams, a Harvard University alumni, boycotted the ceremony. Adams lost the Presidential election to Jackson in 1832. In his diary, Adams called Jackson, who had no college education: **"A barbarian who could not write a sentence of grammar and hardly could spell his own name."**

John Quincy Adams
Library of Congress

War President has to Look at Globe to See What U.S. Captured: In 1898, during the Spanish-American War, President William McKinley received a cable from Admiral George Dewey telling him that the U.S. had captured Manila, the Capital of the Philippines. McKinley did not know where the Islands were and had to look at a globe to find them. He said: **"I could not have told where those damned islands were within 2,000 miles."**

William McKinley
Library of Congress

Waterworks: Lyndon B. Johnson, as a master politician, knew that a President must be an ally of FBI Director J. Edgar Hoover because of his potential to destroy adversaries. Johnson said: **"I would rather have him inside the tent pissing out than outside the tent pissing in."**

J. Edgar Hoover
Lyndon Baines Johnson Library and Museum

Is the World Flat or Round? Lyndon B. Johnson enjoyed telling the following story about a prospective teacher who was in desperate need of a job: **"The schoolteacher came to apply for a job during the Depression in my little town of Johnson City [Texas]. The school board [pretended] to be divided on whether the world was flat or round, and they asked him how he taught it. The poor fellow needed a job so much he said, 'I can teach it either way.'"**

Lyndon B. Johnson
Lyndon Baines Johnson Library and Museum

Presidents

The French Tutor: In a 1838 diary entry, future President Rutherford B. Hayes, at the time a student at a preparatory school in Middletown, Connecticut, said of his teacher: **"The French tutor is a passionate old fellow. He looks more like a plump feather bed than anything else I know of!"**

Rutherford B. Hayes
Library of Congress

Another Fish Story? Calvin Coolidge was a recreational angler. As President, he vacationed at the Cedar Island Lodge in Wisconsin. After a failed fishing excursion, Coolidge was asked how many trout there were in the river. His response was: **"About forty-five thousand. I haven't caught them all yet, but I've intimidated them."**

Calvin Coolidge fishing in Wisconsin
Wisconsin Historical Society

Wilson Holds Senate in Low Regard: In 1919 Woodrow Wilson was inflamed that the U.S. Senate did not ratify the Treaty of Versailles, which he had helped to negotiate to end WWII. Wilson said the U.S. Senate: **"Have no use for their heads except to serve as a knot to keep their bodies from unraveling."**

Woodrow Wilson
Library of Congress

The 'Chocolate Eclair' Analogy: As Assistant Secretary of the U.S. Navy, Theodore Roosevelt viewed President William McKinley as an indecisive leader. He said: **"McKinley had no more backbone than a chocolate eclair."** In 1900 Roosevelt became McKinley's Vice Presidential Running Mate.

Theodore Roosevelt
Library of Congress

Presidents

Leaving JFK's Shadows: John F. Kennedy appeared at a Democratic Party fundraiser in Boston and made light of the efforts by his brother, U.S. Senator Ted Kennedy, to come out of his shadows. John F. Kennedy joked: **"He's going out on his own. Instead of being Teddy Kennedy now, he is changing his name to Teddy Roosevelt."**

John and Ted Kennedy set Sail
John F. Kennedy Presidential Library and Museum

Good Save: The last state that Bill Clinton visited as President was Nebraska. When asked in September of 2000 if the President would visit the state and why he had visited every other state, White House Press Secretary Joe Lockhart explained: **"He's saving the best for last."**

Bill Clinton
William J. Clinton Presidential
Library and Museum

Teddy Roosevelt Unplugged: President Benjamin Harrison did not support the particular version of Civil Service Reform favored by Theodore Roosevelt, then a Civil Service Commissioner. In response, Roosevelt blasted the President, branding him: **"a cold-blooded, narrow-minded, prejudiced, obstinate, timid old psalm-singing Indianapolis politician."** Harrison retorted that the young Roosevelt: **"wanted to put an end to all the evil in the world between sunrise and sunset."**

Theodore Roosevelt
Library of Congress

A Jefferson Partisan: At a 1962 White House Dinner honoring Nobel Piece Prize Winners from the Western Hemisphere, President John F. Kennedy averred: **"I think this is the most extraordinary collection of talent, of human knowledge, that has ever been gathered together at the White House, with the possible exception of when Thomas Jefferson dined alone."**

Thomas Jefferson
Library of Congress

Presidents

Heavy Memoranda: When presented with a memorandum from economic advisor Leon Henderson, Franklin D. Roosevelt admitted: **"Are you laboring under the impression that I read these memoranda of yours? I can't even lift them."**

Franklin D. Roosevelt
Franklin D. Roosevelt Presidential
Library and Museum

Davy Crocket Rips Van Buren: Former U.S. Representative David "Davy" Crockett (Whig-TN) was a vociferous critic of Democratic President Martin Van Buren. He said of Van Buren: **"It is said that at a year old he could laugh on one side of his face and cry on the other, at one and the same time."**

David "Davy" Crockett
Photograph by Chester Harding

President Needs to Enroll in World Religions 101: In a 1962 address to the Pageant of Peace Ceremony, John F. Kennedy said: **"Moslems, Hindus, Buddhists, as well as Christians, pause from their labors on the 25th day of December to celebrate the Pageant of Peace Ceremony, celebrate the birthday of the 'Prince of Peace.'"** Kennedy also called Christmas **"universal."**

John F. Kennedy
Lyndon Baines Johnson Library and Museum

If You Fight for the Flag, You Should Not Be Killed by It: In 2012, former President Bill Clinton spoke at a memorial dedication to former Vice President Hubert Humphrey in St. Paul, Minnesota. An American Flag fell behind him. Clinton picked it up and recounted: **"I once saw a State Senator of mine get hit by the American Flag and he said you know I risked my life in WWII and I don't think I should get killed by it."**

Bill Clinton
Official Photograph

Presidents

Above the Law: In a 1977 interview discussing the Watergate matter, Journalist David Frost asked President Richard M. Nixon: **"So, what in a sense you're saying is that there are certain situations . . . where the president can decide that it's in the best interests of the nation . . . and do something illegal?"** Nixon Responded: **"Well, when the president does it, that means that it is not illegal."**

Richard M. Nixon
Library of Congress

Rhetorical Hyperbole: In 1894, when Theodore Roosevelt was serving as President of the Board of the New York City Police Commissioners, he took great offense at opponents of the plan that he had suggested in order to vigorously enforce a law mandating that saloons by closed on Sunday. He called these opponents: **"Lynchers and whitecrappers"** (White Hooded Klansman.)

Theodore Roosevelt
Norman Photographic Company
Albany, New York

"He or Her?" or "He or She?" In an address promoting the No Child Left Behind Initiative, George W. Bush told a crowd in Townsend, Tennessee: **"You teach a child to read, and he or her will be able to pass a literacy test."**

George W. Bush
White House Photograph by Eric Draper

Chester A. Arthur on the Record: Chester A. Arthur was criticized for his private life, which included the excessive imbibing of alcohol. When a member of a Temperance group asked him about this, Arthur retorted: **"Madam, I may be President of the United States, but my private life is nobody's damned business."**

Chester A. Arthur
Library of Congress

Presidents

Calvin Coolidge: A Man of Few Words: When Vice President Calvin Coolidge ("Silent Cal") visited Channing Cox (his successor as Governor of Massachusetts), Cox asked for advice. Cox complained that people talked to him all day and that he could not get out of his office until late at night. Coolidge gave the following reason for Cox's time management problem when talking to people: **"You talk back."**

Channing Cox
Official Photograph

Not an Insult One Would Normally Hear at the School Yard: Theodore Roosevelt was a harsh critic of Woodrow Wilson. The two had run against each other in 1912, and there was no love lost between the two Presidents. Roosevelt once branded Wilson: **"A Byzantine logothete backed by flubdubs and mollycoddles."** (Translation: A logothete is an administrator; a flubdud means non-sense; mollycoddle means pampered.)

Theodore Roosevelt
Library of Congress

Whisky River, Don't Run Dry: Abraham Lincoln was pleased with the success record of General Ulysses S. Grant. However, One critic of Grant told the President Grant was a **"drunkard"** and told the President he could give him proof. This did not deter from Lincoln's opinion of Grant. Lincoln said: **"You needn't waste your time getting proof; you just find out, to oblige me, what brand of whiskey Grant drinks, because I want to send a barrel of it to each one of my generals."**

Ulysses S. Grant (L), Abraham Lincoln (R)
Library of Congress, The Alfred Whital Stern
Collection of Lincolnian

President Mocks Intellectuals: In an address to California Republicans in 1954, President Dwight D. Eisenhower mocked **"wise cracking intellectuals."** He mustered uproarious applause when he defined an intellectual as **"a man who takes more words than necessary to tell more than he knows."**

Dwight D. Eisenhower
Harry S. Truman Library and Museum

10

Presidents

Johnson Derides Ford: Future President Gerald R. Ford was U.S. House Minority Leader when President Lyndon B. Johnson was in the White House. Ford was a constant partisan critic of Johnson, and delivered the Republican response to Johnson's State of the Union Address in 1967. Johnson often mocked Ford in private, telling his associates that Ford had been the Center on the University of Michigan Football team, and jokingly said of Ford: **"He's a nice guy, but he played too much football with his helmet off."**

Gerald R. Ford on the Gridiron
Gerald R. Ford Library & Museum

The Beltway is an Island Unto itself: Believing that the Nation's Capital is set apart form the rest of the nation, Andrew Johnson said: **"Washington, D.C. is 12 square miles bordered by reality."**

Andrew Johnson
Library of Congress

That Is About Right: In a 1995 speech in Galesburg, Illinois, Bill Clinton said: **"Being president is like running a cemetery: You've got a lot of people under you and nobody's listening."**

Bill Clinton
William Jefferson Clinton Library

FDR Defines Conservatism the Way he Sees It: During a radio address to *The New York Herald Tribune* forum in 1939, Franklin D. Roosevelt observed: **"A conservative is a man with two perfectly good legs who, however, has never learned to walk forward."**

Franklin D. Roosevelt
Franklin D. Roosevelt Presidential Library and Museum

Presidents

A Vacuous Mind is a Terrible Thing to Waste: U.S. Representative John Sherman (R-OH) had little use for Democratic President James Buchanan: He quipped: **"The Constitution provides for every contingency in the executive, except a vacancy in the mind of the President."**

John Sherman
Photograph by Mathew Brady

Jesus Christ? In 1963 German Chancellor Ludgwig Ehrhard visited President Lyndon B. Johnson at his ranch near Stonewall, Texas. The Chancellor said to the President: **"I understand you were born in a log cabin, Mr. President."** Johnson responded: **"No Mr. Chancellor, I was born in a manger."**

Lady Bird Johnson (L) Lyndon B. Johnson (C) and Ludwig Ehrhard (R)
Lyndon Baines Johnson Library and Museum

Still Applies Today: In 1936, former President Herbert Hoover, warning that borrowed money must be paid back by future generations, told the Nebraska Republican Convention: **"Blessed are the young, for they will inherit the national debt."**

Herbert Hoover
Library of Congress

The Big Guy Swims: William Howard Taft had a summerhouse in Beverly, Massachusetts. The 335-Pound President went swimming in Beverly Harbor. A neighbor asked a friend if he wanted to go into the water. The friend joked: **"Perhaps we'd better stay out of the water. The President is using the ocean."**

William Howard Taft
White House Web Site

Presidents

Sons of Bitches Deserve a Place at the Table: President Calvin Coolidge had to make many appointments. An advisor objected to one of his proposed appointments saying that the man was a **"son of a bitch."** Coolidge said: **"Don't they deserve to be represented too?"**

Calvin Coolidge
Library of Congress

Can't He Do Better Than That? Millard Fillmore died after having a stroke in his beloved Buffalo, New York in 1874. These last words were spoken to his physician and were about the soup he was eating: **"The nourishment is palatable."**

Millard Fillmore
Beinecke Rare Books and Manuscripts
Library, Yale University

The First Case of Presidential Telephobia? Calvin Coolidge refused to use the telephone as President. He said: **"If you don't say anything, you won't be called on to repeat it."**

Calvin Coolidge Reluctantly Tries Using the Telephone
Library of Congress

A "Tin Ear" President: Ulysses S. Grant once said he only knew two songs. **"One of them is 'Yankee Doodle' and the other isn't."**

Ulysses S. Grant
Library of Congress

Presidents

Robbers in the Senate: Prior to the ratification of the Seventeenth Amendment to the U.S. Constitution, U.S. Senators were elected by their respective state legislatures. Consequently, many Senators garnered their offices by bribing members of the Legislature to vote for them. This was "an open secret" in the nation's capital. One night, First Lady Francis Folsom Cleveland was startled and thought she heard burglars in the White House. She exclaimed to her husband, President Grover Cleveland: **"Wake up Grover, wake up, there are robbers in the house."** Woken from his deep sleep, the President retorted: **"I think you are mistaken my dear. There are no robbers in the House, but there are lots in the Senate!"**

Grover and Frances Cleveland with "Baby Ruth"
Library of Congress

Proud To Be a Politician: In 1958, former President Harry S. Truman told the Reciprocity Club in Washington D.C: **"I'm proud that I'm a politician. A politician is a man who understands government, and it takes a politician to run a government. A statesman is a politician who's been dead 10 or 15 years."**

Harry S. Truman
Harry S. Truman Library and Museum

President Likes Cannabis: During the Mexican-American War, future President Franklin Pierce (who was a brigadier general in the U.S. army) sent a letter home to his family in which he said that cannabis is **"about the only good thing"** in the war.

Brigadier General Franklin Pierce
Library of Congress

The Importance of Bloviating: The term "bloviating" was popularized by Warren G. Harding, who called it: **"The art of speaking for as long as the occasion warrants without saying anything."**

Warren G. Harding
Library of Congress

Presidents

Burying the Hatchet, Big Time: As an ex-president, Bill Clinton has struck up an unlikely friendship with Christopher S. Ruddy, a former vociferous critic of Mr. Clinton. Ruddy is now CEO of conservative *NewsMax Media.* In 1994, Ruddy published *The Strange Death of Vincent Foster: An Investigation* where he linked Mr. Clinton to the death of Deputy White House Council and lifetime Clinton friend, Vincent Foster. Clinton and Ruddy became allies in the fight against poverty. Mr. Ruddy now says: **"I am a great admirer of President Clinton. He has not only redefined the post-presidency, but has served as an exemplary goodwill ambassador for our country throughout the whole world. His efforts transcend politics and deserve support."**

Bill Clinton
William J. Clinton Presidential
Library and Museum

Whoops: Immediately before a 1984 weekly radio address, Ronald Reagan joked: **"My fellow Americans. I've signed legislation that will outlaw Russia forever. We begin bombing in five minutes."** He later found out his microphone was on and that his statement was broadcast worldwide.

Ronald Reagan
Ronald Reagan Presidential Library and Museum

Don't Forget the Fact that He was President: Thomas Jefferson's grave at Monticello in Charlottesville, Virginia says nothing of his Presidency. It reads: **"Here was Buried Thomas Jefferson Author of the Declaration of American Independence of the Statute of Virginia for Religious Freedom and Father of the University of Virginia."**

Thomas Jefferson's Grave
Library of Congress

In Favor of Women: In a 1964 press conference announcing the appointment of ten women to prominent positions in the government, Lyndon B. Johnson remarked: **"I want to make a policy statement. I am unabashedly in favor of women."**

Lyndon B. Johnson with the Women in his life. (L-R) Lynda Johnson, Luci Johnson, and Lady Bird Johnson
Lyndon Baines Johnson Library and Museum

Presidents

Leading a Country or Raising a Daughter? Alice Roosevelt, the daughter of Theodore Roosevelt, exhibited rebellion proclivities. She had a pet snake and smoked cigarettes. She often barged into the Oval Office and offered her father political advice. On one occasion, when she did this, Theodore Roosevelt told his friend Owen Wister, known as the founding father of the genre "Western Fiction:" **"I can be president of the United States — or — I can attend to Alice. I cannot possibly do both."**

Alice Roosevelt
Library of Congress

Double Dealing: Bob Strauss was a rare commodity in American Politics. He was a Democratic Party Chairman, yet he advised Republican and Democratic Presidents. He managed Jimmy Carter's failed 1980 re-election effort. Knowing that Strauss would likely be active in the administration of his Republican successor, Carter joked: **"Bob Strauss is a very loyal friend. He waited a whole week after the election before he had dinner with Ronald Reagan."**

Bob Strauss (R) Pictured with George H.W. Bush (L): on Cover of *Texas Monthly*

President Has an Eye for the "Young Ladies:" The youngest First Lady in American history was Frances Folsom Cleveland. In 1885, when she was just 21 years old, she married President Grover Cleveland in the White House. President Cleveland was 49 at the time. Cleveland remains the only President to be married in the White House. Folsom was the daughter of Cleveland's late former law partner, Oscar Folsom. When Cleveland was still a bachelor, Folsom asked him when he would get married. Cleveland looked at the 11-year old Frances and said: **"I'm only waiting for my wife to grow up."** True to his word, after Oscar Folsom died in a horse-and-buggy accident, Cleveland became Frances's official guardian, and at 21 married her.

Grover Cleveland and Frances Folsom
Library of Congress

Legal Advice from Abraham Lincoln: A Lawyer by trade, Abraham Lincoln coined the axiom: **"A man who acts as his own attorney has a fool for a client."**

Abraham Lincoln
Library of Congress

Presidents

Bush calls Himself a Media Creation: In a 1989 interview with *The Midland Reporter Telegram* (five years before his successful run for Governor of Texas), George W. Bush said: **"You know, I could run for governor and all this but I'm basically a media creation. I've never really done anything. I've worked for my dad. I worked in the oil industry. But that's not the kind of profile you have to have to get elected to public office."**

George W, Bush
Official Portrait as Governor of Texas

Not Exactly Inspiring "Last Words:" Warren G. Harding died in 1923 after developing a respiratory illness. He was on his way back from a voyage to Alaska where he promoted colonization of the sparsely populated territory. He was at the Palace Hotel in San Francisco with his wife Florence who was reading him the newspaper. Harding's immortal last words were: **"Could you please read that again?"**

Warren G. and Florence Harding
Library of Congress

Bold Stand: After he delivered a speech, a woman came up to Calvin Coolidge and said: **"Oh, Mr. Coolidge, what a wonderful address! I stood up all through it!"** Coolidge replied to her: **"So did I."**

Calvin Coolidge
Library of Congress

Joy to the World! At a 1992 press conference in Canberra, Australia, George H.W. Bush observed: **"We're enjoying sluggish times, and not enjoying them very much."**

George H.W. Bush
George Bush Library and Museum

17

Presidents

Consummate Campaigning: Lyndon B. Johnson was fond of telling a story he heard in his childhood about a man who was about to suffer a public hanging. **"The sheriff told the condemned man that under the state law he would be allowed five minutes to choose whatever words he cared to speak as his last act. The prisoner promptly responded and said, 'Mr. Sheriff, I haven't got anything to say, so just get on and get it over with.' But a man way back in the audience jumped up and said, 'Well, if he doesn't want those five minutes, Sheriff, I'd like to have them. I'm a candidate for Congress.'"**

Lyndon B. Johnson
Lyndon Baines Johnson Library and Museum

"I Plead Guilty to Being Drunk:" Jimmy Carter enjoyed telling audiences the story about: **"an old man who was arrested and taken before the judge for being drunk and setting a bed on fire. And he said, 'Judge, I plead guilty to being drunk, but the bed was on fire when I got in it.'"**

Jimmy Carter
Jimmy Carter Library and Museum

How Dare you Vote Against This Treaty: Woodrow Wilson did not have much respect for those members of the U.S. Senate who opposed the ratification of the Treaty of Versailles, which would have allowed the U.S. to join the League of Nations. Wilson called these dissenting Senators: **"pygmy minds."** The treaty failed to secure ratification in the U.S. Senate.

Woodrow Wilson Returns from the Versailles Peace Conference
Library of Congress

Elegant Arthur: Democrat Woodrow Wilson made the following statement regarding "Elegant" Chester A. Arthur, one of his Republican Predecessors: **"Chester A. Arthur was the only President to sport muttonchop whiskers. He is a non-entity with side-whiskers."** Arthur earned the moniker "Elegant Arthur" for his fancy clothes and sense of fashion.

Chester A. Arthur
Library of Congress

Presidents

I look Better Than That: In 1967, Lyndon B. Johnson was presented with his official portrait painted by artist Peter Hurd. Johnson was displeased with the portrait. He said it was **"the ugliest thing I ever saw."** Hurd was not offended and mentioned that he only had a half-hour to draw the painting and that the President kept falling asleep. The rejected portrait garnered a record amount of visitors at the Diamond Museum in Snyder, Texas.

Portrait of Lyndon B. Johnson drawn by Peter Hurd

Presidential Backbone: President James Garfield took the side of James G. Blaine rather than U.S. Senator Roscoe Conkling (R-NY) on the appointment of William H. Robertson as the Collector of Customs of the Port of New York. Former President Ulysses S. Grant, an ardent ally of Conkling, said of Garfield: **"He is not possessed of the backbone of an angleworm** [earthworm]."

William H. Robertson
Engraving by George Edward Perine

The President and the Mummy: At a Democratic Fundraiser, U.S. Senator Joe Lieberman (D-CT) joked about Bill Clinton's appearance at the Washington National Geographic Society. At that event, Clinton viewed the preserved Incan mummy Princess of Ampato. She was killed in the fifteenth century. Lieberman joked, **"She dated Bob Dole"** (former U.S. Senator and Republican Presidential nominee). When Bill Clinton took to the podium he told the crowd: **"I don't know if you've seen that mummy. But you know, if I were a single man, I might ask that mummy out. That's a good-looking mummy. That mummy looks better than I do on my worst days."**

Bill Clinton
Official Photograph

Good Economics: At a 1974 farewell party for Herbert Stein (the Chairman of the Council of Economic Advisers), President Gerald R. Ford quipped: **"I think an economist has been described as a person who tells you there will definitely not be a hurricane and then shortly thereafter helps you repair and rebuild the roof."**

Gerald R. Ford
Gerald R. Ford Presidential
Library & Museum

Presidents

Humble Beginnings is Always a Plus: Lyndon B. Johnson was fond of telling friends about his humble background. One time while he was giving a tour of his birthplace, Johnson City, Texas, and showed an old cabin to his visitors and told them it was his birthplace. Johnson's mother, Rebekah Baines Johnson, said to him: **"Why Lyndon, you know you were born in a much better house closer to town which has been torn down.** Johnson replied: **"I know mama, but everybody has to have a birthplace."**

Rebekah Baines Johnson
Lyndon Baines Johnson Library and Museum

Bizarre Small Talk: In 1977, British Journalist David Frost secured the first set of interviews with former President Richard M. Nixon since his resignation in 1974. Literally seconds before the interview started, Nixon asked Frost: **"Well did you do any fornicating this weekend?"** Frost did not answer the question, instead beginning the program.

TV Guide Cover From 1977 on the Nixon-Frost Interviews

Preacher Comes Out Against Sin: After attending a Sermon one Sunday, a reporter asked President Calvin Coolidge what the preacher had talked about. Coolidge replied: **"Sin."** The reporter asked what he said about it. Coolidge deadpanned: **"He was against it."**

Calvin Coolidge and wife Grace Egressing from the First Congressional Church
Library of Congress

He's Got the Whole World In his Hands: When Air Force One landed, a young Air Force officer said to President Lyndon B. Johnson: **"Sir, your helicopter is over here."** Johnson replied: **"Son, they're all my helicopters."**

One of President Lyndon B. Johnson's Helicopters
Lyndon Baines Johnson Library and Museum

Presidents

Political Addiction: Lyndon B. Johnson was known to live for politics. He had few hobbies or outside interests. He once said: **"I seldom think of politics more than eighteen hours a day."**

Lyndon B. Johnson
Lyndon Baines Johnson Library and Museum

Bush being Bush: Boston Red Sox slugger Manny Ramirez did not attend the White House reception honoring the 2007 World Series Champion Boston Red Sox. George W. Bush made light of Ramirez's truancy when honoring the team by joking, **"I guess his grandmother died again. Just kidding. Tell him I didn't mean it."**

Manny Ramirez
Photograph by Google Man

As Cold as Ice: Benjamin Harrison had the reputation of being a distant and cold man. U.S. Senator Thomas Platt (R-NY) said of the President: **"Outside the White House and at dinner, he could be a courtly gentleman. Inside the Executive Mansion, in his reception of those who solicited official appointments, he was as glacial as a Siberian stripped of furs. During and after an interview, if one could secure it, one felt even in the torrid weather like pulling on his winter flannels, galoshes, overcoat, mitts and earlaps."**

Benjamin Harrison
Library of Congress

He Doesn't Like Ike: Harry S. Truman thought little of his successor, Dwight D. Eisenhower, though the two made a rapprochement and became friends as former Presidents. Truman once said of Eisenhower: **"The General doesn't know any more about politics than a pig knows about Sunday."**

Harry S Truman (L) and Dwight D. Eisenhower (R)
Harry S. Truman Library and Museum

Presidents

Kidnapping the President: In 1882, Chester A. Arthur was aboard a boat off the Massachusetts town of Marblehead with the intention of speaking in neighboring Salem. After landing in Marblehead where the boat was moored, a persistent Marblehead resident, Captain Benjamin Pitman, asked the President to speak in Marblehead. On three occasions the President declined. Finally, it is said that the Marblehead resident jumped into the driver's seat of President Arthur's carriage and brought him the half-mile to Downtown Marblehead, where he gave a brief address. Arthur later said laughingly: **"I can never forget the time that I was kidnapped in Marblehead."**

Chester A. Arthur
Library of Congress

Past Coolidge's Bedtime: Calvin Coolidge was known to sleep about 12 hours a day. When he was attending a Broadway show, actor Groucho Marx spotted Coolidge in the audience. He broke out of his character, looked at Coolidge and said: **"Isn't it past your bedtime Calvin?"**

Groucho Marx
ABC Photograph

Presidential Backbone: President James Garfield took the side of James G. Blaine rather than U.S. Senator Roscoe Conkling (R-NY) on the appointment of William H. Robertson as the Collector of Customs of the Port of New York. Former President Ulysses S. Grant, an ardent ally of Conkling, said of Garfield: **"He is not possessed of the backbone of an angleworm."** (An Earthworm)

William H. Robertson
Engraving by George Edward Perine

Presidential Freudian Slip: During President Richard M. Nixon's 1974 State of the Union Address, at which time he was enveloped by the Watergate scandal which would bring down his Presidency later that year, he declared: **"I urge the Congress to join me in mounting a major new effort to replace the discredited 'president."** He meant to say: **"replace the 'discredited' present system."**

Richard M. Nixon
Library of Congress

Presidents

Bush Mocks Clinton: At the unveiling of the official portrait of former President Bill Clinton in 2004, President George W. Bush poked fun for Clinton for his role as co-Chairman of the hapless campaign of Democratic Presidential nominee George McGovern in 1972. **"People in Bill Clinton's life have always expected him to succeed, and more than that, they wanted him to succeed, meeting those expectations took more than charm and intellect. It took hard work and drive and determination and optimism. I mean, after all, you've got to be optimistic to give six months of your life running the McGovern campaign in Texas."** McGovern garnered just 33.24% of the vote in the Lone Star State, losing to Republican President Richard M. Nixon.

Bill Clinton
Official Portrait

Coolidge's Advice to Successor, Play Dead: As he left office, Calvin Coolidge gave the following advice to his successor, Herbert Hoover, about how to handle visitors to the White House: **"If you keep dead still, they will run down in three or four minutes. If you even cough or smile, they will start up all over again."**

Calvin Coolidge (L), Herbert Hoover (R)
Library of Congress

Killer Trees? In 1981, President Ronald Reagan said: **"Trees cause more pollution than automobiles do."** He was referring to the fact that in hot weather, trees release organic hydrocarbons, which are linked to smog. After this statement, Presidential Press Secretary James Brady joked to Reporters: **"Watch out for the killer trees."**

Ronald Reagan
Official Portrait

One War at a Time: in 1861, the U.S. Navy seized two Confederate officials. They were sailing toward England. England called for their release. President Abraham Lincoln agreed to release them, quipping: **"One war at a time."**

Abraham Lincoln
Library of Congress

Presidents

Content with the Situation: In a 1982 interview, former First Lady Lady Bird Johnson was asked by Louis Rudolph (co-producer of the *NBC* mini-series *LBJ: The Early Years*) about the sexual affairs of her husband Lyndon B. Johnson. Mrs. Johnson answered: **"You have to understand, my husband loved people. All people. And half the people in the world were women."**

Lady Bird and Lyndon B. Johnson
Lyndon Johnson Library and Museum

Beware! The Future is Near: In a 1984 address before the United Nations, President Ronald Reagan said: **"This Chamber has heard enough about the problems and dangers ahead. Today let us dare to speak of a future that is bright and hopeful and can be ours only if we seek it. I believe that the future is far nearer than most of us would dare to hope."**

Ronald Reagan
National Archives

Roosevelt Faces Cannibalism Charge: After reading a column by esteemed essayist H.L Mencken about the opportunism of President Franklin D. Roosevelt, liberal leader and clergyman Gerald L.K. Smith commented: **"If he [Roosevelt] became convinced tomorrow that coming out for cannibalism would get him votes he sorely needs, he would begin fattening a missionary in the White House back yard come Wednesday."**

Gerald L.K. Smith
Library of Congress

Good Enough For God: The family of Abraham Lincoln's wife, Mary Todd Lincoln, was patrician and had the reputation of being snobby. When the family officially took off the 'd' in Todd (to become "Tod"), Abraham joked: **"One D was good enough for God but not for the Todds."**

Abraham Lincoln
Library of Congress

Presidents

Just Give Me Something, Anything, Even Your Clothes: When future President James Madison was U.S. Secretary of State under President Thomas Jefferson, a job seeker came to his office and asked Madison if he would appoint him Governor of a Western territory. Madison told him he would not. The man then asked for lower-level positions, but they were already filled. The frustrated man then asked Madison: **"Do you have any clothes to spare?"**

James Madison
Library of Congress

As Time Goes By: In 1960, some Republicans praised Franklin D. Roosevelt. The Democratic Party nominee, John F. Kennedy observed of this phenomenon: **"They're [Republicans] even beginning to say a few kind words about Franklin Roosevelt. Twenty years from now they might even speak a good word for Harry Truman, but I guarantee you that Harry Truman will never say a good word about Republicans."**

Harry S. Truman (L), John F. Kennedy (R)
Harry S. Truman Library and Museum

Sweet Nothings: At a 1987 symposium on "Humor and the Presidency" held at the Gerald R. Ford Museum in Grand Rapids, Michigan, former President Gerald R. Ford recounted a speech he gave during his Presidency in Omaha, Nebraska: **"After the speech I went to a reception elsewhere in town. A sweet old lady came up to me, put her gloved hand in mine, and said, 'You spoke here tonight' 'Oh, it was nothing' I replied modestly. 'Yes' the little old lady nodded, 'that's what I heard.'"**

Gerald R. Ford
Lyndon Baines Johnson Library and Museum

Subsidizing Problems: Ronald Reagan, a critic of government power, was fond of saying: **"Government does not solve problems, it subsidizes them."**

Ronald Reagan
Ronald Reagan Presidential Foundation and Library

Presidents

Maxwell House Coffee: In the 1930's. Maxwell House began to circulate a story that their slogan: **"Good to the Last Drop"** was coined by President Theodore Roosevelt. The story went that in 1907, the President was visiting the Hermitage (The Nashville, Tennessee estate of President Andrew Jackson) when he was served Maxwell House coffee. According to legend, Roosevelt said: **"Good to the Last Drop."** However, this quote was later found apocryphal, and the company has since said that former President of General Foods, Clifford Spiller, originated the slogan. According to the Tennessee media, which covered Roosevelt's trip, he did actually get served a cup of Maxwell House coffee, but his actual quote was: **"This is the kind of stuff I like to drink, by George, when I hunt bears."**

Theodore Roosevelt
Library of Congress

George H.W. Bush and Bill Clinton Tell Racy Jokes: During a public discussion with Former Presidents George H.W. Bush and Bill Clinton before the National Automobile Dealers Association in 2009, the presidents were asked how they dealt with protestors. Bush said: **"One time we thought we outsmarted the crowd. We set a decoy limousine off into a direction as I snuck out the back entrance. As we rounded the corner, I'll never forget it, I saw one of the ugliest and angriest woman I've ever seen in my entire life. Boy she was really bad. She charged my car with a sign. I don't know why the Secret Service let her get that close. Right next to that window. 'Stay out of my womb.' No problem lady."** When Bill Clinton got up to speak, he averred: **"You know, he gets away with telling jokes I couldn't get away with telling. Can you imagine what they would do to me if they told that joke he told up here? Some people can do things other people can't. It reminds me of the story of two dogs who watch kids break-dancing and one dog says to the other, if we did that, they'd worm us."**

George H.W Bush (L), Bill Clinton (R)
George Bush Presidential
Library and Museum

26

Presidents

Father Honest about Son: In 1936, when John F. Kennedy applied to Harvard University, his father, Joe Kennedy, wrote a letter to the Dean of Freshmen, Delmar Leighton, informing him that: **"Jack has a very brilliant mind for the things in which he is interested, but lacks application in those in which he is not interested. This is, of course a bad fault."** Kennedy was accepted and earned a degree in International Affairs in 1940.

Joseph Kennedy Sr.
John F. Kennedy Presidential
Library and Museum

In Honor of "C" Students: In 2001, President George W. Bush delivered the Commencement Address at his alma mater, Yale University. In the speech, he ribbed himself and Vice President Dick Cheney, joking: **"To those of you who received honors, awards, and distinctions, I say, 'well done.' And to the "C" students, I say, 'You too can be President of the United States. A Yale degree is worth a lot, as I often remind Dick Cheney—who studied here but left a little early. So now we know: If you graduate from Yale, you become President; if you drop out, you get to be Vice President."**

George W. Bush as a Student at Yale University
George Bush Library and Museum

Lincoln's Legal Advice: In 1850, future President Abraham Lincoln wrote notes for a law lecture. In the notes, he offers this insightful advice: **"If in your own judgment you cannot be an honest lawyer, resolve to be honest without being a lawyer."**

Abraham Lincoln
Library of Congress

Humor in Time of Tragedy: In 1981, Ronald Reagan was shot in front of the Washington Hilton Hotel after speaking to the AFL-CIO. When he was in the emergency room, he whispered to his wife Nancy: **"Honey, I forgot to duck."** This was a line originally uttered by boxer Jack Dempsey. (Reagan survived the shooting)

Nancy Reagan (L) with Ronald Reagan (R)
Four Days Following the Shooting

Presidents

President Says Most Opera is Boring: During 1951 remarks at a Ceremony observing National Music Week, President Harry S. Truman, a music connoisseur and amateur piano player, told the assembled crowd of musicians: **"There is usually one aria or one song in nearly every great opera that is worth listening to – most opera music is boring. I don't want you to say that out loud. It might hurt the Metropolitan Opera."**

Harry S. Truman (C) Plays the Piano With Margaret Truman (L) & Bess Truman (R)
Harry S. Truman Library and Museum

Much Worry About Nothing: In 1881, President-elect James Garfield observed: **"I remember the old man who said he had a great many troubles in his life, but the worst of them never happened."**

James Garfield
Library of Congress

A Universal Language: In a 1983 speech honoring the conservative publication *National Review,* Ronald Reagan said: **"I feel duty-bound to prove that I, too, am a linguist with all of the languages that have been up here. So, in the language of my forefathers, 'I'll have another drink of that fine Irish whiskey.'"**

Ronald Reagan at his Ranch
Ronald Reagan Presidential
Foundation and Library

NO WAY! When he was five years old, Franklin D. Roosevelt accompanied his father, businessman James Roosevelt I, to the White House to visit President Grover Cleveland. After being introduced, Cleveland looked at the young Roosevelt and said: **"My little man, I am making a strange wish for you. It is that you may never be President of the United States."**

A Young Franklin D. Roosevelt (L) with James Roosevelt I (R)
Franklin D. Roosevelt Presidential
Library and Museum

Presidents

In the Doghouse: In 1992 George H.W. Bush delivered an address in Fredericksburg, Virginia on the nation's economy. Before the address, he visited Fredericksburg Hardware. Bush said in the address: **"I told Barbara [Bush] I was coming down to a hardware store this morning. She told me I'd better come back with the tools to fix Millie's doghouse or else I'd be in one myself."** Millie was the Bush's dog.

Barbara Bush (L) Millie Bush (C) and George H.W. Bush (R)
George Bush Presidential Library & Museum

My Dog is Bigger than Your Dog: During a 2014 interview with his daughter, Jenna Bush Hagar, on *The Today Show* on *NBC*, former President George W. Bush related a story about when Russian President Vladimir Putin visited the U.S. Bush showed his small Scottish terrier named Barney to Putin. Putin said to Bush: **"You call that a dog?"** When Bush visited Putin in Russia, the Russian President showed him his hound and said he was: **"bigger, stronger, and faster than Barney."**

Vladimir Putin (L), George W. Bush (R)
White House Photograph by Paul Morse

A Reagan Tongue Twister: Speaking at a rally for Republican candidates in Irving, Texas in 1982, Ronald Reagan said: **"You can't drink yourself sober, you can't spend yourself rich, and you can't pump the prime without priming the pump. You know something? I said that backwards. I didn't say that right at all. You can't prime the pump without pumping the prime is the way it should have been said the first time. It's a tongue-twister."**

Ronald Reagan
The Ronald Reagan Presidential Foundation and Library

Polk Takes on Congress: Though Democrat James K. Polk served in office with a democratically-controlled U.S. Congress, he sometimes got impatient with the Congress. In an 1846 diary entry, Polk wrote: **"The passion for office among members of Congress is very great, if not absolutely disreputable, and greatly embarrasses the operations of the Government. They create offices by their own votes and then seek to fill them themselves."**

James K. Polk
Photograph by Mathew Brady

Presidents

An Hour Speech is No Big Deal: In 1918, a member of the U.S. Congress complimented Woodrow Wilson on his short speeches and asked him how long they take him to prepare. Wilson responded: "It depends. **If I am to speak ten minutes, I need a week for preparation; if fifteen minutes, three days; if half an hour, two days; if an hour, I am ready now.**"

Woodrow Wilson
Library of Congress

Child's Play: U.S. House Minority Leader Gerald R. Ford (R-MI) was out front in opposing President Lyndon B. Johnson's Model Cities Program. For his part, Johnson did not think much of Ford's intellectual dexterity. Johnson said to an aide: "**You've got a little baby boy. Well, you take his little building blocks and go up and explain to Jerry Ford what we're trying to do.**"

Gerald R. Ford Speaks. Lyndon B. Johnson and First Lady, Lady Bird Johnson Claps
Gerald R. Ford Presidential Library and Museum

Power to the Common-Looking People: According to the diary of his personal secretary John Hay, Abraham Lincoln was at a party when he saw two of his fellow partygoers commenting on Lincoln's appearance. One man said to another: "**He is a very common-looking man.**" Lincoln went up to the man and said: "**The Lord prefers common-looking people. That is the reason he makes so many of them.**"

Abraham Lincoln
Library of Congress

He Had Me Fooled: During a 2002 speech in Nashville, George W. Bush confused the African Proverb: "Fool me once, shame on you; fool me twice, shame on me." Bush said: "**There's an old saying in Tennessee - I know it's in Texas, probably in Tennessee - that says, fool me once, shame on - shame on you. Fool me - you can't get fooled again.**"

George W. Bush
White House Photograph by Chris Greenberg

Presidents

Girls, Girls, Girls: John F. Kennedy, known for his sexual prowess, once confided to British Prime Minister Harold Macmillan: **"If I don't have a woman for three days, I get terrible headaches."**

John F. Kennedy (L), Harold Macmillan (R)
John F. Kennedy Presidential Library and Museum

Brainless President: Democrat Woodrow Wilson had little respect for the intellectual acumen of his Republican successor Warren G. Harding. He said: **"Harding is incapable of thought, because he has nothing to think with."** Wilson also said of Harding: **"He has a bungalow mind."**

Woodrow Wilson (L), Warren G. Harding (R)
National Archives and Records Administration

How Coolidge Really Felt About Hoover: Although Calvin Coolidge campaigned for his Commerce Secretary, Herbert Hoover, in Hoover's successful bid to succeed Coolidge as President, Coolidge had a low opinion of Hoover's advice to him. As Coolidge left office, Coolidge said of Hoover: **"That man has offered me unsolicited advice for six years, all of it bad."**

Calvin Coolidge (L), Herbert Hoover (R)
Library of Congress

Poking Fun of John Adams: Thomas Paine, who wrote the 1776 pamphlet *Common Sense*, was a vociferous critic of John Adams. He enjoyed belittling the President. He once deadpanned: **"Some people talk of impeaching John Adams, but I am for softer measures. I would keep him to make fun of him."**

Thomas Paine
Oil Painting by Augusta Milliere

Presents

Former President Jackson Calls President Harrison an Imbecile: Former President Andrew Jackson, a Democratic-Republican, was distraught that the nation elected Whig William Henry Harrison as President in 1840. After Harrison's inauguration, Jackson said: **"The Republic may suffer under the present imbecile chief, but the sober second thought of the people will restore it at our next Presidential election."**

William Henry Harrison
Library of Congress

George W. Ball's Portentous Advice: In 1961, George W. Ball, Undersecretary of State for Economic and Agricultural Affairs, advised President John F. Kennedy that a continued commitment in Vietnam could rise to 300,000 U.S. troops. Kennedy said Ball was: **"Crazier than hell."** U.S. troop levels reached 543,00 by 1969.

George W. Ball
Official Photograph

Politics Makes Me Sick: William Howard Taft did not like politics. His dream was to become Chief Justice of the United States, not President. It took much persuasion on the part of President Theodore Roosevelt and Taft's wife Nellie to get Taft, then Secretary of War, to declare his presidential candidacy. He served just one term, losing re-election in 1912 with just 23% of the vote. Taft averred: **"Politics when I am in it makes me sick."**

William Howard Taft
Library of Congress

Comparing President Grant to a Horse: Former Georgia Governor Joseph Brown belittled President Ulysses S. Grant, stating: **"The people are tired of a man who has not an idea above a horse or a cigar."**

Joseph Brown
Library of Congress

32

Presidents

Not Showing His Hand: Franklin D. Roosevelt liked to keep his plans close to his vest. He once told U.S. Treasury Secretary Henry Morgenthau Jr: **"I never let my right hand know what my left hand does."**

Franklin D. Roosevelt (L) with Henry Morgenthau Jr. (R)
Franklin D. Roosevelt Presidential Library and Museum

An Irish Joke? In a 1999 dedication of a new U.S. embassy in Ottawa, Canada, Bill Clinton said: **"I spend an enormous amount of time trying to help the people in the land of my forebears in Northern Ireland get over 600 years of religious fights. And every time they do it, they are like a couple of drunks walking out of a bar for the last time. When they reach the swing doors, they turn right around and go back in and say, 'I just can't quite get there."'** Clinton later issued a statement apologizing for using **"a metaphor that was inappropriate."**

Bill Clinton
William J. Clinton Presidential Library

President Acts Like a Six-Year-Old: British Diplomat Sir Cecil Spring-Rice was a good friend of Theodore Roosevelt. He was the best man at his wedding to Edith Carrow. When he became President, many went to Rice, asking for any insights about Roosevelt. Rice would answer: **"You must always remember the President is about six [years old]."**

Cecil Spring-Rice
Project Gutenberg

President Grant, A No Brainer: Massachusetts Governor William Claflin was the Chairman of the Republican National Committee. Interestingly, he had little respect for Republican President Ulysses S. Grant. Claflin was a critic of his handling of the Presidency. He averred: **"Early in 1869** (The year Grant assumed the Presidency) **the cry was for no politicians, but the country did not mean no brains."**

William Claflin
Portrait by Brady-Handy Studio

Presidents

Speaking Frankly about George W. Bush: In 2005, George W. Bush suggested that "intelligent design" should be taught in schools alongside creationism. This precipitated U.S. Representative Barney Frank (D-MA) to quip: **"People might cite George Bush as proof that you can be totally impervious to the effects of Harvard and Yale education."**

Barney Frank
Official Photograph

Aristotle and My Dear Old Daddy: Lyndon B. Johnson was adamant that the General Public understand his speeches. He would often modify the speeches written for him. On one occasion, the White House Speechwriter quoted Greek Philosopher Aristotle. Johnson thought his audience would not know who Aristotle was, so he crossed out Aristotle and wrote: **"As my dear old daddy used to say."**

Aristotle
Ludovisi Collection (Photograph by Jastrow)

Presidential Baggage Boy: The day after Harry S. Truman returned to Independence, Missouri after leaving the Presidency, a reporter asked him now that he was retired, what is the first thing he plans to do. Truman responded: **"I took the suitcases to the attic because the boss** [Former First Lady Bess Truman] **didn't want them downstairs."**

Bess Truman (L), Harry S. Truman (R)
Harry S. Truman Library and Museum

Take That: In 1929, some Southerners expressed disenchantment that First Lady Lou Hoover had invited an African-American woman to be a guest at the White House. Some segregationist members of the Texas Legislature called for her husband, Herbert Hoover, to be impeached for this act. The President commented to his wife: **"One of the chief advantages of orthodox religion is that it provides hot hell for the Texas Legislature."**

Herbert and Lou Hoover
Library of Congress

Presidents

Win One For The Gipper: When Ronald Reagan was asked by a reporter about Actor Clint Eastwood's candidacy for Mayor of Carmel, California, he responded: **"What makes him think a middle-aged actor who's played with a chimp could think he has a future in politics?"**

Pin Supporting Clint Eastwood's Bid for Mayor of Carmel, California

Nixon v. Rather: At a 1974 news conference during the Watergate Affair, which was held in front of an audience in Houston, Texas, *CBS* White House Correspondent Dan Rather said: **"Thank you Mr. President, Dan Rather of CBS News."** The crowd reacted with a mix of cheers and boos. President Richard M. Nixon joked: **"Are you running for something?"** Rather retorted: **"No sir, are you?"**

Dan Rather
U.S. Air force Photograph

On Caving: During the 1995 Budget negotiations, U.S. House Minority Leader Dick Armey complained to President Bill Clinton that his mother-in-law was scared by the Democrats' claims that the Republicans want to cut Medicare. Clinton responded to Armey: **"I don't know about your mother-in-law, but I do know that a lot of poor seniors will die if these Medicaid cuts are put into effect. I will never sign your Medicaid cuts! I don't care if my poll numbers go down to five percent! If you want to pass your budget, you're going to have to put somebody else into this chair."** Vice President Al Gore praised the President for drawing a line in the sand and told him he should say that in public. But Gore told him: **"Just one little thing. When you said you don't care if your popularity goes down to five percent, I think it would sound better if you said, 'I don't care if my popularity goes down to zero.'"** Clinton looked at Gore and said: **"No, that's not right Al. If I go down to four percent, I'm caving."**

Al Gore (L) and Bill Clinton (R)
William J. Clinton Presidential Library

Presidents

Corrupt Office Seekers Need Not Apply: When Grover Cleveland assumed office in 1885, he was inundated with a cavalcade of Democratic office seekers, some with corrupt pasts. Having run for President as a reformer, Cleveland refused to appoint corrupt politicos to administration posts. He said facetiously to one corrupt office seeker: **"Do you want me to appoint another horse thief for you?"**

Grover Cleveland
Library of Congress

The Teflon President: In 1983, U.S. Representative Patricia Schroder (D-CO) called Ronald Reagan: **"The Teflon President."** She said, **"He has been perfecting the Teflon-coated presidency. He sees to it that nothing sticks to him."** Schroder later said in *USA Today* that she came up with the moniker **"while fixing eggs for my kids. He had a Teflon coat like the pan."**

Patricia Schroeder
Official Photograph

Carter Loses in Plains, Georgia: In 1976, about a month after his brother Jimmy Carter was elected as President, Billy Carter, a local gas service station owner, lost in his bid to become Mayor of Plains, GA. Billy Carter secured 71 votes, losing to incumbent A.L. Blanton. After hearing of his loss, Billy Carter told reporters: **"I see Plains going straight to hell. If the people want it to go the Hell, I'll back out and let it go."** A reporter asked him if he had plans for higher office. Billy Carter responded: **"Yes, I'm going to build an office upstairs so I can live a little higher."** Before the election, Billy had said: **"As of right now, I have two votes, mine and Jimmy's. I'm sure of Jimmy because he said he is gonna vote for me, and Jimmy never tells a lie."** Jimmy had promised never to tell a lie during his Presidential campaign.

Jimmy Carter (L) with Billy Carter (R)
White House Photograph

Does Ford Really Have Super Powers? Gerald R. Ford was an avid baseball fan. However, he once explained in error how he watches the games. He said: **"I watch a lot of baseball on radio."**

Gerald R. Ford
Baseball Hall of Fame

Presidents

A Protective Father: In 1950, First Daughter Margaret Truman sang at Constitution Hall. In Washington, D.C. *Washington Post* music critic Paul Hume wrote that she "**cannot sing very well, is flat a good deal of the time.**" In response, Harry S. Truman fired off a letter to Hume reading in part: "**It seems to me that you are a frustrated old man who wishes he could have been successful. When you write such poppycock, as were in the back section of the paper you work for, it shows conclusively that you're off the beam and at least four of your ulcers are at work. Some day I hope to meet you. When that happens you'll need a new nose, a lot of beefsteak for black eyes, and perhaps a supporter below!**"

Margaret Truman (R) with her Conductor (L) Before The Show
Harry S, Truman Library and Museum

Beyond Two Wrongs Don't Make a Right: Norman Cousins, the Editor of *Saturday Review,* told *The Daily Telegraph* in 1969, "**President** [Richard M.] **Nixon's motto was, if two wrongs don't make a right, try three.**"

Norman Cousins
NASA Photograph

Bail To The Chief: As Richard M. Nixon was on his last legs preparing to resign because of the Watergate affair, U.S. Senator Howard Baker (R-TN) said: "**I suppose we shall sing Bail to the Chief.**"

Howard Baker
Official Photograph

I Like Ike: When a visitor asked Dwight David Eisenhower II, the grandson of President Dwight D. Eisenhower, his name, David replied: "**Dwight David Eisenhower.**" The visitor said: "**If you are Dwight David Eisenhower, then who is he?**" (Pointing to the President). David replied: "**That's Ike.**" The presidential retreat "Camp David" is named for Dwight David Eisenhower II.

David Eisenhower
The Eisenhower Presidential Library and Museum

Presidents

Borrowed Brains: In 1955, Dwight D. Eisenhower, in referring to his Special Assistant on Foreign Affairs, Nelson Rockefeller, told his Personal Secretary Ann Whitman: **"He is too used to borrowing brains instead of using his own."** Rockefeller's personal staff was considered highly intelligent.

Nelson Rockefeller
Department of Health Education and
Welfare Photograph

Blamed For the Great Depression? After leaving the presidency, Herbert Hoover quipped: **"Once upon a time my political opponents honored me as possessing the fabulous intellectual and economic power by which I created a world-wide depression all by myself."**

Herbert Hoover with Dog King Tut
Library of Congress

At least He Still Has His Own Monument: Calvin Coolidge was having a conversation about the effects of a book written by Rupert Hughes Titled *George Washington: The Human Being and the Hero*. The book gave a negative patina of George Washington. Coolidge looked out the window and observed: **"I see his monument is still there."**

Washington Monument
Library of Congress

Political Name Calling: Theodore Roosevelt supported the election of William Howard Taft to succeed him as President. However, Roosevelt, who was a progressive, became disillusioned with the leadership of the more conservative Taft. Roosevelt called Taft **"Dumber than a guinea pig, a fathead."**

Theodore Roosevelt (L)
William Howard Taft (R)
Library of Congress

Presidents

President Uses the Term "Stupid:" In a 1954 letter written to his brother Newton Eisenhower, Dwight D. Eisenhower upbraids conservatives who want to abolish the social safety net. He writes: "There is a tiny splinter group, of course, that believes you can do these things. Among them are H.L. Hunt, a Texas oil tycoon, a few other Texas oil millionaires, and an occasional politician or businessman from other areas. Their number is negligible and they are stupid."

Dwight D. Eisenhower
The Eisenhower Presidential
Library and Museum

Nixon the Sportscaster: In a 1971 interview with sportscaster Frank Gifford, President Richard M. Nixon said: **"I have often thought that if I had my life to live over again and did not go into politics I would like to have your job, you know, be a sportscaster or writer."**

Richard M. Nixon
Library of Congress

Truman Gets Testy: At the end of a 1958 Press conference, a reporter asked: **"Is there anything we have overlooked, Mr. President?"** Truman responded: **"I don't believe there is. If I could think of any, why, would I give it to you."**

Harry S. Truman at a Press Conference
Harry S. Truman Library and Museum

President Admits He is Not Jesus Christ, and Flatly Refuses to Raise Predecessor From the Dead: After the Pearl Harbor attack in 1941, Franklin D. Roosevelt asked financier Bernard Baruch for advice on ways to consolidate the country in light of WWII. Baruch recommended that Roosevelt ask his predecessor Herbert Hoover for help. However, Hoover was unpopular because the Great Depression began under his watch. Hoover had also been a vociferous critic of Roosevelt's policies. Roosevelt told Baruch: **"I'm not Jesus Christ. I'm not raising him from the dead."**

Herbert Hoover (L) with Franklin D. Roosevelt (R)
Library of Congress

Presidents

Presidential Maxim For a Happy Marriage: When Princess Margaret of Great Britain (accompanied by her husband Lord Snowdon, Antony Armstrong-Jones) visited the White House in 1965; Lyndon B. Johnson gave Lord Jones some unsolicited advice for a happy marriage. Johnson told him: **"I've learned that there are only two things necessary to keep your wife happy. First, let her think she's having her way. And second, let her have it."**

Lyndon B. Johnson and Wife Lady Bird entertain Princess Margaret Rose and her Husband Lord Armstrong Jones of Snowden
Lyndon Baines Johnson Library and Museum

Geography 101? In 2001, after a meeting of the Organization of the American States, George W. Bush asked Brazilian President Fernando Henrique Cardoso: **"Do you have blacks too?"** National Security Advisor Condoleezza Rice informed Bush that: **"Brazil probably has more blacks than in the USA."**

Fernando Henrique Cardoso
Photograph by Agencies Braszil

Library of Congress Favors Original Edition of Bible: After Calvin Coolidge learned that the Library of Congress had purchased an original *Gutenberg Bible*, Coolidge deadpanned: **"I should think that an ordinary copy of the King James Version would have been good enough for those Congressmen."**

Librarian of Congress Herbert Putnam with the *Gutenberg Bible*
Library of Congress

That's Big: Theodore Roosevelt drank a gallon of coffee per day. His son, Theodore Roosevelt Jr., became U.S. Assistant Secretary of the Navy. His son joked that the President's Coffee mug was **"more in the nature of a bathtub."**

Theodore Roosevelt Jr.
Official Photograph

Chapter II

Vice Presidents

Vice Presidents

No Love for the Job: When Republican Calvin Coolidge garnered the GOP Vice Presidential nomination in 1920, incumbent Vice President Thomas Riley Marshall telegraphed Coolidge: **"Please accept my sincere sympathy."**

Thomas Riley Marshall
Library of Congress

How Morbid: Nelson Rockefeller, who once held great power as Governor of New York, felt bored in the job of Vice President. He summed up his official duties this way: **"I go to funerals. I go to earthquakes."**

Nelson Rockefeller
Library of Congress

A Good Sea Story: Vice President Alben Barkley, who served under President Harry S. Truman, made light of the irrelevancy of his office. He was fond of telling this joke: **"There was a mother who had two sons. One went to sea; the other became vice president; and neither was heard from again."**

Alben Barkley
Harry S. Truman Library and Museum

The Bureaucratic Senate: Vice President Henry Wilson, who served under President Ulysses S. Grant, made the following comment about the U.S. Senate that he in fact presided over: **"I believe if we introduced the Lord's Prayer here, senators would propose a large number of amendments to it."**

Henry Wilson
Library of Congress

Vice Presidents

The Vice President Ain't a Drunkard Vice President Andrew Johnson was drunk at the 1865 Presidential Inauguration. Johnson had taken "medicinal" whiskey to cure a bout of Malaria. He slurred his Inaugural Address. President Abraham Lincoln later defended Johnson, saying: **"I have known Andrew Johnson for many years. He made a slip the other day, but you need not be scared; Andy ain't a drunkard."**

Andrew Johnson
Library of Congress

Blue Grass Bourbon: Vice President Alben Barkley, known for his storytelling ability, said: **"A good story is like fine Kentucky bourbon. It improves with age and, if you don't use it too much, it will never hurt anyone."**

Kentucky Bourbon
Photograph by Greg Duncan

Nothing Like a Good Five-Cent Cigar: While U.S. Senator Joseph Bristow (R-KS) was speaking on the U.S. Senate floor about what the country needs, Vice President Thomas Riley Marshall, while presiding over the Senate, deadpanned: **"What this country really needs is a good five-cent cigar."**

Thomas Riley Marshall
Library of Congress

Tell Us How You Really Feel, John: Vice President John Adams was less than thrilled with the lack of power in his job. In a letter to his wife, Abigail Adams, he called the Vice Presidency: **"The most insignificant office that ever the invention of man contrived or his imagination conceived."**

John Adams
Library of Congress

Vice Presidents

Fun With Alliteration: In an address to the California Republican State Convention delivered on September 11, 1970, Vice President Spiro Agnew excoriated the American news media, saying: **"In the United States today, we have more than our share of the nattering nabobs of negativism. They have formed their own 4-H Club – The hopeless, hysterical hypochondriacs of history."** Speechwriter William Safire wrote these words for Agnew.

Spiro Agnew
Official Photograph as Governor of Maryland

Vice President States Position That is Difficult to Argue With: In an address to employees of NASA in 1990, Vice President Dan Quayle asserted: **"For NASA, space is still a high priority."**

NASA Symbol

Beam Me Out of Here, Scotty: In 1927, U.S. Senator and future Vice President Alben Barkley (D-KY) asked Vice President Charles Dawes if he liked his job. Dawes, who was Vice President under Calvin Coolidge, did not sugarcoat his boredom with his role as Vice President. He told Barkley: **"I can do only two things here. One of them is to sit up here on this rostrum and listen to you birds talk without the ability to reply. The other is to look at the newspapers every morning to see how the President's health is."**

Charles G. Dawes
Library of Congress

Big Difference Between Michael Jordan and Michael Jackson: While speaking at a fundraiser in Washington, D.C. in 1998, Vice President Al Gore took a moment to discuss Basketball legend Michael Jordan. Gore said: **"I tell you that Michael Jackson is unbelievable, isn't he. He's just unbelievable."**

Al Gore
Executive Office of the President

Vice Presidents

Cheney Not Down with Rap: Vice President Dick Cheney shocked the nation when he told *The Washington Times* in December of 2008 that he is not a rap fan: **"I have trouble even following it."**

Dick Cheney
White House Photograph by David Bohrer

Is This the U.S. Senate or the Jerry Springer Show? In 2004, Vice President Dick Cheney, while serving in his constitutional role as President of the U.S. Senate, was on the Senate floor for the official Senate photograph. After the photograph, U.S. Senator Patrick Leahy (D-VT) greeted Cheney. In response, Cheney said to Leahy: **"Go f*** yourself."** Cheney was indignant at Leahy for excoriating him in his role as ranking member of the U.S. Senate Judiciary Committee for the alleged profiteering of Halliburton (formerly led by Cheney) in Iraq.

Patrick Leahy
Official Photograph

He'd Rather be Number One: In 1796, Thomas Jefferson, the newly sworn-in Vice President, found his job unchallenging, but thought otherwise of the Presidency, which he would assume four years later. In a letter to his friend Elbridge Gerry (who would later become Vice President himself), Jefferson wrote: **"The Second Office of this government is honorable and easy, the first, but a splendid misery."**

Thomas Jefferson
Library of Congress

Gore Humor: Former Vice President Al Gore, in alluding to the disputed 2000 Presidential election, often begins speeches joking: **"I'm Al Gore, and I used to be the next President of the United States."**

Al Gore
Photograph by Breuwi

Vice Presidents

Supplying Red Meat to the Republican Base: In a speech delivered to the Midwest Regional Republican Committee in Des Moines, Iowa in 1968, Vice President Spiro Agnew waged war on the so-called elites, stating: **"Perhaps the place to start looking for a credibility gap is not in the offices of the Government in Washington but in the studios of the networks in New York!"**

Spiro Agnew
Library of Congress

That About Sums Him Up: Vice President Hubert Humphrey got to know President Lyndon B. Johnson pretty well. He summed up the President this way: **"He loved women, he loved a good earthy story. There was nothing delicate about him. He was like a cowboy making love."**

Lyndon B. Johnson (L) with Hubert Humphrey (R)
Lyndon Baines Johnson Library and Museum

Roosevelt's Spare Tire: When John Nance Garner left his position as Speaker of the U.S. House of Representatives to assume the Vice Presidency under President Franklin D. Roosevelt, Garner said: **"Worst damn fool mistake I ever made was letting myself be elected Vice President of the United States. Should have stuck with my old chores as Speaker of the House. I gave up the second most important job in the government for one that didn't amount to a hill of beans. I spent eight long years as Mr. Roosevelt's spare tire. I might still be Speaker if I didn't let them elect me Vice-President."**

John Nance Garner in Happier Days as Speaker of the U.S. House of Representatives
John Nance Garner Papers, 1874-1968, Dolph Briscoe Center for American History, University of Texas at Austin.

Vice Presidents

Camp Quayle: During a trip to American Samoa, Vice President Dan Quayle used an interesting way of describing the locals. He told the American Samoans: **"You all look like happy campers to me. Happy campers you are, happy campers you have been, and, as far as I am concerned, happy campers you will always be."**

Dan Quayle
Official Photograph

Waging a War Against Intellectuals: Following the 1969 Moratorium to end the War in Vietnam, Vice President Spiro Agnew revved up conservative populist indignation against intellectuals: He told a Republican Party fundraiser in New Orleans: **"A spirit of national masochism prevails, encouraged by an effete corps of impudent snobs who characterize themselves as intellectuals."**

Spiro Agnew
Official Photograph

Who are These Buggers? Three days before assuming office, incoming President Bill Clinton and Vice President Al Gore took a tour of Monticello, the former home of Thomas Jefferson. Gore saw some busts and asked the museum's curator: **"Who are these people?"** The curator explained: **"This is George Washington on the extreme right, with Benjamin Franklin close behind."**

Monticello
Photograph by Martin Falbisoner

That's How the Game is Played: As House Minority Leader, Tip O'Neill (D-MA) had a friendship with his counterpart U.S. House Minority Leader Gerald R. Ford. When Ford was sworn in as Vice President in 1974 upon the resignation of Vice President Spiro Agnew, O'Neill was singing Ford's praises. Before the swearing-in ceremony, O'Neill said to Ford: **"Christ, Jerry, isn't this a wonderful country? Here we can talk like this and you and I can be friends, and eighteen months from now I'll be going around the country kicking your ass."**

Gerald R. Ford (L) with Tip O'Neill (R)
Library of Congress

Vice Presidents

Great Analogy: U.S. Senator Barry Goldwater (R-AZ) once commented about Vice President Hubert Humphrey: **"He talks so fast that listening to him is like trying to read *Playboy Magazine* with your wife turning the pages."**

Playboy Magazine

Just Let the Man Golf: Former Vice President Dan Quayle, a Republican and an avid golfer, offered a rare defense of Barack Obama and his propensity to hit the links. He said on *FOX Business Network*: **"I'm glad he's out playing golf. I happen to be a golfer. I think presidents deserve down time. And believe me, he is in constant communication with what's going on. I mean, what do you want him to do, stay in his house and be on the phone with the ambassador to Japan all the time?"**

Dan Quayle
Photograph by Gage Skidmore

Socratic Wisdom: In 1939, Freshman U.S. Representative Wilber Mills (D-AR) met Vice President John Nance Garner and admitted his ignorance of politics and governance. He said: **"I just don't know anything."** Garner replied: **"Shake hands with me, boy. That makes you the smartest man who ever came to Washington."**

John Nance Garner
Harry S. Truman Library and Museum

Democratic Vice President Not Popular in the House of Labor: While President Franklin D. Roosevelt was revered by many in the Labor Movement, Vice President John Nance Garner was castigated by the labor movement for his more business-oriented views. John F. Lewis, the President of the United Mine workers of America and the Congress of Industrial Organizations, testifying before the U.S. House Labor Committee, called Garner: **"a labor-baiting, poker-playing, whiskey-drinking evil old man."**

John L. Lewis
Library of Congress

49

Vice Presidents

Oops, Wrong State: In a 1998 stump speech for Hubert "Skip" Humphrey III and Roger Moe, the Democratic Farmer Labor Party nominee for Governor and Lieutenant Governor of <u>Minnesota</u>, Vice President Al Gore declared: **"They will be the education team <u>Missouri</u> needs."** (Emphasis added) Gore was in Minnesota at the time.

Al Gore
Photograph by Tom Raftery

Now That's Poor: Commenting on the poverty his family suffered when growing up in Wheel, Kentucky, future Vice President Alben Barkley commented: **"We were so poor that we had to use hoot owls for watchdogs."**

Hoot Owl
Photograph by Terren

Quick-Witted Andrew Jackson Smacks Down Vice President: Vice President John C. Calhoun broke with President Andrew Jackson over the issue of nullification (The right of a State to nullify a federal law which that state deems unconstitutional). Calhoun, a native South Carolinian, supported it, while Jackson opposed it. Calhoun publicly said that he would even support his state's succession from the Union if necessary, to which Jackson responded: **"John Calhoun, if you secede from my nation, I will secede your head from the rest of your body."**

Andrew Jackson
Library of Congress

Vice President is Naked: After leaving the Vice Presidency in 1969, Hubert Humphrey told *Time Magazine* that the job of Vice President: **"Is like being naked in the middle of a blizzard with no one to even offer you a match to keep you warm."**

Hubert Humphrey
Lyndon Baines Johnson Library and Museum

Vice Presidents

Vice President Prepares for Silence: In 1913, Vice President Thomas Riley Marshall began his Inaugural Address by stating: **"I believe I'm entitled to make a few remarks because I'm about to enter a four-year period of silence."** (Vice Presidents no longer deliver Inaugural Addresses.)

Thomas Riley Marshall
Library of Congress

This is a Job For a Technocrat: When Bill Clinton announced that Vice President Al Gore, known as a technocratic policy wonk, would undertake his initiative to reinvent government, Clinton said: **"I asked him to do it because he was the only person that I could trust to read all 150,000 pages in the Code of Federal Regulations."**

Bill Clinton (L) with Al Gore (R) announcing Their Reinvent Government Initiative
William J. Clinton Presidential Library

How True That Is: In an address to the United Negro College Fund (UNCF), Vice President Dan Quayle, when trying to state the slogan of the organization: **"A Mind is a Terrible Thing to Waste"** lost his train of thought and said: **"When you take the UNCF model that, what a waste it is to lose one's mind, or not to have a mind is being very wasteful, how true that is."**

Dan Quayle
Official Photograph

The Book on Mediocrity: Charles G. Dawes, who served as Vice President under Calvin Coolidge, observed: **"Mediocrity requires aloofness to preserve its dignity."**

Charles G. Dawes
Official Photograph

Chapter III

Cabinet Members

Cabinet Members

A Horse is a Horse, of Course, of Course: While Governor of the Philippines, William Howard Taft, who weighed well over 300 pounds, one day sent a message to U.S. Secretary of War Elihu Root, which read: **"Went on a horse ride today; feeling good."** Root Replied: **"How's the horse?"**

William Howard Taft
Library of Congress

Mending Fences: The phrase **"Mend fences"** was coined by U.S. Treasury Secretary John Sherman in 1879. He told an audience in his native Ohio: **"I have come home to look after my fences."** While Sherman likely meant that he was coming home to look after the fences on his farm, the line came to mean that he was trying to consolidate political support in his home state.

John Sherman
Library of Congress

Pomposity Defined: William Gibbs McAdoo, who served as U.S. Treasury Secretary under the administration of Woodrow Wilson, said of President Warren G. Harding (who was known for his verbose prose): **"His speeches left the impression of an army of pompous phrases moving over the landscape in search of an idea; sometimes these meandering words would actually capture a straggling thought and bear it triumphantly as a prisoner in their midst, until it died of servitude and overwork."**

William Gibbs McAdoo
Library of Congress

Oops: Ronald Reagan played host to the U.S. Conference of Mayors in 1981 at the White House. He walked up to one attendee of the event and said: **"How are you Mr. Mayor? How are things in your city?"** Unbeknownst to Reagan, the guest was not a Mayor, but Samuel Pierce, the Reagan Administration's Secretary of Housing and Urban Development.

Samuel Pierce
Official Photograph

Cabinet Members

Way Too Many Unknowns: At a 2002 Press Briefing, U.S. Secretary of Defense Donald Rumsfeld was asked about the evidence that Iraq had reconstituted its Weapons of Mass Destruction program and whether Iraq was linked to Al-Qaeda. Rumsfeld responded accordingly: **"... There are known known's. There are things we know that we know. There are known unknowns. That is to say, there are things that we now know we don't know. But there are also unknown unknowns. There are things we do not know we don't know."** After leaving office, Rumsfeld published a book titled: *"Known and Unknown: A Memoir."*

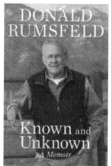

Known and Unknown: A Memoir
By Donald Rumsfeld

In Defense of Bribery: In 1791, U.S. Secretary of State Thomas Jefferson wrote in a letter to Maryland resident Charles Carol: **"The most economical as well as the most humane conduct towards the Indians is to bribe them into peace and to retain them in peace by eternal bribes."**

Thomas Jefferson
Portrait by Charles Wilson Peale

Before the Freedom of Information Act: In 1975, U.S. Secretary of State Henry Kissinger told the Turkish Foreign Minister, Melih Esenbel: **"Before the Freedom of Information Act, I used to say at meetings, 'The illegal we do immediately; the unconstitutional takes a little longer.' But since the Freedom of Information Act, I'm afraid to say things like that."**

Henry Kissinger
Executive Office of the President

Mocking the Pope is not Good Politics: At a 1974 World Food Conference in Rome, U.S. Secretary of Agriculture Earl Butz used a fake Italian accent to mock Pope Paul VI for his steadfast opposition to human population control. Butz said: **"He no play the game, he no make the rules."**

Earl L. Butz
Official Photograph

Cabinet Members

Hey! What's That You're Smoking? In 1978, President Jimmy Carter visited the battleground state of North Carolina. His Secretary of Health, Education, and Welfare, Joe Califano, was an outspoken critic of tobacco, a major cash crop in the state. Carter told his audience: **"I had planned today to bring Joseph Califano with me, but he decided not to come. He discovered that not only is North Carolina the number-one tobacco-producing state, but that you produce more bricks in the nation as well. Joe did encourage me to come though. He said it was time for the White House Staff to start smoking something regular."**

Joseph Califano
Lyndon Baines Library and Museum

Breaking the Code No More: In 1929, U.S. Secretary of State Henry Stimson announced the shutdown of the State Department's Cryptanalytic unit, the unit that tries to break the codes of enemy communications. In closing down this intelligence unit Stimson joked to his analysts: **"Gentlemen don't read each other's mail."**

Henry Stimson
Harris & Ewing Collection, Library of Congress

Words of Wisdom: John W. Gardner, who served as Secretary of Health, Education, and Welfare under President Lyndon B. Johnson, told a Commencement Address at Cornell University in 1968: **"Pity the leader caught between unloving critics and uncritical lovers."** Gardner had resigned his position in protest of U.S. involvement in the Vietnam War.

John Gardner
Photograph from White House Fellows Release

It Will Still Stain: In 1987, after being acquitted on charges of larceny, former U.S. Secretary of Labor Raymond James Donavan asked assembled members of the media: **"Which one of these offices do I go to get my reputation back?"**

Raymond James Donavan
U.S. Department of Labor Photograph

Cabinet Members

Attorney General: A Gateway to a Career in Law: At a Gridiron Dinner in 1961, John F. Kennedy joked about his nomination of his brother Robert F. Kennedy as U.S. Attorney General. At that time, Robert F. Kennedy had a fairly light legal résumé. In fact, he had never even practiced law. Some critics charged that he was only nominated because he was the brother of the President. John said jokingly that he nominated his brother **"so he might get a little experience first."**

**Robert Kennedy (L) John F. Kennedy (R)
With Brother Ted Kennedy (C)**
Executive Office of the President

Lots of Bull: British Prime Minister Winston Churchill said U.S. Secretary of State John Foster Dulles **"was a bull who always carried a China Shop around."**

John Foster Dulles
Official Portrait by Paul Gratz

Big Heels to Fill: In an address to employees of the U.S. State Department, after assuming the post of Secretary of State, John Kerry made light of the fact that he would be succeeding Hillary Clinton. He said: **"The big question before the country and the world is: 'Can a man actually run the State Department?' I don't know … as the saying goes, I have big heels to fill."**

John Kerry
Official Photograph

Strictly Non-Partisan: General George Marshall, who served as U.S. Secretary of State during the administration of President Harry S. Truman made it a point to be strictly non-partisan. In fact, he did not even vote. When a reporter asked him his political affiliation, Marshall replied: **"My father was a Republican, my mother was a Democrat. I am an Episcopalian."**

George Marshall
Harry S. Truman Library and Museum

Cabinet Members

Is There Anyone I Missed? In a 1985 speech delivered before the U.S. Chamber of Commerce, U.S. Agricultural Secretary James Watts said that he was being advised by an advisory panel on the issue of leasing coal mining. He said of the panel: **"We have every kind of mixture you can have. I have a black. I have a woman, two Jews and a cripple and we have talent."** The remark drew laughter at the event. However, there was outrage by Civil Rights groups by the insensitivity of the remark. Watts later issued an apology for making the statement.

James Watt
Official Photograph

Bet on Clay: Lucretia Clay, the wife of U.S. Secretary of State Henry Clay (1825-1829), came to accept her husband's perpetual gambling. A patrician Bostonian once asked her: **"Doesn't it distress you to have Mr. Clay gamble?"** Lucretia replied: **"Oh Dear No. He Always Wins."**

Henry and Lucretia Clay
Official Portrait

A Proclivity Toward Blonds: When *The New York Times* asked failed U.S. Defense Secretary nominee John Tower about his *1942 Beaumont High School Yearbook* description of him liking baseball and blonds, Tower retorted: **"Really, my preference generally has run to brunettes, although I happen to be lashed to a blond."** The Reporter then asked the following follow-up question: **"Does that bother Ms. Heyser, who is a blond?"** Tower then answered: **"Oh, she knows it. One night when I went to pick her up, she showed up at the door in a black wig. She said, 'Does this turn you on?' And I said, 'It might - on somebody else.'"**

John Tower
Official Photograph

The Gift of Potato Chips: In 2010, Australian comedian radio hosts Hanis & Andy scored an interview with U.S. Secretary of State Hillary Clinton. The duo gave Clinton a gift, a bag of potato chips. Clinton responded: **"I cannot tell you how much this means to me."**

Hillary Clinton
Official Photograph

Cabinet Members

The Definition of Hell: Getting The National Energy Act of 1978 supported by President Jimmy Carter through the U.S. Congress proved a protracted and arduous process. U.S. Energy Secretary James Schlesinger said: **"I understand what Hell is. Hell is endless and eternal sessions of the Natural Gas Conference."**

James Schlesinger Depicted on the Cover of *Time Magazine*

Here We Go Loop-de-Loop: In 2013, when Barack Obama nominated Jack Lew to be U.S. Treasury Secretary, he noted to the assembled press Lew's loopy signature: **"Jack assures me that he is going to work to make at least one letter legible in order not to debase our currency."**

Jack Lew
Official Photograph

Jack Lew's Real Signature

A Clean Sweep: In 1972 Richard M. Nixon was re-elected in a 49-state landslide. The day after the election, Chief of Staff H.R. Haldeman ordered a meeting of the President's Cabinet and called for the resignation of all Cabinet members. He told them: **"You are all a bunch of burned-out volcanoes."**

H.R. Haldeman
Official Photograph

Monkey Business: During a 2014 interview with Greta Van Susteran on the Fox News Program *On the Record*, former U.S. Secretary of Defense Donald Rumsfeld derided Barack Obama for not receiving a status of forces agreement with Afghanistan. He said: **"A trained ape can get a status of forces agreement. It does not take a genius."**

Donald Rumsfeld
Official Photograph

Cabinet Members

Eye of the Tiger: In 1987, en route to China, Helena Shultz, the wife of U.S. Secretary of State George Shultz, revealed to reporters that the Secretary had a tiger tattoo on his posterior. He got the tattoo while a student at Princeton, home of the Princeton Tigers. Mrs. Schultz said: **"When the children were young, they used to run up and touch it and he would growl and they would run away."** When Johanna McGreary of *Time Magazine* asked the Secretary about the tattoo, Shultz responded: **"My gosh I have been investigated by the FBI, the IRS, by the Senate Intelligence Committee. My mail is opened. I don't have any secrets left. That's the only thing I have left, what is on my rear end."**

George Schultz
Official Photograph

Princeton Tiger

Sticking it to Charles de Gaulle: In 1966, French President Charles de Gaulle announced that France was egressing from NATO and said that all American troops must leave France. Lyndon B. Johnson ordered U.S. Secretary of State Dean Rusk to ask De Gaulle: **"Does That include all the U.S. troops buried on French soil from the liberation of France?"** De Gaulle did not answer the question.

Dean Rusk (L) with Lyndon B. Johnson (R)
Lyndon Baines Johnson Library and Museum

Yachting For Facts: U.S. Agricultural Secretary David Franklin Houston served with U.S. Secretary of State William Jennings Bryan under the administration of President Woodrow Wilson. Houston had a low opinion of Bryan's intellect and the underpinnings of his arguments. He said of Bryan: **"One could drive a schooner through any part of his argument and never scrape against a fact."**

David Franklin Houston
Photograph by Harris and Ewing

Cabinet Members

Cameron the Corrupt: In 1861, newly elected President Abraham Lincoln nominated Simon Cameron to the post of U.S. Secretary of War. He made this appointment based on a political bargain with the Republican Party leaders. Once confirmed by the U.S. Senate, Lincoln asked U.S. Representative Thaddeus Stevens (R-PA) about the honesty of his new Secretary of War. Stevens had served with Cameron as a member of the Pennsylvania Congressional Delegation. Stevens was well aware of Cameron's corruption, and responded to Lincoln by saying: **"You don't mean to say you think Cameron would steal? No, I do not believe he would steal a red-hot stove."** When Lincoln told him that Cameron was offended by the comments and wanted an apology, Stevens replied: "**I believe I told you he would not steal a red-hot stove. I will now take that back.**" Cameron was forced to leave office because of his notorious corruption.

Simon Cameron
Library of Congress

"Halitosis of the Intellect:" In 1933, U.S. Interior Secretary Harold Ickies said of U.S. Senator Huey Long (D-LA), who at that time was pushing legislation to place all federal spending under federal control: **"He is suffering from halitosis of the intellect; that's presuming he has an intellect."**

Harold Ickes
Official Photograph

Congress is Just as Stupid as the People: In a 1971 interview with Theodore A. Wilson and Richard D. McKenzie, Dean Acheson, former U.S. Secretary of State during the Truman administration, blasted the American people: **"People say, If the Congress were more representative of the people it would be better. I say the Congress is too damn representative. It's just as stupid as the people are; just as uneducated, just as dumb, just as selfish."**

Dean Acheson
Harry S. Truman Library and Museum

She Can't Climb Trees: In 1933, Frances Perkins became the first female member of a Presidential Cabinet. She served as U.S. Secretary of Labor for the entire term of Franklin D. Roosevelt. When she was asked by a reporter if being a woman hampered her ability, she replied: **"Being a woman has only bothered me in climbing trees."**

Frances Perkins
Official Portrait

Cabinet Members

No Love Lost Here: When future U.S. Secretary of State John Foster Dulles was a lawyer at Sullivan & Cromwell, he chose not to hire future U.S. Supreme Court Justice William O. Douglas, saying he **"didn't seem sharp enough."** Douglas later recalled the job interview saying: **"I was so struck with Dulles' pomposity that when he helped me on with my coat as I was leaving the office, I turned and gave him a quarter tip."** Douglas later said, **"I'm not sure I want to go to Heaven. I'm afraid I might meet John Foster Dulles there."**

John Foster Dulles
Official Photograph

It is Claimed That the Founding Fathers Authorized Electronic Surveillance: In defending the warrantless wiretapping program of George W. Bush, U.S. Attorney General Alberto Gonzalez said: **"President Washington, President Lincoln, President Wilson, President Roosevelt have all authorized electronic surveillance on a far broader scale."**

Alberto Gonzales
Official Photograph

Out of Left Field: Prior to visiting New Zealand in 1998, U.S. Secretary of State Madeline Albright exclaimed: **"I've never been to New Zealand before. But one of my role models, Xena, the Warrior Princess, comes from there."**

Madeleine Albright
Official Photograph

Taking Power: After President Ronald Reagan was shot and incapacitated in 1981, U.S. Secretary of State Alexander Haig told reporters: **"I am in control here."** Actually, the U.S. Constitution delegates that authority to the Vice President. Haig later asserted that he wasn't talking about transition. **"I was talking about the Executive branch, who is running the government. That was the question asked. It was not, 'Who is in line should the President die?'"** Vice President George H.W. Bush was in Fort Worth, Texas at the time, and thus could not immediately be available to take charge of the Executive branch.

Alexander Haig
Official Photograph

Chapter IV

Presidential Campaigns

Presidential Campaigns

Defining Hell: President Harry S. Truman was delivering a campaign speech in Harrisburg, Illinois in 1948 when an audience member yelled: **"Give em' hell Harry."** Truman's rejoinder was: **"I don't give them hell, I just tell the truth about them and they think it's hell."**

Harry S. Truman
Harry S. Truman Library and Museum

Two John Kerry's: Speaking at the 2004 Republican National Convention in New York City, Vice President Dick Cheney, in trying to characterize Democratic Presidential nominee John Kerry as a flip-flopper, said: **"Senator Kerry says he sees two Americas. It makes the whole thing mutual -- America sees two John Kerrys."**

Dick Cheney
Official Photograph

Not so Sober Advice: In 1856, President Franklin Peirce lost his own Party's nomination for reelection to James Buchanan who was serving as Ambassador to the United Kingdom. When he found out that he had lost, Pierce deadpanned: **"There's nothing left to do but get drunk."**

Franklin Pierce
Library of Congress

President of What: In 1974, Jimmy Carter told his mother, Lillian Carter, that he would seek the Presidency. She responded: **"President of What?"**

Jimmy Carter (L), Lillian Carter (R)
National Archives and Records
Administration

Presidential Campaigns

A Bucket of Warm Spit: When Johnson was offered the Vice Presidential nomination by Democratic Presidential nominee John F. Kennedy in 1960, Johnson talked to former Vice President John Nance Garner, who did not like the job and rued the day he relinquished his previous job as Speaker of the U.S. House of Representative to assume the office. Garner said to Johnson: **"The Vice Presidency isn't worth a bucket of warm spit."**

John Nance Garner
Library of Congress

Not a Country Club Republican: Before serving in elective office, U.S. Senator Barry Goldwater applied for membership in a Phoenix country club. However, Goldwater was blackballed from joining because his father was Jewish. Goldwater responded with the following remark: **"Since I'm only half-Jewish, can I join if I only play nine holes?"** Ironically, when he won the Republican nomination for President in 1964, he wrested it away from the hegemonic Country Club Wing of the Republican Party.

Barry Goldwater on the Cover of
Time Magazine

Born With a Silver Foot: Texas State Treasurer Ann Richards made a name for herself in 1988 when she delivered the keynote address at the Democratic National Convention in Atlanta. Poking fun at the Republican Presidential nominee, George H.W. Bush, who came from patrician stalk, Richards joked: **"Poor George, he can't help it. He was born with a silver foot in his mouth."**

Ann Richards
Official Photograph as Governor of Texas
By James Tennison

Presidential Candidate Urges Students to Chug-a-lug Alcohol: In 2008, Democratic Presidential aspirant Mike Gravel, speaking to students at Phillips Exeter Academy in Exeter, New Hampshire, offered the High School students some unsolicited advice: **"Go get yourself a fifth of Scotch or a fifth of gin and chug-a-lug it down and you'll find you lose your senses a lot faster than you would smoking some marijuana."**

Mike Gravel
Photograph by George Rebh

Presidential Campaigns

Are You Ready for some Football? During the heated Republican Presidential Primary between President Gerald R. Ford and former California Governor Ronald Reagan, Ford's media advisor, Don Penny, told the President that he was not as charismatic as Reagan and needed more one-liners in his speeches. The quick-witted Ford delivered one. **"Governor Reagan and I do have one thing in common: We both played football. I played for Michigan; he played for Warner Brothers."** (Reagan was a former actor and played George Gipp, a famous Notre Dame football player, in the Warner Brothers Movie: *Knute Rockne—All American*).

Ronald Reagan and Gerald R. Ford
Gerald R. Ford Presidential Library and Museum

Alternative History: In a 2011 speech to Iowans for Tax Relief, prospective Republican Presidential candidate Michele Bachmann, in referring to the nation's founding documents said: **"The very founders that wrote those documents worked tirelessly until slavery was no more."** Actually, many of the founders were slave owners, and slavery did not end until the Civil War.

Michele Bachmann for President
Bumper Sticker

Luke-Warm Endorsement From Ike: During the 1960 Presidential election, outgoing Republican President Dwight D. Eisenhower was asked by a reporter to name one decision in which his Vice President, Richard M. Nixon (the Republican Presidential nominee), had participated. Eisenhower answered: **"If you give me a week, maybe I'll think of one."**

Dwight D. Eisenhower (L)
Richard M. Nixon (R)
Eisenhower Presidential Library and Museum

Not Just Peanuts: Jimmy Carter operated a peanut farm and used it to his political advantage in 1976. His campaign plane was called: "Peanut One" and his campaign slogan was: **"Not Just Peanuts."** He wanted voters to focus on his role as an officer in the U.S. Navy, as the Governor of Georgia, as well as his role as a peanut farmer.

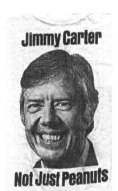

Jimmy Carter Not Just Peanuts T-shirt

Presidential Campaigns

Humphrey Plays Tonto: During the 1968 Presidential campaign, Republican Vice President Spiro Agnew compared Democratic Vice Presidential nominee Hubert Humphrey to Tonto (the sidekick of The Loan Ranger in the 1950s television series by the same name) for his role as loyal Vice President to President Lyndon B. Johnson. Agnew told a rally in Las Vegas: **"After playing Tonto for so long, apparently Mr. Humphrey isn't comfortable playing the Loan Ranger. In fact, with all of Humphrey's efforts to break away from the administration, perhaps Dick Nixon and I should keep quiet and let Mr. Humphrey and Mr. Johnson fight it out."**

Lyndon B. Johnson and Hubert Humphrey
Lyndon Baines Johnson Presidential Library

The Olympic Tax & Spend Competition: During the 1988 Presidential race, Republican George H.W. Bush used an Olympic analogy against his Democratic opponent, Michael Dukakis. He said: **"My opponent ranks first in spending increases -- Second in tax hikes. If this were the Olympics, his composite score would make him the gold medal winner in the tax-and-spend competition."**

Olympic Rings

You Could At Least Give the Appearance the Election is Legitimate: In a letter written to his son John F. Kennedy during his 1960 Presidential race, Joseph P. Kennedy Sr. wrote: **"Dear Jack. Don't buy a single vote more than necessary. I'll be damned if I'm going to pay for a landslide."**

Joseph P. Kennedy Sr.
Photograph by Larry Gordon

George McGovern "Exposes" Himself: In 1972, while campaigning for Democratic Presidential nominee George McGovern, Rhode Island Governor Frank Licht asserted: [Republican President Richard M.] **Nixon has been sitting in the White House while George McGovern has been exposing himself to the people of the United States."**

Frank Licht
Official Photograph

Presidential Campaigns

No Sugarcoating This One: After garnering just 3.5% of the vote in the New Hampshire Presidential Primary in 1984, U.S. Senator Ernest "Fritz" Hollings announced he would drop out of the race. Hollings told reporters and supporters: **"Well: Nothing happened to me on the way to the White House."**

Campaign Pin for the Hollings
Presidential Campaign

Texas Governor: A Good Looking Rascal: In a 2011 address to the International Association of Firefighters in New York City, Bill Clinton made fun of the campaign announcement of Texas Governor Rick Perry for the Republican Presidential nomination: **"I got tickled by watching Governor Perry announce for president. He's a good-looking rascal. And he's saying 'Oh, I'm going to Washington to make sure that the federal government stays as far away from you as possible … while I ride on Air Force One and that Marine One helicopter and go to Camp David and travel around the world and have a good time.'"**

Rick Perry
Official Photograph

John Kerry the Comedian: In a 2004 Presidential debate, Democrat John Kerry joked: **"Being lectured by the President** [George W. Bush] **on fiscal responsibility is a little bit like Tony Soprano** [a mobster in the hit television program, *The Sopranos*] **talking to me about law and order in this country."**

John Kerry
Official Photograph

Hornblower: When President Jimmy Carter delivered his acceptance speech at the Democratic National Convention in 1980; he made a major faux pas. He was paying tribute to the late former Vice President Hubert Horatio Humphrey and mistakenly referred to him as: **"Hubert Horatio Hornblower Humphrey."** Humphrey's full name was Hubert Horatio Humphrey. Horatio Hornblower was a fictional character in novels by author Cecil Scott Forester.

Jimmy Carter (L) with Hubert Humphrey (R)
Library of Congress

71

Presidential Campaigns

If you Want to Become President, Stay Out of Arizona: In his failed 2000 bid for the Republican nomination for the Presidency, U.S. Senator John McCain (R-AZ) would often end his speeches with a poke at previous Presidential candidates from his home state of Arizona who lost their Presidential bids, including U.S. Senator Barry Goldwater, U.S. Representative Mo Udall, and Governor Bruce Babbitt. McCain would say: **"Arizona may be the only state where mothers don't tell their children they can grow up to be President. I want to change that."** McCain, like the aforementioned Arizonans, lost the Presidential election.

John McCain on the Cover of
Newsweek **Magazine**

Is Acting a Prerequisite to the Presidency? During the 1980 Presidential campaign, a reporter asked Republican Presidential nominee Ronald Reagan: **"How can an actor run for President?"** Reagan responded: **"How can a President not be an actor?"**

Ronald Reagan
Ronald Regan Presidential
Foundation and Library

Duke Takes On Mitt: In a 2012 forum with students at the University of California at Davis, former Massachusetts Governor Michael Dukakis did not have any kind words to say about Mitt Romney, one of his Gubernatorial successors who was the Republican Presidential nominee. Dukakis said of Romney: **"He's Smart, he's slick, he's a fraud, simple as that . . . I think he'd be a disaster in the White House. I'm trying to be as subtle as I possibly can here."**

Michael Dukakis
Official Photograph

No New Bombers! In 1968, during the height of the Vietnam War, George Wallace, the nominee of the American Independence Party, asked the following question: **"Why does the Air Force need expensive new bombers? Have the people we've been bombing over the years been complaining?"**

George Wallace
Library of Congress

Presidential Campaigns

The Best Way to Get From Boston to Oklahoma: In 1976, the Cab Drivers Union endorsed U.S. Senator Fred Harris (D-OK) in his bid for the Democratic Presidential nomination. Harris tells a story of a friend of his from Oklahoma who was visiting Massachusetts to campaign for Harris in the Massachusetts Primary. The friend saw that the cab driver had literature in the cab supporting Harris. The friend asked, **"Where's he from."** [Referring to Harris] The Cab Driver responded: **"Oklahoma."** The friend then jokingly asked: **"Where is Oklahoma?"** The Cab Driver responded: **"Well I think you go west on Commonwealth Avenue."**

Campaign Button for Cabbies for Fred Harris

Playing it Too Safe Can Be Dangerous: In 1948, Republican Presidential nominee Thomas E Dewey tried to sit on a comfortable lead by avoiding making controversial statements. One line he often used was: **"You know that your future is still ahead of you."** Dewey's future was that he lost the election in an historic upset to Democratic President Harry S. Truman.

Harry S. Truman (L), Thomas E. Dewey (R)
Harry S. Truman Library and Museum

Times are Tough: Speaking before a Chamber of Commerce Luncheon in Charleston, West Virginia during that state's heated 1960 Democratic Presidential primary, Robert F. Kennedy, the brother of candidate John F. Kennedy, said he was in the state **"to help my brother get a job."**

Robert F. Kennedy
Lyndon Baines Johnson Library and Museum

Kerry Digs Quayle: In a speech at the 2000 St. Patrick's Day Breakfast in South Boston, U.S. Senator John Kerry joked about Republican Presidential nominee George W. Bush. He quipped: **"A lot of people are asking whether Governor** [George W.] **Bush is smart enough to be President, and one of the most hurtful things is that** [Former Vice President] **Dan Quayle is one of those people."**

John Kerry
Official Photograph

Presidential Campaigns

Be Careful What You Wish For: New York Republican Party boss and U.S. Senator Thomas C. Platt, a rival of New York Governor Theodore Roosevelt, successfully urged the Republican Party to select Roosevelt as the running mate to President William McKinley in 1900. Platt did this to get Roosevelt out of the Governorship because Roosevelt was challenging the Platt political machine in New York. Platt thought that with Roosevelt gone, Lieutenant Governor Benjamin Barker Odell Jr. would become the Governor and would be more compliant to Platt's political machine. The thinking was that Roosevelt would be rendered inconsequential in that the Vice Presidency has little power. As circumstances would have it, President McKinley was assassinated in 1901, during the first year of his second term in office, and Roosevelt became president. Upon hearing the news, a shocked Platt exclaimed: **"Oh God, now that dammed cowboy is president of the United States."** To add insult to injury, Governor Odell following in the steps of Theodore Roosevelt, became a crusader for reform, shunning the Thomas C. Platt political machine.

Thomas C. Platt
Library of Congress

A Biting Zinger: During the 1988 Vice Presidential debate, Republican Dan Quayle suggested that he had more experience than John F. Kennedy had in 1960 when he was elected President. In what became one of the most remembered lines in Presidential debate history, the Democratic nominee Lloyd Bentsen deadpanned: **"Senator, I served with Jack Kennedy. Jack Kennedy was a friend of mine. Senator, you're no Jack Kennedy."** Quayle called the remark **"uncalled for."**

Lloyd Bentsen
Official Photograph

Comparing Politics to War and Mud Wrestling: Arguing for reforming the American Political system, 1996 Reform Party nominee H. Ross Perot observed: **"War has rules. Mud wrestling has rules. Politics has no rules."**

H. Ross Perot
U.S. Department of Veteran's Affairs

Presidential Campaigns

Presidential Candidate Declares he Won't Eat Like a Rabbit: In a 2007 interview with Tara Mckelvey, former Arkansas Governor Mike Huckabee, a candidate for the Republican Presidential nomination, was asked about losing 110 pounds. Huckabee responded: **"It isn't rocket science. Diets fail because you lose weight and then it's, 'Oh, thank goodness this is over.' I did every diet: Atkins. Cabbage-soup diet. Dean Ornish. But I couldn't live the rest of my life like a rabbit."**

Mike Huckabee
Official Photograph

Presidential Verbal Gaff: During a campaign rally in 1988, Republican Presidential nominee George H.W. Bush made the following malapropism: **"For seven and a half years I've worked alongside President Reagan. We've had triumphs. Made some mistakes. We've had some sex...uh...setbacks."**

George H.W. Bush
George Bush Presidential Library and Museum

You Don't Shoot Santa Clause: During the 1936 Presidential campaign, former New York Governor Al Smith supported Republican Presidential nominee Alfred Landon over his fellow Democrat, President Franklin D. Roosevelt. However, Smith thought that Roosevelt had won over many voters through his New Deal domestic programs. He conceded: **"You don't shoot Santa Clause."**

Franklin D. Roosevelt (L), Al Smith (R)
Franklin D. Roosevelt Presidential Library and Museum

Keeping It Simple: After the 1968 Presidential Election, Chicago Mayor Richard J. Daley was asked why Democratic Party Presidential nominee Hubert Humphrey did not win Illinois. Daley replied: **"He didn't get enough votes."**

Richard J. Daley
Official Photograph

Presidential Campaigns

Presidential and Vice Presidential Nominees Did Not Even Know Each Other: Before the days of Presidential primaries, Presidential nominees were selected at Party conventions. Vice Presidential nominees were also selected at the convention. Unlike today, the Presidential nominee did not select his runningmate. In 1876, Ohio Governor Rutherford B. Hayes secured the Republican Presidential nomination. Out of reverence to U.S. Senator Roscoe Conkling, (R-NY), the omnipotent Republican kingmaker, the Republican high command allowed the delegation of his home state to select the Vice Presidential nominee. They chose U.S. Representative William Wheeler (R-NY). Hayes had literally never even heard of his new Runningmate. Upon hearing that Wheeler had secured the Republican Nomination for Vice President, Ohio Governor Rutherford B. Hayes, replied: **"I am ashamed to say: 'Who is Wheeler?'"** The two became personal friends and once elected, Wheeler was a frequent guest of Hayes at social occasions.

Rutherford B. Hayes and William Wheeler
Presidential Campaign Poster
Library of Congress

In Dire Need of Drama: The 1924 Republican National Convention was essentially a coronation of President Calvin Coolidge. His Republican challenger, U.S. Senator Hiram Johnson (R-CA), had little chance. The lack of drama at the convention spawned Humorist Will Rogers, who was covering the convention as a Nationally syndicated columnist, to quip: **"The only excitement occurred when a delegate lost his hotel room key."**

Will Rogers
Library of Congress

Other-Worldly: During a 1984 debate of aspirants for the Democratic Presidential nomination, U.S. Senator John Glenn (D-OH) boasted of his role as an astronaut, to which U.S. Senator Ernest "Fritz" Hollings (D-SC) retorted: **"But What have you done in 'this' world?"**

Ernest "Fritz" Hollings
Official Photograph

Presidential Campaigns

Know the Fans, Not the Owners: In 2008, Republican Presidential candidate Mitt Romney was interviewed by Alabama Sports Talk Radio Host Paul Finebaum. Romney was asked his thoughts on the possibility that quarterback Peyton Manning could be traded to the Denver Broncos. Romney's response was: **"Well, you know I'm surprised to hear that Denver's thinking about him. They're — I don't want him in our neck of the woods** [New England]. **Let's put it that way. I don't want him to go to Miami or to the Jets. But I've got a lot of good friends, the owner Miami Dolphins, and the New York Jets — both owners are friends of mine."**

Mitt Romney
Official Photograph

Profound: Speaking at a campaign rally in Troy, Ohio in 1988, less than a month before the General Election, Republican Vice Presidential nominee George H.W. Bush told the crowd: **"It's no exaggeration to say the undecided's could go one way or another."**

George H.W. Bush on Campaign Trail in 1988
George Bush Presidential Library

Living in a Bubble: In a lecture to the Modern Language Association, just subsequent to the 1972 Presidential election, Pauline Keel, a film critic for *The New Yorker Magazine* and a resident of Berkeley, California, told the audience: **"I live in a rather special world. I only know one person who voted for** [Republican Richard M.] **Nixon. Where they are I don't know. They're outside my kin. But sometimes when I'm in a theater I can feel them."**

Pauline Kael on the Cover of her Autobiography, *Pauline Kael: A Life In The Dark*

Learning Spanish the Hard Way: In 2012, Former New Hampshire Governor John H. Sununu handled questions at a Spanish-language news conference at the Republican National Convention. After the press conference Sununu told Mark Finkelstein of *Newsbusters.org* how he became fluent in Spanish. Sununu's mother, Victoria Dada, was born in El Salvador. Sununu said: **"As a boy, when I was bad, my mother would chew me out in Spanish. And since I was bad a lot, I learned a lot of Spanish!"**

John H. Sununu
Official Portrait

Presidential Campaigns

Weird Admission: In 1995, speaking at a Clinton campaign fundraiser in Houston, Bill Clinton, in referring to the Budget Reconciliation Act that he signed in 1993 (which raised taxes on Americans earning more that $200,000 a year), told the well-healed donors: **"Probably there are people in this room still mad at me at that budget because you think I raised your taxes too much. It might surprise you to know that I think I raised them too much, too."**

Bill Clinton
William J. Clinton Presidential Library
and Museum

Tough Time with Numbers: As he ended a speech at Saint Anslem College in Manchester, New Hampshire, Republican Presidential candidate Rick Perry, assuming he would win the nomination, told the young audience: **"Those of you that will be 21 by November the 12th, I ask for your support and your vote. Those of you who won't be, work hard."** The problem is that the legal voting age is 18, not 21, and the election is November 6, not November 12.

Rick Perry on the Cover of *Parade Magazine*

Indian Throws Support for Biden: While exploring a Presidential run in 2006, then U.S. Senator Joe Biden (D-DE) was approached by an Indian-American who informed Biden that he was supporting him. Biden answered: **"In Delaware, the largest growth in population is Indian-Americans moving from India. You cannot go to a 7-11 or a Dunkin Donuts unless you have a slight Indian accent. I'm not joking."**

Joe Biden
Official Photograph

Mississippi Men Don't Cook: In 1984, Democratic Vice Presidential nominee Geraldine Ferraro was the first woman to be placed on a National Ticket by a major political party. She was asked by Mississippi Agricultural Secretary Jim Buck Ross, **"Can you bake a blueberry muffin?"** Ferraro replied: **"Sure can. Can you?"** Ross responded: **"Down here in Mississippi the men don't cook."**

Geraldine Ferraro
Official Photograph

Presidential Campaigns

Rum, Romanticism, and Rebellion: A few days before the 1884 Presidential election, Republican Presidential nominee James G. Blaine made a campaign appearance in New York. At this event, Presbyterian Minister Samuel Burchard, a Blaine supporter, excoriated the Democrats as the Party of: **"Rum, Romanticism, and Rebellion."** Blaine sat silently during this tirade and made no effort to disassociate himself from these volatile remarks. Unfortunately for the unsuspecting Blaine, many Irish voters took umbrage by the use of the word **"rum,"** believing that the Minister was perpetuating a stereotype that Irish-Americans (who were mostly Democrats) were alcoholics. This galvanized the Irish vote against Blaine in the swing state of New York, where Democrat Grover Cleveland eked out a razor-thin victory, defeating Blaine by just 1,047 votes. New York proved to be the state that made the electoral difference in a very close Presidential election.

James G. Blaine
Library of Congress

Being Blunt: At the funeral of his former Chief of Staff Tom D'Amore, former U.S Senator Lowell Weicker (R-CT), a liberal Republican, told the story of D'Amore meeting with a local editor in New Hampshire telling him about a possible bid by Weicker for the Republican Presidential nomination in 1980. Weicker went on to say that the editor told D'Amore: **"Mr. D'Amore, let me tell you something. We got Communists here in New Hampshire, and believe me, 'our' Communists don't even like your Communists."**

Lowell Weicker
Official Photograph

In Defense of the Three-Martini Lunch: In 1976, Democratic Presidential nominee Jimmy Carter charged that: **"The working class was subsidizing the $50 martini lunch."** His opponent in the race, President Gerald R. Ford (after loosing the election), told the National Restaurant Association: **"The three-martini lunch is the epitome of American efficiency. Where else can you get an earful, a bellyful and a spoonful at the same time?"**

A Three-Martini-Lunch
Photograph by Hayford Peirce

Presidential Campaigns

Someone Needs To Do Her American History Homework: In 2011, Republican Presidential aspirant Michele Bachmann spoke to a crowd in Concord, New Hampshire. In the address, she said: **"You're the state where the shot was heard around the world at Lexington and Concord, and you put a marker in the ground and paid with the blood of your ancestors."** She was referring to the first shot fired during the Revolutionary War, which did not happen in Concord New Hampshire, but in Concord, Massachusetts.

Michele Bachmann
Official Photograph

Radios and Doorknobs: During the 1928 Presidential election, radio became an essential tool for candidates to use to reach a wide audience. Republican nominee Herbert Hoover reluctantly used the medium, although he did not like it. When he was asked if he got a thrill from speaking on radio, Hoover replied: **"The same thrill I get when I rehearse an address to a doorknob."**

Herbert Hoover
Herbert Hoover Presidential Library and Museum

Deceptive Dirty Tricks: After the first Presidential debate between Democrat John F. Kennedy and Republican Richard M. Nixon, Democratic Strategist and political prankster Dick Tuck hired an elderly woman to wear a Nixon button and embrace Kennedy in front of TV cameras. She said, **"Don't worry, son! He beat you last night, but you'll get him next time."**

John F. Kennedy and Richard M. Nixon
Richard M. Nixon Foundation

Partisanship Gone Wild: During the 1976 Vice Presidential Debate, Republican Bob Dole asserted that all major wars in the Twentieth Century were started by Democratic Presidents: **"I figured it up the other day: If we added up the killed and wounded in Democrat wars in this century, it would be about 1.6 million Americans — enough to fill the city of Detroit."** Dole later said he regretted making this remark.

Walter Mondale (L), Bob Dole (R) Debating
Gerald R. Ford Library and Museum

Presidential Campaigns

Nice Problem to Have: In an interview with *Politico,* Republican Presidential nominee John McCain was asked how many houses he and his wife Cindy owned? He could not come up with an answer. He said: **"I think — I'll have my staff get to you. It's condominiums where — I'll have them get to you."** In the aggregate, the couple owned seven properties.

John McCain
Official Photograph

Thee Efficient Use of Nuclear Weapons: In 1968, at a press conference announcing that American Independent Party nominee George Wallace had selected General Curtis Lemay as his Vice Presidential runningmate, Jack Nelson of *The Los Angeles Times* asked Lemay if nuclear weapons would be necessary to win the war in Vietnam. Lemay bellicosely responded: **"We can win this war without nuclear weapons."** However, he then added, **"But I have to say, we have a phobia about nuclear weapons. I think there may be times when it would be most efficient to use nuclear weapons."**

General Curtis Lemay
National Museum of the U.S. Air Force

Madonna's Base Guitar Player: When asked on ABC's *This week* if he thought Republican Presidential nominee apparent Mitt Romney would ask him to be his Vice Presidential runningmate in 2012, former Arkansas Governor Mike Huckabee replied: **"I think there is greater likelihood that I'll be asked by Madonna to go on tour as her base player than I'll be picked to be on the ticket."**

Mike Huckabee
Official Portrait

Even Anarchists Qualify For Discounts: Before the start of the 2004 Republican National Convention in New York City, Mayor Michael Bloomberg said he welcomed the protesters who would descend upon his city. He even said protestors who sport badges reading: "Peaceful Activist" will qualify for hotel and restaurant discounts. Bloomberg said at a Press Conference: **"Its no fun to protest on an empty stomach . . . . They will still get a discount, even the anarchists."**

Michael Bloomberg
Official Photograph

Presidential Campaigns

Hell Raiser: In June of 1996, Republican Presidential candidate Pat Buchanan was disallowed from attending the Washington State Republican Convention because he did not endorse the prospective nominee, former U.S. Senate Majority Leader Bob Dole (R-KS). Accordingly, Buchanan held a convention of his own with his supporters in San Diego and stated: **"We're going to fight until Hell freezes over. You all come down to San Diego** [Where the Republican National Convention was scheduled to be held] **and bring your ice skates."**

Pat Buchanan on the Cover of *Time* *Magazine*

Small-Town Mayor Takes on Community Organizer: In her 2008 speech accepting the Republican nomination for Vice President, Sarah Palin referred to her days as Mayor of Wasilla, Alaska, and compared this experience with Democratic Presidential nominee Barack Obama's days as a community organizer. Palin said sarcastically: **"I guess a small-town mayor is sort of like a community organizer, except that you have actual responsibilities."**

Sarah Palin Speaking at the 2008 Republican National Convention
Photograph by T toes

Maine is Not Always a Good Barometer: Up Until 1957, Maine held its Gubernatorial and Congressional elections in September. During Presidential years, the state became a bellwether for the pending election in November. If the state voted for a member of one party for Governor, the thinking was that the nation would vote for the Presidential nominee of the same party in the Presidential election. In 1936, Maine voted overwhelmingly for Republican candidates in the September election. However, in the Presidential election, only Maine and staunchly Republican Vermont voted for the Republican nominee Alfred Landon over Democrat Franklin D. Roosevelt. James Farley, the Postmaster General, and Roosevelt's campaign manager joked: **"As Maine Goes, So Goes Vermont."**

James Farley
Official Photograph

Leaches and Insurance Companies: During a 2004 Presidential campaign speech in De Moines, Iowa, Dennis Kucinich said: **"Many years ago doctors would bleed patients with leeches. Today, the insurance companies do that."**

Dennis Kucinich
Official Photograph

Presidential Campaigns

Is it "Ditch?" In 1984, Barbara Bush, the wife of Vice President George H. W. Bush, was asked by *The New York Times* to give her opinion of Bush's opponent for re-election, Democratic Vice Presidential nominee Geraldine Ferraro (D-NY). Mrs. Bush responded: **"I can't say it, but it rhymes with 'rich.'"**

Barbara Pierce Bush
George Bush Presidential Library and Museum

Words in the Margin Not Meant to Be Uttered: Campaigning for a full term in 1976, Gerald R. Ford mistakenly read words in the margin of his speech ("with emphasis"): **"I say to you this is nonsense with emphasis!"**

Gerald R. Ford
Gerald R. Ford Presidential Library and Museum

We Are Eggheads, Hear us Roar: In 1952, the Democratic Presidential nominee, Adlai Stevenson, was derided by his critics as too much of an intellectual. They chided him as an "egghead." Stevenson wore that moniker with pride, declaring: **"Eggheads of the world unite, you have nothing to lose but your yolks."**

Adlai Stevenson
Library of Congress

Presidential Candidate Gets Humbled, Big Time: In 1975, Democratic Presidential candidate Mo Udall walked into a barbershop to greet residents. He said: **"I'm Mo Udall, and I'm running for President.** The barber looked back at him and retorted: **"Yeah, I know, we were just laughing about that yesterday."**

Campaign Pin supporting Mo Udall for President

Presidential Campaigns

William Jennings Bryan finally gets it: In 1908, after losing the Presidency for a third time, Democratic nominee William Jennings Bryan deadpanned: **"I'm beginning to think those fellows don't want me in there."**

William Jennings Bryan
Library of Congress

This Buds For Newt: In 2011 there was a mass exodus of campaign consultants from Newt Gingrich's presidential campaign. The campaign was overspending. As one of the advisors, David Carney, explained the situation: **"We were living a Cadillac campaign on a Bud Light budget."**

Newt Gingrich
Official Portrait

Ouch: In 2008, during a commercial break, while being interviewed on *Fox News*, the Reverend Jesse Jackson made the following off-hand comment about Democratic Presidential nominee Barack Obama **"See, Barrack's been talking down to black people on this faith-based...I want to cut his nuts off."** Unbeknownst to Jackson, the microphone was still on.

Jesse Jackson
Library of Congress

From George W. to George W: In his speech accepting the Republican Party's Presidential nomination in Philadelphia in 2000, George W. Bush paid homage to the city for hosting the Constitutional Convention in 1787. He exclaimed: **"Ben Franklin was here. Thomas Jefferson. And, of course, George Washington -- or, as his friends called him: "George W."**

George W. Bush
White House Photograph by Eric Draper

Presidential Campaigns

Big Time Open Microphone: At a campaign rally in Naperville, Illinois in 2000, where the Republican nominees for President and Vice President (George W. Bush and Dick Cheney) were on the podium waving to the assembled crowd and getting ready to speak, Cheney noticed Adam Clymer of *The New York Times* with other member of the press in the crowd. Cheney said to Bush: **"There's Adam Clymer, Major League Asshole from *The New York Times*."** Bush responded: **"Oh yeah, he is, big time."** Unbeknownst to them, the microphone picked up the conversation and it became front-page news. The reason Bush and Cheney had such a negative view of Clymer is that he wrote an article concluding that Cheney donated just 1% of the money he had earned in the energy industry to charity.

Dick Cheney and George W. Bush
White House Photograph by David Bohrer

Finally, Some Downtime: In his 1996 concession speech, failed Republican Presidential nominee Bob Dole told the crowd of assembled supporters: **"Tomorrow will be the first time in my life I don't have anything to do."**

Bob Dole
Robert J. Dole Archive and Special Collections

Well, Ok: During a speech in Dodge, Iowa in 1952, Democratic Presidential nominee Adlai Stevenson, in referring to the campaign of his Republican opponent, Dwight D. Eisenhower, told the audience: **"The Republicans have a 'me too' candidate running on a 'yes but' platform, advised by a 'has-been' staff."**

Adlai Stevenson
Library of Congress

At least he's Honest: In 1940, U.S. Senator Arthur Vandenberg (R-MI) ran for the Presidency by campaigning for delegates at the Republican National Convention. He did not participate in the Republican primaries, viewing them as inconsequential. He said: **"Imagine killing yourself for Vermont."** Vandenberg lost the nomination to fellow Republican Wendell Willkie.

Arthur Vandenberg
Official Photograph

85

Presidential Campaigns

President Vows to Whip Senator's Ass: In 1979 President Jimmy Carter told a gathering of Democratic members of the U.S. Congress that if U.S. Senator Ted Kennedy were to challenge him for the Democratic Party nomination for President, **"I'll whip his ass."** When Kennedy was told of this comment, he retorted: **"I always knew the White House would stand behind me, but I didn't realize how close they would be."** Kennedy did challenge Carter, and lost.

Ted Kennedy (L), Jimmy Carter (R)
The National Archives and
Records Administration

Roosevelt Plays Both the Weight and Castrated Rooster Cards: During the last days of the 1932 Presidential campaign, Democratic Presidential nominee Franklin D. Roosevelt referred to his Republican opponent, Herbert Hoover, as a: **"fat, timid capon."**

Herbert Hoover (L)
Franklin D. Roosevelt (R)
Franklin D. Roosevelt
Presidential Library and Museum

He May have Been Right, But He Was Never President: In 1839, U.S. Senator Henry Clay (Whig-KY) tried to stick to the middle of the road on the contentious issue of slavery. His position did not propitiate Northerners who thought Clay was sympathetic to the institution of slavery, nor Southerners who thought Clay was an opponent of Slavery. Yet Clay intransigently held to his centrist position. Clay maintained: **"I would rather be right than President."** Clay had been the Presidential nominee of the Democratic-Republican Party in 1824 and the nominee of the National Republican Party in 1832. He still harbored Presidential ambitions, and was nominated by the Whig Party in 1844. He lost, making Clay, along with Democrat William Jennings Bryan, the only two candidates to be nominated by a major political party three times and to lose all three Presidential races.

Henry Clay
Library of Congress

Presidential Campaigns

Starting a Fight: While campaigning for U.S. Representative Patrick Kennedy (D-RI), Bill Clinton took a shot at Republican nominee-apparent George W. Bush. He told the crowd: **"Nearest I can tell, the message of the Bush campaign is: 'How bad can I be? I've been governor of Texas, my daddy was president, I own a baseball team.'"** George H. W. Bush was offended by the attack on his son, and responded: **"I'm going to wait a month. If he continues like that, then you [The Media] give me a call - I'll give you the home number - and I'm going to tell the nation what I think about him as a person."** George W. Bush said: **"I welcome the criticism. It's amazing that the President of the United States would spend time trying to be a political pundit. He's so desperate to have his legacy intact by getting Al Gore elected that he'll say anything."** Clinton later became friends with both George H. W. Bush and George W. Bush.

George W. Bush (L), Bill Clinton (R)
William J. Clinton Presidential Library

Foreign Policy Experience?: During a 2007 interview with Radio Talk Show Host Don Imus, Republican Presidential candidate Mike Huckabee quipped: **"I may not be the expert as some people on foreign policy, but I did stay at a Holiday Inn Express Last night."**

Holiday Inn Express Logo

Cheney Shows a Sense of Humor: During the 2000 Vice Presidential debate in Danville, Kentucky, Democratic nominee Joe Lieberman joked about how most of the country is better off now than they were four years ago and then said to Cheney (Who made a fortune as the CEO of Halliburton and was awarded a $34 million retirement package): **"I know, Dick, that you're better off than you were 8 years ago too."** Cheney opined: **And I can tell you, Joe, that the government had absolutely nothing to do with it."** Lieberman responded: **"I can tell my wife is out there, she wants me to go out in the private sector."** Cheney replied: **"I'm trying to get you there Joe."**

Dick Cheney
White House Photograph by David Bohrer

Serious Condition: U.S. Senator George Aiken (R-VT) saw many of his colleagues run for President during his 34 years in the U.S. Senate. Senator Aiken observed: **"When the Presidential bug gets into your veins, the only thing that will get it out is embalming fluid."**

George Aiken
Official Photograph

Presidential Campaigns

Watch Who You Praise: In 1920, Franklin D. Roosevelt, who at the time was U.S. Assistant Secretary of the Navy, praised Herbert Hoover for his role as U.S. Food Administrator during WWI. **"He Certainly is a wonder, and I wish we could make him President. There couldn't be a better one."** Hoover went on to become President in 1929 and lost his re-election bid in 1932, ironically to Roosevelt.

Herbert Hoover and Franklin D. Roosevelt
Library of Congress

Damage Control: Presidential Candidate Banishes Runningmate to Southeast Asia: At an appearance at Yale University in 1968, Independence Party Vice Presidential nominee Curtis Lemay was asked about the issue of population growth. He called himself: **"a warmonger in the battle against the dissipation of our natural resources."** He then suggested he favored abortion as a means of birth control, proclaiming: **"This view was contrary to the view of his Presidential runningmate George Wallace."** To get the gaffe-prone, politically tone-deaf Lemay out of the news, the Wallace campaign sent him on a "fact finding mission" to Vietnam.

Curtis Lemay
Official Photograph

The Presidency Is No Big Deal: In the 1900 Presidential election, Democratic activists convinced the enormously popular U.S. Navy Admiral George Dewey to seek the Democratic Presidential nomination. The Admiral was fresh from victory in the Spanish-American War. However, Dewey's candidacy imploded when he said publicly: **"I am convinced that the office of the President is not such a very difficult one to fill."**

Admiral George Dewey
Library of Congress

Candidate Asks Heckler to Kiss His Ass: When Democratic Presidential nominee George McGovern was harassed by a heckler in Battle Creek, Michigan, he whispered in his ear: **"Listen, you son of a bitch, why don't you kiss my ass."** His supporters then manufactured campaign buttons with the acronym "KMA" emblazoned on them. U.S. Senator James Eastland (D-MS) later told McGovern: **"That was the best line in the campaign."**

George McGovern
Library of Congress

Presidential Campaigns

Ready to Rumble: In 1988, Vice President George H. W. Bush was sitting next to NBC news anchorman Tom Brokaw in New York City. Dole was interviewed by satellite from New Hampshire. The two were on the air at the same time. Brokaw asked Bush if he had anything to say to Dole. Bush responded: **"No, just wish him well and [we'll] meet again in the South."** Brokaw then asked Dole if he had anything to say to Bush. Dole was inflamed by an advertisement the Bush campaign was running accusing him of "straddling on taxes." Dole responded: **"Yeah, tell him to stop lying about my record."**

Bob Dole (L), George H. W. Bush (R)
Robert J. Dole Archives and Special Collections

Diaper Dewey: In 1940, Manhattan District Attorney Thomas E. Dewey was the early frontrunner in the race for the Republican Presidential nomination. However, he was only 36-years-old. When the young Dewey declared his candidacy, U.S. Interior Secretary Harold Ickies quipped: **"Dewey has thrown his diapers into the ring."** Dewey lost the nomination to Wendell Willkie.

Thomas E. Dewey
Library of Congress

Creative Use of the Trilogy Technique: As the Republican Presidential nominee in 1980, Ronald Reagan galvanized his conservative base with the following memorable line used against his main opponent President Jimmy Carter: **"A recession is when your neighbor looses his job, a depression is when you lose yours. A recovery is when Jimmy Carter loses his."**

Jimmy Carter (L), Ronald Reagan (R)
Jimmy Carter Presidential Library and Museum

Money is the Mother's Milk of Politics: U.S. Senator Mark Hanna (R-OH) managed William McKinley's successful bid for the Presidency in 1896. McKinley wildly outspent his Democratic opponent William Jennings Bryan. Hanna commented after the campaign: **"There are two things that are important in politics. The first is money and I can't remember what the second one is."**

Mark Hanna
Library of Congress

Presidential Campaigns

The Pope's Son? In 1928, Franklin D. Roosevelt, the Democratic nominee for Governor of New York and a supporter of New York Governor Al Smith's bid for the Presidency, received a letter from a voter saying she had heard that **"If Governor Smith is elected president, the Pope's son will be his secretary."**

Al Smith (L), Franklin D. Roosevelt (R)
Franklin D. Roosevelt Presidential Library and Museum

Fly Swatter Politics: In a campaign speech in Ames Iowa in 1976, President Gerald R. Ford mocked statements by his Democratic opponent Jimmy Carter. Carter had said he would cut the nation's defense budget. Ford told the crowd: **"Teddy Roosevelt once said, 'Speak softly and carry a big stick.' Jimmy Carter wants to speak loudly and carry a fly swatter."**

Jimmy Carter (L), Gerald R. Ford (R)
Gerald R. Ford Presidential Library and Museum

President Calls Opponents "Bozos:" At a 1992 campaign rally in Warren, Michigan, President George H.W. Bush lashed out at his Democratic opponents Bill Clinton and Al Gore exclaiming: **"My dog Millie knows more about foreign affairs than these two bozos."** Bush lost the election.

Millie
George Bush Presidential Library and Museum

Kemp Bashes Dole's Intellectual Prowess: U.S. Representative Jack Kemp (R-NY) was an arch adversary of U.S. Senator Bob Dole (R-KS). This was exhibited in 1988 when the two men were candidates for the Republican Presidential nomination. Kemp said of Dole: **"When his library burned down, it destroyed both books. He hadn't finished coloring in the second."** In 1996, Dole selected Kemp as his Vice Presidential Runningmate.

Campaign button for the Dole-Kemp Campaign

90

Presidential Campaigns

Newt Garners Endorsement From Inside Federal Penitentiary: In 2012, Republican Presidential candidate Newt Gingrich mustered the endorsement of a former colleague, former U.S. Representative Randy "Duke" Cunningham (R-CA). Cunningham made his endorsement from the Federal Penitentiary in Tucson, Arizona, where he was serving time for federal charges of conspiracy to commit bribery, mail fraud, tax evasion, and wire fraud. Cunningham said **"Newt, a voice out of the past. Down but not out and still fighting. First I do not want anything from you but have been watching the debates. I have 80% of inmates that would vote for you. They might not be able to but their extended families will."**

**United States Penitentiary
Tucson, Arizona**
Federal Bureau of Prisons

No More Mister Nice Guy: During a 2003 Democratic Presidential debate, moderator George Stephanopoulos asked candidate Joe Lieberman if he was too nice to take on George W. Bush in the General election. Lieberman quipped: **"I'd like to come over and strangle you George."**

Joe Lieberman
Official Photograph

Senator Eagleton's Secret Statements: In 1972, as liberal insurgent U.S. Senator George McGovern (D-SD) was winning vital Democratic Presidential Primaries, many establishment Democrats were worried that if McGovern were to garner the nomination, his liberal views would lead to an electoral landslide for Republican President Richard M. Nixon. This would bring other Democrats down with him. One of McGovern's Senate Colleagues, Thomas Eagleton, revealed to Columnist Robert Novak (as an undisclosed source): **"The people don't know McGovern is for amnesty, abortion and legalization of pot. Once Middle America - Catholic Middle America, in particular - finds this out, he's dead. Amnesty, Acid, and Abortion."** Once McGovern mustered the nomination, his opponents called McGovern the candidate of: **"Amnesty, Acid, and Abortion."** Without knowing that Eagleton was the originator of that quote, McGovern selected Eagleton to be his running mate. After just 18 days on the ticket, McGovern bowed to public pressure to "Dump Eagleton" when it was revealed that Eagleton had gone through electroshock therapy to cure a bout of clinical depression. Nixon would go on to trounce McGovern in the General Election. Novak did not reveal the source of the quote until 2008, after Eagleton's death.

Campaign Button for the short-lived George McGovern-Thomas Eagleton Campaign

Presidential Campaigns

No Room at the Holiday Inn: After flirting with a run for the Democratic Presidential nomination in 1976, U.S. Senator Walter Mondale (D-MN) decided not to pursue the nomination. He said it was because: **"I don't want to spend the next few years at Holiday Inns."** However, as luck would have it, Mondale was chosen by the eventual nominee, former Georgia Governor Jimmy Carter, as his Vice Presidential runningmate.

Walter Mondale
Official Photograph

A Splintered Party: The 1924 Democratic National Convention in New York City proved a divisive affair, with a resolution to condemn the Ku Klux Klan rejected by one vote. Unable to agree on a nominee, the convention issued 103 ballots until choosing former U.S. Solicitor General John W. Davis as their Presidential nominee. The humorist Will Rogers observed: **"New York had invited the delegates as visitors, not to live there."** He also observed: **"I belong to no organized party, I am a Democrat."**

Will Rogers
Library of Congress

Tweeter, Twitter, Lets call the whole thing off: In 2012, Republican Presidential candidate Rick Perry mistakenly referred to the social networking site "Twitter" as "Tweeter" in a videotaped message to a crowd of conservative bloggers and social networkers in Minneapolis: **"You can always follow me on Tweeter."**

Rick Perry
Official Photograph

Japan Won the Cold War? At a campaign event with voters at the Episcopal Church in Lewiston Maine in 1992, Democratic Presidential candidate Paul Tsongas argued jokingly that Japan was the real winner in the Cold War. He told the voters: **"The Cold War is over. Japan Won."** Tsongas was referring to the fact that the Japanese automotive industry was on the rise while the U.S. auto industry was experiencing a nosedive.

Pin from the 1992 Paul Tsongas for President Campaign

Presidential Campaigns

The Right to Drink Raw Milk: Running for the 2012 GOP Presidential nomination on a Libertarian message of Personal Freedom, U.S. Representative Ron Paul (R-TX) told a crowd at the Peterborough, New Hampshire Town Hall: **"I would like to restore your right to drink raw milk anytime you like."**

Ron Paul
Official Photograph

Taking on the Hippies: In 1968, when George Wallace, the nominee of the American Party, was heckled by young hippies, he responded: **"You come up when I get through and I'll autograph your sandals for you. That is, if you got any on. . . . You need a good haircut. That's all that's wrong with you . . . . There are two four-letter words I bet you folks don't know: work and soap."** He got an uproarious ovation from his mostly blue color supporters in the crowd.

George Wallace
Library of Congress

Linguistic Legerdemain: During a debate in the 1988 race for the Democratic Presidential nomination, U.S. Representative Richard Gephardt (D-MO) turned to U.S. Senator Al Gore (D-TN) and tried to blast him for moving to the right to secure Southern votes. Gephardt said: **"When you started this race, you decided you needed a Southern political strategy. So you decided that you'd better move to the right on defense and [on] a lot of other issues. And lately you've been sounding more like Al Haig than Al Gore."** (Al Haig was U.S. Secretary of State in the Reagan administration and was also a GOP Republican Presidential Candidate). Without missing a beat, Gore said: **"That line sounds more like Richard Nixon than Richard Gephardt."**

Bumper sticker from the 1988 Presidential Campaign of Al Gore

Kerry Compares His Candidacy to Bobsled Team: In his 1992 address announcing he was dropping out of the race for the Democratic Presidential nomination, U.S. Senator Bob Kerry (D-NE) said: **"I feel a little like the Jamaican bobsled team. We had a lot of spirit, but unfortunately, we didn't get a lot of medals."**

Jamaican Bobsled Team Insignia

Presidential Campaigns

Truman Disses Kennedy: Former U.S. President Harry S. Truman supported U.S. Senator Stuart Symington (D-MO) in his bid for the Democratic Presidential nomination in 1960. Truman urged U.S. Senator John F. Kennedy (D-MA) to reconsider his bid for the nomination. Truman stated publicly about Kennedy: **"I have no doubt about the political heights that you are destined to rise, but I am deeply troubled about the situation we are up against in the world now and in the immediate future. That is why I hope someone with the greatest possible maturity and experience may be available at this time. May I urge you to be patient?"** Truman maintained that the Democratic National Convention was manipulated so that Kennedy would muster the nomination. In protest, Truman refused to attend the Convention as a delegate. When asked whom he would support if Symington lost the nomination, Truman deadpanned: **"I have no second choice."** Once Kennedy secured the nomination, Truman became a loyal foot soldier, barnstorming the country campaigning for Kennedy.

John F. Kennedy (L), Harry S. Truman (R)
Harry S. Truman Library and Museum

Linguistic Creativity: In 1976, members of the media were saying that the Iowa caucuses would **"winnow out'** candidates who perform poorly. U.S. Senator Fred Harris (D-OK), who was not considered a leading candidate for the Democratic Presidential nomination, outperformed expectations by finishing in fourth place. Harris thus one-upped the media, and in the process coined the following term: **"winnowing in."** Harris told the media: **"The winnowing-out process has begun and we have just been 'winnowed in.'"**

Fred Harris
Official Photograph

Truman Chides Dewey: In a speech in Phoenix, Republican Presidential nominee Thomas E. Dewey asserted: **"America's future, like yours in Arizona, is still ahead of us."** His Democratic opponent, Harry S. Truman, chided Dewey for making this remark. During a campaign address in New York City, Truman said: **"Well I hope the future will last a long time for all of you, and I hope it will be a very happy future – and I hope it won't be a future under Republicans, either."**

Harry S. Truman and Thomas E. Dewey Shaking Hands
Harry S. Truman Library and Museum

94

Presidential Campaigns

John McCain and the Beach Boys: During a 2007 campaign appearance in Murrells, South Carolina, Republican Presidential candidate John McCain was asked by an audience member: **"When do we send them an airmail message to Tehran?"** McCain began singing: **"That old Beach Boys song, Bomb Iran, Bomb – Bomb -- Bomb."** The actual name of the song was "Barbara Ann."

John McCain
Official Photograph

Not a Good Start: At a 2008 ceremony in Springfield, Illinois, Democratic nominee-apparent Barack Obama announced that he has chosen U.S. Senator Joe Biden as his choice for a Vice Presidential running mate. Senator Biden then said of Obama: **"One man stands ready to deliver change we desperately need. A man I'm proud to call my friend. A man who will be the next president of the United States, Barack 'America.'"**

Joe Biden
Official Photograph

Did I Say That? During the 1976 Presidential debate between Republican Gerald R. Ford and Democrat Jimmy Carter, Max Frankel of *The New York Times* suggested that because of The Helsinki Accords: **"The Russians have dominance in Eastern Europe."** Ford mendaciously asserted: **"There is no Soviet domination over Eastern Europe and there never will be under a Ford administration."** Frankel gave Ford a chance to correct his misstatement, but instead Ford doubled-down, exclaiming: **"I don't believe Mr. Frankle that the Yugoslavians consider themselves dominated by the Soviet Union. I don't believe that the Romanians consider themselves dominated by the Soviet Union. I don't believe that the Poles consider themselves dominated by the Soviet Union. Each of those countries is independent, autonomous. It has its own territorial integrity and the United States does not concede that those countries are under the domination of the Soviet Union."** After this statement, the President's team went into damage control mode and asserted that the President simply meant that the U.S. would never recognize Soviet control of Eastern Europe. But the damage was done, and this gaffe was one of the reasons Ford lost this razor-thin election.

**Jimmy Carter (L) and Gerald R. Ford (R)
at the 1976 Presidential Debate**
Executive Office of the President

Presidential Campaigns

No Hedging Here: In 1964, Republican Presidential nominee Barry Goldwater justified his selection of Republican Party Chairman and U.S. Representative William E. Miller (R-NY) as his Vice Presidential Runningmate by telling reporters: **"One of the reason I chose Miller is that he drives** [President Lyndon B.] **Johnson nuts."**

William E. Miller
Official Photograph

What are You Saying Hubert? In a 1968 interview with *Playboy Magazine,* Democratic Presidential Nominee Vice President Hubert Humphrey, in defending the policies of the administration of President Lyndon B, Johnson in Vietnam, stated: **"No sane person in the country likes the war in Vietnam and neither does President Johnson."**

Lyndon B. Johnson (L)
Hubert Humphrey (R)
Lyndon Baines Johnson Library and Museum

Sad But True: While delivering the Keynote Address at the 1948 Democratic National Convention, U.S. Senator Alben Barkley (D-KY) said: **"What is a Bureaucrat? A bureaucrat is a Democrat who holds an office a Republican wants."** This keynote address captivated the audience and Barkley was nominated as the Vice Presidential nominee with President Harry S. Truman.

Alben Barkley
Harry S. Truman Library and Museum

Three Letter Word, J-O-B-S: In 2008, Democratic Vice Presidential nominee Joe Biden, in referring to Republican Presidential nominee John McCain, told an Athens, Ohio audience: **"Look, John's last-minute economic plan does nothing to tackle the number one job facing the middle class, and it happens to be, as Barack** [Obama] **says, a three-letter word: jobs. J-O-B-S."**

Joe Biden
Official Photograph

Presidential Campaigns

Way Too Much Information: As a guest on MSNBC's *Morning Joe* in 2008, Republican Presidential candidate Mike Huckabee told an offbeat story: **"When we were in college we used to take a popcorn popper -- because that was the only thing they would let us have in the dorms -- and fry squirrels in the popcorn popper."**

Mike Huckabee
Photograph by Greg Michaud

Where George McGovern's Energy Came From: During the 1972 Presidential campaign, Actress Shirley MacLaine asked Democratic Presidential candidate George McGovern why he: **"never gets tired."** McGovern's response was: **"The secret is telling the truth. If you always tell the truth you don't have to use up energy trying to remember what you said in other places."**

Shirley MacLaine
Movie Photograph

Hunting Tale: In 2007, Republican Presidential aspirant Mitt Romney told a voter: **"I purchased a gun when I was a young man. I've been a hunter pretty much all my life."** It was later revealed that Romney had only hunted twice in his life. Romney later said: **"I'm not a big-game hunter. I've made that very clear. I've always been a rodent and rabbit hunter. Small varmints, if you will."**

Mitt Romney
Official Photograph

A Talking Horse and a Charismatically Challenged Presidential Candidate: 1988 Democratic Presidential candidate Bruce Babbitt's television appearances were flat and uncharismatic. However, he worked on trying to improve his charisma by reviewing his past television performances. He told the *New York Times*: **"If they can teach Mr. Ed to talk on television, they can teach me."** (*Mr. Ed* was a 1950s TV sitcom featuring a talking horse.)

Bruce Babbitt
Official Photograph as Governor of Arizona

Presidential Campaigns

McCain States He Will Veto Beer: When showing his seriousness about eliminating earmarks, 2008 Republican Presidential nominee John McCain declared: **"I will veto every single beer."** He meant to say he will veto every **"bill."**

John McCain
Official Photograph

I'm Easy: In 1995, Republican Presidential candidate Bob Dole, knowing how much Republicans revere former President Ronald Reagan, told a Republican crowd: **"I'll be another Ronald Reagan if that's what you want me to be."**

Ronald Regan (R) with Bob Dole (L)
Robert J. Dole Archive and Special Collections

"Giv'em Hell, Harry!"--Uncensored: While campaigning for 1960 Democratic Presidential nominee John F. Kennedy, former U.S. President Harry S. Truman asserted that: **"If Nixon had to stick to the truth, he'd have very little to say. You don't set a fox to watching the chickens just because he has a lot of experience in the henhouse...Nixon has never told the truth in his life...He is against the small farmer. He is against small business, agriculture, public power. I don't know what the hell he's for, and that bird has the nerve to come to Texas and ask you to vote for him. If you do, you ought to go to Hell.** In response, Kennedy joked: **"I've asked President Truman to please not bring up the religious issue in this campaign . . ."**

Richard M. Nixon (L), Harry S. Truman (R)
Harry S. Truman Library and Museum

Slip of the Tongue: Campaigning for the Republican Presidential nomination in 2000, George W. Bush told the Greater Nashua, New Hampshire Chamber of Commerce: **"I know how hard it is for you to put food on your family."**

George W. Bush
White House Photograph by Pete Souza

Presidential Campaigns

How Best to Handle a Bad Attendance Record: In 1960, U.S. Senate Majority Leader Lyndon B. Johnson (D-TX), who had a sterling attendance record, tried to make missed Senate votes a campaign issue when running against U.S. Senator John F. Kennedy (D-MA) for the Democratic Presidential nomination. During a debate, Johnson challenged Kennedy for being on the campaign trail during a six-day Senate debate on Civil Rights legislation. Johnson exclaimed: **"It was my considered judgment that my people had sent me to the Senate to perform the duties of a United States Senator for which I was paid $22,500 a year."** Kennedy adroitly responded: **"It is true that Senator Johnson made a wonderful record in answering those quorum calls and I want to commend him for it."** The issue died.

Lyndon B. Johnson (L), John F. Kennedy (R)
Lyndon Baines Johnson Library and Museum

Donkey Kicking: In 2003, Democratic Presidential candidate Al Sharpton received uproarious applause when he told the Democratic State Convention in Columbia, South Carolina: **"I'm going to slap the donkey until the donkey kicks and we are going to kick George Bush out of the White House."**

Al Sharpton
Photograph by David Shankbone

Pancake Diplomacy: At the 1992 Republican National Convention, Pat Buchanan, who failed to garner the nomination, spoke in favor of the victor, President George H. W. Bush. Buchanan mocked the Democratic nominee, Bill Clinton, for his dearth of foreign policy experience. Buchanan declared: **"Bill Clinton's foreign policy experience stems mainly from having breakfast at the International House of Pancakes."**

International House of Pancakes Official Logo

Sistah Souljah Rebuked by Bill Clinton: In her single, *The Final Solution: Slavery's Back in Effect*, Souljah says: **"If black people kill black people every day, why not have a week and kill white people?"** Souljah was invited to address the Rainbow PUSH Coalition run by Civil Rights activist Jesse Jackson. Arkansas Governor Bill Clinton, the likely presidential nominee for the Democratic Party, addressed the coalition. Clinton told the crowd: **"If you took the words 'white' and 'black,' and you reversed them, you might think David Duke** [Former Ku Klux Klan Grand Wizard and Louisiana Gubernatorial candidate] **was giving that speech."**

Bill Clinton
William J. Clinton Presidential Library and Museum

Presidential Campaigns

The Existential Question: In 1992, former Vice Admiral James Stockdale, the Vice Presidential Runningmate of Independent Presidential candidate H. Ross Perot, was not known to many voters. At the Vice Presidential debate, Stockdale acknowledged this, and began his opening statement with the existential question: **"Who am I. Why am I here?"** Stockdale was a former Prisoner of War in Vietnam.

James Stockdale
U.S. Navy Photograph

It Hurts So Good: In 1984, after loosing the Presidency in a 49 state-landslide, Democrat Walter Mondale asked George McGovern, the only other Democratic Presidential nominee to loose 49 states (in 1972): **"When does it stop hurting?"** McGovern replied: **"When it does, I'll let you know."**

Button From Walter Mondale's 1984 Presidential Campaign

Truman Lets Nixon Have It: Former President Harry S. Truman had little respect for Richard M. Nixon. When Nixon was the Republican Presidential nominee in 1960, the former President said: **"Richard Nixon is a no-good lying bastard. He can lie out of both sides of his mouth at the same time, and if he ever caught himself telling the truth, he'd lie just to keep his hand in."**

Richard M. Nixon (L)
Harry S. Truman (R)
Harry S. Truman Library and Museum

Really? At a 1992 campaign rally for the re-election of George H.W. Bush, Michigan Governor John Engler introduced the president by saying: **"My friends, its with a great deal of pride that I present to you a president who wants to cut jobs, who wants to cut taxes and cut jobs, who wants to stop the regulations and cut the jobs."**

John Engler
Official Photograph

Presidential Campaigns

Just Say Nothing: 1920 Republican Presidential nominee Warren G. Harding was prone to verbal gaffes, yet he looked Presidential and his message of **"a return to normalcy"** was striking a resonant chord with the American Electorate. U.S. Senator Boise Penrose (R-PA), a supporter of Harding, suggested to the Harding campaign team: **"Don't let him make any speeches. If he goes out on a tour, somebody's sure to ask him questions, and Warren's just the sort of damn fool to answer them."**

Boise Penrose
Official Photograph

Presidential Ham: In 1840, Whig Presidential nominee William Henry Harrison was viewed by his opponents as a ham that loves the limelight. After winning the election, U.S. Senator John C. Calhoun (D-SC) commented: **"He seems to enjoy this election as a mere affair of personal vanity."**

William Henry Harrison
Photograph by Albert Sand Southorth and Josiah Johnson Hawes

Great Phrase, We Will Make It Work Somehow: In 1919, journalist Talcott Williams asked U.S. Senator Boise Penrose (R-PA): **"What is going to be the great keynote of the Republican Party in the next presidential election?"** Penrose replied: "Americanism." Williams asked Penrose what that meant. Penrose responded: **"Dam'd if I know, but I tell you Talcott, it is going to be a damn good word with which to carry an election."** The party's 1920 Presidential nominee, Warren G. Harding, adopted the phrase, delivering an address surveying American history called: **"Americanism."**

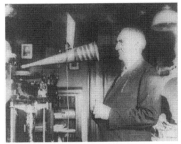

Warren G. Harding Delivering a Taped Address Called "Americanism"
Library of Congress

Willkie Takes One on the Chin: At the 1940 Republican National Convention, candidate Wendell Willkie, who had recently converted from the Democratic Party, encountered former U.S. Senator James E. Watson (R-IN). Watson said to Willkie: **"I don't mind the Church converting a whore, but I don't like her to lead the choir the first night."**

James E. Watson
Official Photograph

Presidential Campaigns

As Partisan as it Gets: During the 1948 Presidential election, in support of President Harry S. Truman, U.S. Representative John F. Kennedy waded into extreme partisan territory when he made the following statement about the Republican Party: **"They follow the Hitler Line – no matter how big the lie; repeat it often enough and the masses will regard it as true."**

John F. Kennedy (L) and Harry S. Truman (R) in His Later Years
National Archives and Records Administration

Candidate Calls Himself a Horse's Ass: While campaigning for President in 1991, U.S. Senator Bob Kerry (D-NE) posed next to a horse. He pointed to the horse and said: **"Here you have a horse's head."** He then pointed to himself and said: **"and here you have a horse's ass."**

Bob Kerry
Official Photograph

57 State Gate: At a campaign event in Beaverton, Oregon, Democratic Presidential candidate Barack Obama meant to say that he had visited 47 states. Instead, he said he visited 57 states. His political opponents had a field day with this, suggesting that Obama legitimately thought there were 57 states in the U.S. The actual quote is: **"It is wonderful to be back in Oregon. Over the last 15 months, we've traveled to every corner of the United States. I've now been in 57 states. I think [I have] one left to go. Alaska and Hawaii. I was not allowed to go to even though I really wanted to visit, but my staff would not justify it."**

Barack Obama
U.S. Air force Photograph

Orange Hair? In 1976, Gerald R. Ford joked of his Republican Primary opponent: **"Ronald Reagan doesn't dye his hair, he's just prematurely orange."**

Ronald Reagan (L), Gerald R. Ford (R)
Gerald R. Ford Presidential Library and Museum

Presidential Campaigns

Sock it To Nixon: In 1968, both the Republican and Democratic nominees, Richard M. Nixon and Hubert Humphrey, were invited to appear on the television show *Rowan and Martin's Laugh-In.* Nixon scored political points by showing his humorous side by declaring: **"Sock it to Me."** This was a catchphrase on the program. Under normal circumstances the person saying this suffered the fate of having water poured on him/her. Nixon did not suffer that fate. Humphrey declined to appear on the program and later said it may have cost him the election.

Richard M. Nixon on *Rowan and Martin's Laugh-In*

You Gotta Know Dewey to Judge Him: The Republican Presidential nominee in 1944 and 1948 was Thomas E. Dewey. He was viewed as prickly, aloof, and distant. U.S. Senator Robert A. Taft (R-OH), who competed with Dewey three times for the Republican Presidential nomination, commented: **"You really have to get to know Dewey to dislike him."**

Thomas E. Dewey
Library of Congress

The Heart Versus the Gut: In 1964, the Presidential campaign slogan of Republican Presidential nominee Barry Goldwater was: **"In your heart you know he's right."** The campaign of Goldwater's opponent, Democratic President Lyndon B. Johnson, retorted: **"In your gut, you know he's nuts."**

Barry Goldwater (L), Lyndon B. Johnson (R)
Lyndon Baines Johnson Library and Museum

Cut Capital Gains: The Panacea: At the 1991 New Hampshire Democratic Party Convention, Presidential candidate Tom Harkin (D-IA) made fun of Republican President George H.W. Bush's emphasis on cutting capital gains taxes. Harkin said: **"Bush's recovery program can be summed up in three words: Cut Capital Gains. That's his answer to everything. Give more tax cuts to the rich. You've got eight million unemployed: Cut capital gains. Stagnant economy: Cut capital gains: Trade deficit: Cut capital gains. Got a tooth ache: Cut capitol gains."**

Tom Harkin for President Bumper Sticker

Presidential Campaigns

Don't Even Joke About That: In 1963, U.S. Senator and prospective Republican Presidential aspirant Barry Goldwater (R-AZ) was discussing the precision of nuclear missiles. He quipped: **"I don't want to hit the moon. I want to lob one into the men's room of the Kremlin and make sure I hit it."** This remark became fodder for Democrats to suggest that Goldwater was trigger-happy and not a rational thinker.

Barry Goldwater 1964 Presidential
Campaign Poster

Getting Off On The Wrong Foot: During the 1932 Democratic National Convention, the Indiana Delegation, led by future Indiana Governor Paul V. McNutt, refused to support Franklin D. Roosevelt's Presidential nomination until the very last ballot. Roosevelt claimed McNutt was rude to him when he asked for support from the Indiana Delegation. McNuttt was elected Governor that year and Roosevelt was elected President. The two Democrats had a rocky relationship, and Roosevelt referred to McNutt as: **"That platinum blond S.O.B. from Indiana."**

Paul V. McNutt
Library of Congress

Political Intervention-Not Divine Intervention: After his razor-thin victory in 1888 (Winning the Electoral Vote but not the National Popular Vote), President-Elect Benjamin Harrison said to Republican National Committee Chairman Matthew Stanley Quay: **"Providence has given us victory."** Quay later said to a news reporter: **"He ought to know that Providence didn't have a damn thing to do with it. Harrison will never know how many men were compelled to approach the penitentiary to make him President."**

Mathew Stanley Quay
Official Portrait

Sage Advice: In 1940, Republican Vice Presidential nominee Charles L. McNary, a long-time U.S. Senator from Oregon and Senate Minority Leader, gave the following advice to his runningmate Republican Presidential nominee Wendell Willkie: **"In politics you'll never get into trouble by not saying too much."**

Charles L. McNary (L), Wendell Willkie (R)
Library of Congress

Presidential Campaigns

Richard J. Daley on the Record: While defending the Chicago Police Force against charges of overzealous behavior toward demonstrators during the 1968 Democratic National Convention in Chicago, Mayor Richard J. Daley told members of the media: **"Gentleman – get this thing straight once and for all – the policeman is not there to create disorder, the policeman is there to preserve disorder."**

Richard J. Daley
Los Angeles Times

The Thinking Person's Vote Will Not Cut It: During the 1952 Presidential election, an enthusiastic supporter approached the Democratic Presidential nominee, Adlai Stevenson, and said: **"Governor, every thinking person will be voting for you."** Stevenson replied: **"Madam that is not enough. I need a majority."**

Adlai Stevenson
Library of Congress

Presidential Candidate Compares Himself to a Greek God: After winning the Presidential primary in his home state of Illinois in 1988, U.S Senator Paul Simon (D-IL) declared: **"The victory is one of the most gratifying in my years of public life. The ancient god of Greek mythology Antilles received his strength by touching the ground. I have renewed my strength by touching the ground of Illinois."**

Paul Simon
Official Photograph

Don't Blame Me: I'm From Massachusetts: Massachusetts was the only state carried by Democrat George McGovern in the 1972 Presidential Election. Republican President Richard M. Nixon took every other state including McGovern's home state of South Dakota. During and after the Watergate Affair, some Massachusetts residents donned a bumper sticker exclaiming: **"Don't blame me. I'm From Massachusetts."**

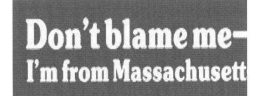

Bumper Sticker

Presidential Campaigns

No Fan of Romney: During his address to the Democratic National Convention in 2012, former Ohio Governor Ted Strickland drew plaudits from the partisan crowd for saying of the Republican Presidential nominee Mitt Romney: **"Mitt Romney has so little economic patriotism that even his money needs a passport."**

Ted Strickland
Official Photograph

Comparing the Vice Presidency to a North Vietnamese Prison Camp: In 2004 there was speculation that Democratic Presidential nominee-apparent John Kerry was considering tapping U.S. Senator John McCain (R-AZ) as his prospective runningmate. Talk show host Conan O'Brien asked McCain if he would have any interest. McCain replied: **"I spent several years in a North Vietnamese prison camp, in the dark, fed with scraps. Do you think I want to do that all over again as vice president of the United States?"**

John McCain
Official Photograph

Equivocating on "Unequivocal" The day after being elected to the U.S. Senate from Illinois in November of 2004, Barack Obama said: **"I can unequivocally say I will not be running for national office in four years, and my entire focus is making sure that I'm the best possible senator on behalf of the people of Illinois."** In February of 2007 he announced his candidacy for the Presidency of the United States.

Barack Obama
Official Photograph

Making light of Candidate's Costly Hair Care: Making light of recent revelations that Democratic Presidential candidate John Edwards had taken $800 out of his campaign war chest for two haircuts, Republican Presidential candidate Mike Huckabee said in a Republican debate: **"We've had a Congress that spent money like John Edwards at a beauty shop."**

Mike Huckabee
Photograph by Greg Skidmore

Presidential Campaigns

Of God and Guns: During the 2008 Presidential campaign, Democratic Presidential aspirant Barack Obama said at a private fundraiser in San Francisco of Americans who lose their jobs after factories in their town shut down: **"It's not surprising then. They get bitter. They cling to guns or religion or antipathy to people who aren't like them, or anti-immigrant sentiment, or anti-trade sentiment, as a way to explain their frustrations."** At an NRA convention in 2011, Texas Governor Rick Perry, seeking the Republican Presidential nomination, asserted: **"I happily cling to my guns and my God, even if President Obama thinks that that is a simpleminded thing in his elitist heart."**

Rick Perry
Official Photograph

No Catholic Scholar: Some Americans were skeptical that 1928 Democratic Presidential nominee Al Smith, who was the first Catholic to be nominated for President, would be a tribune for the Pope. Smith's response was to say: **"I never heard of these bulls and encyclicals and books."**

Poster Promoting Al Smith for President

Clinton Suggests Representative Needs Rabies Shot: One of the harshest Critics of Bill Clinton during the 1992 Presidential campaign was U.S. Representative Robert K. Dornan (R-CA). Clinton told reporters: **"Every time I see Bob Dornan - he looks like he needs a rabies shot."**

Bill Clinton
William J. Clinton Library and Museum

My How Times Have Changed: Gays protested outside the Presidential Campaign offices of U.S. Senator Edmund Muskie (D-ME) during the 1972 Democratic Presidential Primary. They demanded to meet with him. A frustrated Muskie shouted to his staff: **"Goddamn it, if I have to be nice to a bunch of sodomites to be elected President, then f— it."**

Edmund Muskie
Official Photograph

Presidential Campaigns

Voted for It -- Before Voting Against It: While at an appearance at Marshall University in Huntington, West Virginia, a heckler asked Democratic Presidential candidate John Kerry about his vote against an $87 billion appropriation to pay for the wars in Afghanistan and Iraq. Kerry responded: **"I actually did vote for the $87 billion before I voted against it."** Kerry later explained that he had meant to say that he voted for a Democratic version of the appropriation which would have paid for the wars by eliminating tax cuts signed by George W. Bush in 2001 on those making over $200,000. That measure did not pass, and Kerry voted against a subsequent proposal, which would have borrowed the money. Yet the damage was done, and the campaign of Republican President George W. Bush ran advertisements highlighting Kerry's inarticulate quote. This helped Bush's campaign to perfect the master narrative that Kerry is a flip-flopper.

John Kerry
Official Photograph

Unemployed Presidential Candidate: During a 2011 meeting with unemployed Americans in Tampa, Florida, Republican Presidential candidate Mitt Romney said: **"I should tell my story. I too am unemployed."**

Pin Promoting Mitt Romney For President

Cell Phone Goes Off During Political Speech: In 2007, While addressing the National Rifle Association (NRA), the cellular phone of Republican Presidential aspirant Rudy Giuliani went off in his pocket. He answered it and it was his wife. In front of the crowd, Giuliani said: **"Hello, dear. I'm talking to the members of the N.R.A. right now. Would you like to say hello? I love you, and I'll give you a call as soon as I'm finished, O.K.? O.K., have a safe trip. Bye-bye. Talk to you later, dear. I love you."** He was met with uproarious laughter from the audience.

Rudy Giuliani
Photograph by Jason Bedrick

Putting the Cart Before The Horse: In 1940, after the Republicans nominated Wendell Willkie as their Presidential nominee, a reporter asked him if he would meet with Democrat Franklin D. Roosevelt should he win re-nomination for a third Presidential term. Willkie responded: **"Certainly, if I am invited. One should always be courteous to one's predecessor."**

Wendell Willkie
Library of Congress

Presidential Campaigns

Don't Let the Door hit You on the Way Out: In 1976, former President Richard M. Nixon traveled to China as a private citizen. The trip occurred during the New Hampshire Primary season. Nixon's successor, Gerald R. Ford was facing a redoubtable challenge by former California Governor Ronald Reagan. Nixon's trip reminded primary voters that Ford had pardoned the unpopular Nixon. When U.S. Senator Barry Goldwater (R-AZ), a Ford supporter, was asked about Nixon's trip, he averred: **"As far as I'm concerned, Nixon can go to China and stay there."** Despite the Nixon episode, Ford still won the New Hampshire Primary and the GOP Presidential nomination.

Barry Goldwater
Library of Congress

You've Got him already: At the Republican National Convention in 1940, conventioneers began shouting on the sixth ballet: **"We want [Wendell] Willkie!"** to be the Republican nominee. The chairman of the convention, U.S. House Minority Leader Joe Martin (R-MA), could not control the Convention and finally bellowed: **"Well, if you'll be quiet long enough, maybe you'll get him."** That quieted the delegates, and Willkie garnered the nomination.

Wendell Willkie
Library of Congress

You Can Pick on Me, but Leave My Dog Alone: Franklin D. Roosevelt had a Scottish terrier named Fala. His beloved pet was mistakenly left behind when he departed the Aleutian Islands. Not willing to lose his companion, Roosevelt used taxpayer money to send a ship back to retrieve his dog. The Republicans made political hay out of this in 1944, when Roosevelt was seeking an unprecedented fourth term as President. However, Roosevelt made no apology, averring: **"You can criticize me, my wife and my family, but you can't criticize my little dog. He's Scotch and all allegations about spending all this money have just made his little soul furious."** This is now referred to as "The Fala Speech." Roosevelt won that election. The Franklin D. Roosevelt Memorial in Washington, D.C. includes a statue of Fala.

Franklin D. Roosevelt Memorial
National Parks Service

Life on the Campaign Trail: During a 2008 interview with Fox News, Republican Presidential candidate Mike Huckabee, the former Arkansas Governor discussed a hotel he stayed at on the campaign trail: **"It was so bad, I called my wife and said I'm the only guy in this hotel that has sleeves on his shirt and is not completely tattooed from head to toe. It was that bad."**

Mike Huckabee
U.S. Department of Health and Human Services

109

Presidential Campaigns

Showdown State: In the 2012 Presidential campaign, President Barack Obama made no effort to hide his focus on Ohio above the non-battleground states. This is evidenced by a statement he made on *The Tonight Show with Jay Leno* on October 25, 2012. Six days prior to Halloween, the President joked that trick or treaters should come to the White House. He added: **"If anybody comes from Ohio, they can expect a Hershey bar 'This' big** [moving his hands outward]**."**

Barack Obama
White House Photograph

Don't You People Ever Listen? New Jersey Governor Chris Christie was often asked if he would be a candidate for the Republican Presidential nomination. This aggravated Christie. In February of 2011, when the question was posed to him by a reporter at a Press Conference, Christie responded bluntly: **"Short of suicide, I don't really know what I'd have to do to convince you people that I'm not running."**

Chris Christie
Official Photograph

Campaign Advisor Goes Rogue: During the 2008 Presidential Campaign, former U.S. Senator Phil Gramm (R-TX) served as an advisor to the Republican nominee, U.S. Senator John McCain (R-AZ). Gramm told *The Washington Times*: **"We have sort of become a nation of whiners. You just hear this constant whining, complaining about a loss of competitiveness, America in decline despite a major export boom that is the primary reason that growth continues in the economy."** McCain disavowed the remarks, averring: **"I think Senator Gramm would be in serious consideration for ambassador to Belarus, although I'm not sure the citizens of Minsk would welcome that."**

Phil Gramm
Official Photograph

Positive Spin: In 1912, William Howard Taft suffered the worst defeat of any President seeking re-election, garnering just 23.2% of the vote, and winning only 8 electoral votes. Still in good humor, William Howard Taft said: **"I have one consolation. No candidate was ever elected ex-president by such a large majority."**

William Howard Taft
Library of Congress

110

Presidential Campaigns

Cleveland Supporters Have the Last Laugh: During the 1884 Presidential election, the Republicans alleged that Democrat Grover Cleveland had fathered an illegitimate child while a Buffalo attorney with Maria Crofts Halpin Cleveland. However, he did not know for certain if he was the biological father. Ms. Halpin had affairs with other men at the time. Cleveland did pay child support to Halpin, leading to Republicans chanting: **"Ma, Ma, Where's my Pa."** After Cleveland won the election, his supporter returned fire, leading to chants of **"Gone to the White House Ha Ha Ha!"**

A Political Cartoon making light of the allegations that Cleveland had fathered Oscar Folsom Cleveland out of wedlock printed in *Judges Magazine*
Library of Congress

Avoiding Taxes is as American as Apple Pie: In defending 2012 Republican Presidential nominee Mitt Romney's holdings in offshore tax havens, U.S. Senator Lindsey Graham (R-SC) averred: **"It's really American to avoid paying taxes, legally."**

Lindsey Graham
Official Photograph

Southern Hospitality: During the 1968 Presidential campaign, American Party Presidential nominee George Wallace gained political traction by mocking anti-Vietnam War Protesters and government bureaucrats. He warned: **"Well if I get to become President I'm gonna call in a bunch of bureaucrats and take away their briefcases and throw 'em in the Potomac River. And if any demonstrator ever lays down in front of my car, it'll be the last car he'll ever lay down in front of."**

George Wallace
Lyndon Baines Johnson Library and Museum

Jack Daniels is Ok with Pat Buchanan: When asked if he had ever used cocaine, 2000 Reform Party Presidential Candidate Pat Buchanan answered: **"No to marijuana. No to cocaine, and a question mark over Jack Daniels."**

Campaign Bumper Sticker for Pat Buchanan's 2000 Presidential campaign

111

Presidential Campaigns

The New Nixon, Again: During the 1968 Presidential campaign, Democratic nominee Vice President Hubert Humphrey, made fun of the reinvention of his Republican opponent, former Vice President Richard M. Nixon: **"They had a renewal job in 1952** [When Nixon won the GOP Vice Presidential Nomination]. **There was some reason for it too. Then they had another renewal job in 1956** [When Nixon ran for reelection as Vice President]. **Then they had another renovation operation in 1960** [when Nixon was the Republican Presidential nomine]. **Then when he ran for Governor in California in 1962, they renewed him again. Then in 1964, another touchup, and now I read about the new Nixon of 1968. Ladies and gentleman, anybody who had his political face lifted so many times can't be very new."**

Richard M. Nixon (Left)
Hubert Humphrey (Right)
Cover of *Veja Magazine*

Panda Bear or Pander Bear? During the 1992 Presidential election, former U.S. Senator Paul Tsongas accused Bill Clinton of pandering to Connecticut voters by saying he would support a scaled back version of the Sea Wolf Nuclear Submarine Program. Then Tsongas told Florida voters: **"It was a cynical attempt to get votes from Connecticut. The American people are just hearing how cynical and unprincipled Bill Clinton is. He knows full well it will never be built."** At a campaign rally in Fort Lauderdale, Florida, Tsongas held up a teddy bear and said, **"This is my opponent, Pander bear."** Unfortunately for Tsongas, many voters watching the event thought he was saying **"panda bear"** and did not understand why he was calling Bill Clinton a **"panda bear."**

Bill Clinton and Paul Tsongas on the Cover of *Time Magazine*

Presidential Campaigns

Mafia Politics: During a 2004 Presidential debate with President George W. Bush, Democratic Presidential nominee John Kerry suggested that Bush's rhetoric about fiscal responsibility did not match his record. Kerry averred: **"Being lectured by the president on fiscal responsibility is a little bit like Tony Soprano** [who played Mafia member James Gandolfini] **talking to me about law and order in this country."**

John Kerry
Official Photograph

Good Question: U. S Senator Bob Dole (R-KS) was the Republican Vice Presidential nominee in 1976 and the Republican Presidential nominee in 1996. He later said: **"I don't know how many people run for Vice president and President and lose both."**

**Bob Dole During his 1976
Vice Presidential Run**
Robert J. Dole Archive and Special Collections

Harrison Falls Asleep Before Learning he had been Elected President: On election night of 1888, a friend woke Benjamin Harrison and told him that he had been elected President. Harrison was in bed. The friend asked Harrison why he had gone to bed before the final results were in. Harrison replied: **"I knew that my staying up would not change the election result if I were defeated, while if elected I had a hard day ahead of me. So I thought a night's rest was best in any event."**

Benjamin Harrison
Library of Congress

Unsolicited Endorsement: After the Boston Red Sox won the World Series in 2004, Pitcher Curt Schilling appeared with his wife Shonda on ABC's *Good Morning America.* At the end of the broadcast, Schilling told host Charles Gibson: **"And make sure you tell everyone to vote, and vote Bush next week."** After that endorsement, the Bush campaign called Shilling and asked him to campaign with Bush. He did.

Curt Shilling on the Cover of *Sporting News*

Presidential Campaigns

The Country of Solyndra? At a campaign rally in Ames, Iowa in 2011, Texas Governor and Republican Presidential candidate Rick Perry made the following statement about government waste: **"No greater example of it than this administration sending millions of dollars into the solar industry, and we lost that money. I want to say it was over $500 million that went to the country Solyndra."** Perry misspoke. Solyndra was not a "country," but a failed renewable energy company, which won $535 million in federal stimulus funding.

Rick Perry
Official Photograph

A Political Christmas Carol: During the 1988 Presidential campaign, Republican nominee George H.W. Bush proposed tax-deferred savings accounts. His Democratic opponent, Michael Dukakis, made fun of the idea by holding up a $20 bill and exclaiming that the $20 bill represented the amount American families would save from the plan. Dukakis said: **"George Bush plays Santa Claus to the wealthy and Ebeneaser Scrooge to the rest of us."**

Michael Dukakis
Photograph by Hal O'Brien

Edible Words: At a campaign speech in Denver, Colorado in 1952, Democratic Presidential nominee Adlai Stevenson said: **"Man does not live by words alone; despite the fact that sometimes he has to eat them."**

Adlai Stevenson
Harry S. Truman Library and Museum

Sending Politicians to the Moon: During a 2012 Presidential debate in Jacksonville, Florida, U.S. Representative Ron Paul (R-TX) was asked by host Wolf Blitzer about a proposal by one of his opponents, Newt Gingrich, to colonize the moon. Paul responded: **"Well, I don't think we should go to the moon. I think we maybe should send some politicians up there."**

Ron Paul
Photograph by David Carlyon

Presidential Campaigns

The Man Who Did Not Invent the Internet: In March of 1999, as Vice President Al Gore was beginning his quest for the Democratic Presidential nomination against former New Jersey Senator Bill Bradley, he was asked by CNN's Wolf Blitzer: **"Why should Democrats looking at the Democratic nomination -- the process -- support you instead of Bill Bradley** [Gore's opponent for the nomination], **a friend of yours, a former colleague in the Senate? What do you have to bring to this that he doesn't necessarily bring to this process?"** Gore Responded in part: **"During my service in the United States Congress, I took the initiative in creating the Internet."** Gore was referring to his role as the lead sponsor of the 1991 High-performance Computing and Communications Act, which appropriated $600 million for high-performance computing and co-sponsored the Information Infrastructure and Technology Act of 1992. Critics chided Gore for his statement and falsely claimed that Gore had said he **"invented the Internet."** U.S. House Majority leader Dick Armey (R-TX) joked: **"If the Vice President created the Internet then I created the Interstate."**

Al Gore
Official Photograph

Nixon Cuts Down Redwood Tree? In 1956, Democratic Presidential nominee Adlai Stevenson poked fun at Vice President Richard M. Nixon. Stevenson said: **"Nixon is the kind of politician who would cut down a redwood tree, then mount the stump for a speech on conservation."**

Adlai Stevenson
Library of Congress

Dick Cheney Declares Himself a Sex Symbol: At the 2004 Republican National Convention, Republican Vice President Dick Cheney said: **"People tell me that Senator** [Democratic Vice Presidential nominee] **John Edwards got picked for his good looks, his sex appeal, and his great hair. I say to them, 'How do you think I got the job?'"**

Dick Cheney
White House Photograph by David Bohrer

115

Presidential Campaigns

From Campaigning to Dog Walking: In 1997, former Republican Presidential nominee Bob Dole said in an appearance on NBC's *The Today Show*: **"Elizabeth** [Dole's Wife] **is back at the Red Cross, and I'm walking the dog."**

Elizabeth Dole (R) and Bob Dole (L) with a Previous Dog, Leader (C)
Robert J. Dole Archive and Special Collections

Americans are All Over America: In 1936, Republican Presidential nominee Alfred Landon said in a campaign speech: **"Wherever I have gone in this country, I have found Americans."**

Alfred Landon
Official Photograph

Easy Rider: At a 1992 luncheon at the Democratic National Convention in New York, Ann Richards drew laughter by commenting: **"Well, you can put lipstick on a hog and call it Monique, but it's still a pig."** She was referring to feckless government programs.

Ann Richards
Texas State Libraries and Archives Commission

He's Finally in the Money: After raising $4.1 million at a fundraiser for his 1996 bid for the Republican Presidential nomination, U.S. Senator Phil Gramm (R-TX) boasted: **"I have the most reliable friend you can have in American politics, and that is 'ready money.'"**

Campaign Pin For the Phil Gramm for President Campaign in 1996

Presidential Campaigns

Hay, He's a Man: During a Youtube debate hosting the 2008 Democratic Presidential candidates, Jason Coop from Colorado Springs, Colorado asked the candidates to look to the left and tell the audience one thing you like and one thing you dislike about that candidate. U.S. Senator Joe Biden (D-DE) looked to his left and found U.S. Representative Dennis Kucinich (D-OH) and said: **"Dennis, the thing I like best about you is your wife."** Kucinich is married to the former Denise Harper, 31 years his junior.

Denise Harper (L), Dennis Kucinich (R)
Photograph by Bbsrock

Not a Ringing Endorsement of the Wisdom of His Party: At the 1896 Republican National Convention, U.S. House Speaker Thomas Brackett Reed (R-ME) was asked by a reporter if the party would nominate him for President. Reed's reply was: **"They could do worse, and they probably will."** Ultimately, the party nominated former Ohio Governor William McKinley, not Reed. McKinley went on to win the Presidency.

Thomas Brackett Reed
Official Photograph

Doles Gives It Right Back to Cave Man: Before the New Hampshire Primary in 1988, Republican Presidential candidate Bob Dole was confronted by a heckler who said: **"You've voted for tax increases 600 times in your career. How can you defend that?"** Dole responded: **"Check back into your cave."**

Bob Dole Campaigning for President in 1988
Robert J. Dole Archives and Special Collections

Great Strategy to Get off Desert Island: *The Associated Press* asked the 2008 Republican Presidential aspirants the one thing they would want if they were ever stranded on a desert island. U.S. Representative Tom Tancredo (R-CO) adroitly answered: **"A boat."**

Tom Tancredo
Official Photograph

117

Presidential Campaigns

One-Liner Time: During the 1988 Presidential race, Republican nominee George H.W. Bush tried to use the fact that Boston Harbor was the dirtiest harbor in the U.S. against his Democratic opponent, Massachusetts Governor Michael Dukakis. During one of the Presidential debates, after Democratic nominee Michael Dukakis delivered a long answer to a question about the bulging federal budget deficit. Bush quipped: **"Is this the time for one-liners? That answer is about as clear as Boston Harbor."**

George H. W. Bush and Michael Dukakis
George Bush Presidential Library and Museum

Just Can't Stop Running: In 1908, the Democrats nominated William Jennings Bryan for the third time as their Presidential nominee. The Republicans, in support of their Presidential nominee, William Howard Taft, developed the slogan: **"Vote for Taft now, you can vote for Bryan anytime."**

William Jennings Bryan
Library of Congress

Reagan Turns the Tables on the Age Question: During a Presidential debate between President Ronald Reagan and Walter Mondale, Reagan was asked this question by Henry "Hank" Trewitt of *The Baltimore Sun,* **"You already are the oldest President in history, and some of your staff say you were tired after your most recent encounter with Mr. Mondale. I recall, yes, that President Kennedy, who had to go for days on end with very little sleep during the Cuban missile crisis. Is there any doubt in your mind that you would be able to function in such circumstances?"** Reagan answered: **"Not at all Mr. Trewhitt, and I want you to know that also I will not make age an issue of this campaign. I am not going to exploit for political purposes my opponent's youth and inexperience."** Trewhitt then exclaimed: **"Mr. President, I'd like to head for the fence and try to catch that one before it goes over."**

Walter Mondale (L), Ronald Reagan (R)
Ronald Reagan Presidential
Library and Museum

Presidential Campaigns

The Tail of a Yankee Patrician and a Mom and Pop Store in Ohio: In 2004, Democratic Presidential nominee John Kerry entered the Village Grocery Store in Buchanan, Ohio and asked the store owners Paul and Debra McKnight: **"Can I get me a hunting license here?"** He bought the license for $140.

John Kerry
Official Photograph

Human-Fish Relations: In 2000, Republican Presidential candidate George W. Bush addressed a crowd in Saginaw, Michigan, outlining his energy policy. Bush said he was against eliminating energy-producing dams solely because they can endanger the fish population. Bush said: **"I know the human being and fish can exist peacefully."**

George W. Bush
White House Photograph

Tom Delay Provides Creative Defense for Dan Quayle and His Own Lack of Military Experience: In 1988, while defending Republican Vice Presidential nominee Dan Quayle's lack of military service during the Vietnam War, as well as his own lack of military service during that time period, U.S. Representative Tom Delay (R-TX) told the Houston media: **"So many minority youths had volunteered for the well-paying military positions to escape poverty and the ghetto that there was literally no room for patriotic folks like himself."**

Tom Delay
Official Photograph

Not Another Football Analogy? In 1967, Democratic Presidential candidate Eugene McCarthy was quoted in *The Washington Post* as saying: **"Being in politics is like being a football coach. You have to be smart enough to understand the game, and dumb enough to think it's important."**

Eugene McCarthy
Official Photograph

119

Presidential Campaigns

No Hunting Party with Cousin Dick Cheney: During an appearance on NBC's *The Tonight Show with Jay Leno* in 2007, Democratic Presidential candidate Barack Obama was asked about recent revelations that he was the eighth cousin of Republican Vice President Dick Cheney. Obama said: **"The truth is, I am ok with it. You know, now I don't want to be invited to the family hunting party."** In 2006, Cheney accidently shot attorney Harry Whittington on a quail hunt in Kennedy County, Texas.

Barack Obama
White House Photograph by Pete Souza

Lieberman Admits He Never Inhaled: During a 2003 CNN sponsored Democratic Presidential debate, the candidates were asked by a viewer: **"Which, if any of you are ready to admit to using drugs in the past?"** After John Kerry and John Edwards answered **"Yes,"** Joe Lieberman said: **"Well, you know I have a reputation for giving unpopular answers at Democratic debates. I never used marijuana, sorry."**

Joe Lieberman
Official Photograph

Inadvertent Gaffe Corrected: During a 2007 Iowa debate, Democratic Presidential aspirant John Edwards said: **"I want every caucus-goer to know I've been fighting these people and winning my entire life. And if we do this together, rise up together, we can actually make absolutely certain, starting here in Iowa, that we make this country better than we left it."** After an uproarious laughter by the audience, Edwards corrected himself and said: **"Leave it better than we started."**

John Edwards
Official Photograph

George McGovern Created Marriages and Divorces: In 1984, Presidential candidate George McGovern was asked by ABC News Reporter Cokie Roberts if he felt his previous Presidential campaign in 1972 had changed people's lives. McGovern responded: **"Every once in a while I run into somebody who tells me that she met her husband in my campaign or a husband who says I met my wife. I have to tell you, I caused a few divorces too."**

George McGovern
Library of Congress

Presidential Campaigns

The Allusive Competence in Government: In 1976, U.S. Senator Henry "Scoop" Jackson (D-WA) garnered the endorsement of former United States Ambassador to the United Nations, Daniel Patrick Moynihan. Jackson was seeking the Democratic Presidential nomination. At an event in Boston announcing the endorsement, a reporter asked Jackson if Moynihan's wit would counter Jackson's reputation for dullness. Before Jackson could utter a syllable, Moynihan chimed in: **"Don't give me that. The most exciting thing you encounter in government is competence, because it's so rare. This man [Jackson] knows his business."**

Daniel Patrick Moynihan
Official Photograph

Presidential Candidate Compares Tobacco to Milk: In 1996, Republican Presidential nominee-apparent Bob Dole said of cigarettes: **"We know it is not good for kids, but a lot of other things aren't good. Drinking is not good. Some would say milk is not good."** Vice President Al Gore responded: **"Kick the habit, Senator Dole. It not worth stinking up your reputation with the smoky stench of special interest politics and the dangerous din of dishonesty."**

Bob Dole on the Campaign Trail in 1996
Robert J Dole Archives and Special Collections

A House Divided: In 1976, Louisiana's Democratic Governor Edwin Edwards campaigned for his party's nominee former Georgia Governor Jimmy Carter. However, Edwards' wife, Elaine S. Edwards, a one-time Democratic U.S. Senator from Louisiana, bucked party lines by supporting and campaigning for Republican President Gerald R. Ford. Without mentioning that the popular Governor Edwards had endorsed Carter, Ford artfully introduced Mrs. Edwards at a Louisiana campaign rally by asserting: **"Now may I introduce to all of you wonderful people of Louisiana the wife of your great Governor, Elaine Edwards. I thank Elaine very, very much for her personal endorsement. I am grateful, and I have told her in the next four years we won't let her and the State of Louisiana down."** Carter pocketed the state's ten electoral votes with 51.73 percent of the popular vote.

Elaine Edwards
Official Photograph

Defining Marriage Using a Tree Analogy: In 2011, Republican Presidential candidate Rick Santorum openly discussed his opposition to same-sex marriage. He told Douglas Burns of *The Carroll Daily Times Herald*: **"It's like going out and saying, 'That tree is a car.' Well, the tree's not a car. A tree's a tree. Marriage is marriage."**

Rick Santorum
Photograph by Greg Skidmore

Presidential Campaigns

Heckler Puts Presidential Nominee in His Place: In 1896, Democratic Presidential nominee William Jennings Bryan broke precedent and barnstormed the country, campaigning for himself. He delivered over 600 speeches in 27 states. Prior to this, candidates used surrogates to campaign for them, and only spoke to voters who came to their hometowns to visit them. At one stop, Bryan told the audience: **"After the election, I will be sleeping in the White House."** A heckler who supported the campaign of Republican Presidential nominee William McKinley bellowed: **"If you do, you'll be sleeping with Mrs. McKinney."**

Ida McKinley
Library of Congress

"That" Would Be A Story: In 1975, Democratic Presidential candidate Jimmy Carter was asked by a reporter how he would feel if his daughter Amy participated in a premarital affair. Carter responded: **"I would be deeply shocked and disappointed —- because our daughter is only seven years old."**

Amy Carter with her Cat
Executive Office of The President
of the United States

Where's The Beef??? In a 1984 Democratic Presidential Primary debate between former Vice President Walter Mondale and former U.S. Senator Gary Hart, (D-CO) Hart challenged the establishment candidate by talking about his "New Ideas." Mondale was quick to turn to Hart and say: **"When I hear your new ideas, I'm reminded of that ad, 'Where's the beef?'"** This drew laughter from the crowd. The line was taken from a Wendy's commercial, which humorously alleged that its competitors put very little beef in their sandwiches.

Walter Mondale
Official Photograph

Just Blame The Workers: During the 1988 Democratic Presidential Primary, candidate Richard Gephardt said of one of his rivals: **"Governor [Michael] Dukakis has an ad on the air in which he basically blames American workers for our trade problems. I [Gephardt] have a motto in my campaign: 'It's your fight too.' I wonder if his (campaign) has a motto, 'It's your fault too.'"**

Richard Gephardt for President Pin

Presidential Campaigns

Spreading Partisan Manure: In 1896, Democratic Presidential nominee William Jennings Bryan noticed at a campaign stop in Missouri that there was no platform from which to deliver his stump speech. A supporter found a manure spreader and rolled it out for Bryan to stand on. Bryan stood on the spreader and said: **"This is the first time I have ever spoken from a Republican Platform."**

William Jennings Bryan
Library of Congress

Vice President? No Way: In 1980 there was speculation that Independent Presidential candidate John Anderson would ask former U.S. Health, Education, and Welfare Secretary Joseph Califano to be his Vice Presidential running mate. Califano told Civil Liberties attorney Mitchell Rogovin: **"Vice Presidents are candidates for castration."**

Joseph Califano
Lyndon Baines Johnson
Presidential Library and Museum

He Really Does: In 1944, Alice Roosevelt Longworth, the daughter of President Theodore Roosevelt, observed that the Republican Presidential nominee, Thomas E. Dewey **"looks like the little man on the wedding cake."**

Thomas E. Dewey
Harry S. Truman Library and Museum

Presidential Midlife Crisis: In 1996, Republican Presidential candidate Lamar Alexander observed: **"President Clinton zigs and zags. He gets up on both sides of the bed every morning. He's the only President we've ever had who feels it's necessary to act out his midlife crisis in public."**

Lamar Alexander
Official Photograph

Presidential Campaigns

Catchy Tune: In 1884, Republican Presidential nominee James G. Blaine was enveloped in accusations that when he served as Speaker of the U.S. House of Representatives, he had influenced legislation benefitting the railroad companies, and had allegedly profited from the bonds he owned in the railroad companies. Democrats chanted: **"Blaine Blaine, James G. Blaine, The continental liar from the state of Maine."** Blaine lost the election to Democrat Grover Cleveland.

James G. Blaine
Library of Congress

Full of Himself: In 1999, when Business mogul Donald Trump was considering running for the Presidential nomination of the Reform Party, he told Maureen Dowd of *The New York Times*: **"To be blunt, people would vote for me. They just would. Why? Maybe because I'm so good looking. I don't know.** [Talk Show Host] **Larry King calls and says, 'Do my show. I get my highest ratings when you're on.'"**

Donald Trump
Photograph by Cage Skidmore

OK, Can You Name One Magazine or Newspaper? In 2008, Republican Vice Presidential nominee Sarah Palin was asked by NBC reporter Katie Couric: **"When it comes to establishing your world view, what magazines and newspapers did you regularly read before you were tapped for this to stay informed."** Her response was: **"Most of them...all of em...any of em. I have a vast variety of sources where we get our news too. Alaska isn't a foreign country, where, it's kind of suggested and it seems like, 'Wow, how could you keep in touch with what the rest of Washington, D.C. may be thinking and doing when you live up there in Alaska?' Believe me, Alaska is like a microcosm of America'"**

Sarah Palin
Official Photograph

Doggy Humor: During a 2011 debate amongst Republican Presidential aspirants, Gary Johnson brought down the house by stating: **"My next-door neighbor's two dogs have created more shovel-ready jobs than this current administration."** After garnering little attention in the Republican Primary, Johnson became a Libertarian and mustered that party's Presidential nomination. He garnered just less than 1% of the vote in the General Election.

Gary Johnson
Official Photograph

Presidential Campaigns

Vice President Says Atheists Should Not be Regarded as Citizens: In 1987, Vice President George H.W. Bush was visiting Chicago to survey flood damage and to announce townships that would receive disaster relief. During a press conference, Rob Sherman of *American Atheist Magazine* turned the conversation to Atheism and Bush's 1988 bid for the Republican Presidential nomination. Sherman asked: **What are you going to do to win the votes of Americans who are atheists?"** Bush responded: **"I guess I'm pretty weak in the atheist community. Faith in God is important to me."** Sherman followed up: **"Do you support the equal citizenship and patriotism of Americans who are atheists?"** Bush answered: **"I don't know that atheists should be regarded as citizens, nor should they be regarded as patriotic. This is one nation under God."**

George H.W. Bush
George Bush Presidential Library and Museum

Democrat Slams Democrat at Republican National Convention: In 2004, U.S. Senator Zell Miller (D-GA) endorsed Republican President George W. Bush over his own party's Presidential nominee, John Kerry. He delivered the keynote address at the Republican National Convention and belittled his Senate colleague, proclaiming: **"Listing all the weapon systems that Senator Kerry tried his best to shut down sounds like an auctioneer selling off our national security, but Americans need to know the facts . . . This is the man who wants to be the Commander in Chief of our U.S. Armed Forces? U.S. forces armed with what? Spitballs?"**

Zell Miller
Official Photograph

Alliterative School: Dean Acheson, who was serving as U.S. Secretary of State under the administration of Democrat Harry S. Truman, advocated a policy of "containment" of communism. In 1952, Republican Vice Presidential candidate Richard M. Nixon argued that the U.S. should work to roll back, rather than contain communism. He railed against **"Acheson's College of Cowardly Communist Containment."**

Dean Acheson
Lyndon Baines Johnson Library and Museum

Presidential Campaigns

Truman Does Not Want to be Vice President: In 1944, incoming Democratic National Committee Chairman Robert Hannigan told U.S. Senator Harry S. Truman (D-MO) that President Franklin D. Roosevelt wanted him to be his Vice Presidential runningmate. Harry S. Truman responded: **"Tell him to go to Hell! I'm for Jimmy Brynes."** Brynes was the Director of the Office of War Mobilization and a former South Carolina Governor, and U.S. Supreme Court Justice. Truman eventually relented and accepted Roosevelt's request. Roosevelt won re-election and died just 83 days into his fourth term, making Truman President.

Harry S. Truman (L)
Franklin D. Roosevelt, (R)
Harry S. Truman Library and Museum

Chlorofluoro-carbon Abatement Enters a Presidential Debate: In his opening statement in the 1996 Vice Presidential debate, Democrat Al Gore looked at his Republican debate counterpart Jack Kemp, a former NFL Quarterback, and stated: **"I'd like to start by offering you a deal, Jack. If you won't use any football stories, I won't tell any of my warm and humorous stories about chlorofluoro-carbon abatement."**

Al Gore
Photograph by Greg Michaud

Senator Wishes He Could Challenge Talk Show Host To a Duel: In 2004, U.S. Senator Zell Miller (D-GA) was interviewed by Chris Mathews on MSNBC after Miller delivered the Keynote Address at the Republican National Convention. Mathews asked Miller about his speaking at the opposing party's convention, and asked him what he would do if a Republican spoke at the Democratic National Convention. After a moment of bitter crosstalk, Miller complained: **"Get out of my Face. If you are going to ask me a question, step back and let me answer. I wish we lived in the day where you could challenge a person to a duel. Now, that would be pretty good."**

Zell Miller
Official Portrait by Thomas V. Nash

Self-Deprecating Humor: During the 1992 Presidential debate, Independent candidate H. Ross Perot, who has abnormally large ears, said in his closing statement: **"We've got to clean this mess up, leave this country in good shape, and pass on the American dream to them [Our Children]. We've got to collect the taxes to do it. If there's a fairer way, I'm all ears."**

H. Ross Perot
U.S. Department of Veteran's Affairs

Presidential Campaigns

Double Negative: In 1951, President Harry S. Truman was undecided on whether to seek re-election. A reporter asked him if he would go on a whistle-stop campaign in 1952 for the Democratic nominee if it is not Truman. Truman answered: **"I will answer that in a negative way. I will not say that I would not."** After losing the New Hampshire Primary to Estes Kefauver, Truman decided not to seek the nomination in 1952. He did campaign for the Democratic ticket for Adlai Stevenson and John Sparkman. They lost to Dwight D. Eisenhower in the General Election.

Harry S. Truman (L) with John Sparkman (C) and Adlai Stevenson (R)
Harry S. Truman Library and Museum

Another Super Hero? In 2004, Independent Presidential candidate Ralph Nader, who was excluded from Presidential debates because he failed to obtain the requisite 15% poll support to be allowed on stage, told a gathering of the University of Miami's Faculty Club: **"If I could only go through the ducts and leap out onstage in a cape - - that's my dream."**

Ralph Nader
Photograph by Dan LaVange

Flip Flop Charge: The day after a 1992 Presidential debate that was held in East Lansing, Michigan, President George H.W. Bush campaigned in Holland, Michigan. Bush noted that a Michigan furniture company, the Herman Miller Corporation, made the furniture for the debate: Three podiums, one for each of the three candidates. Bush joked: **"Governor [Bill] Clinton has a tendency to take two positions on every issue. So maybe Herman Miller should make a fourth podium, one for Clinton when he's for something and one for Clinton when he's against it."**

George H.W. Bush (L), Bill Clinton (M) H. Ross Perot (R) and Jim Lehrer
George Bush Presidential
Library and Museum

Competent Extremist v. Incompetent Moderate: In 1980, former Watergate Special Prosecutor Leon Jaworski became the honorary chairman of "Democrats for [Ronald] Reagan." When asked about the charges by Democratic Jimmy Carter that Reagan was too extreme, Jaworski replied: **"I would rather have a competent extremist than an incompetent moderate."**

Leon Jaworski
Official Photograph

Presidential Campaigns

I have Some Racist Constituents: In 2008, U.S. Representative John Murtha (D-PA), who represented the Western part of Pennsylvania, was asked by a member of *The Pittsburg Post-Gazette's* Editorial Board if Barack Obama could carry his blue-collar Congressional District in the Presidential race. Murtha exclaimed: **"There's no question West Pennsylvania is a racist area."** After this remark went viral, Murtha apologized. Interestingly, Obama lost the District in November. It was the only District where John Kerry won in 2004 but Obama lost in 2008. Murtha won re-election despite making the controversial remark.

John Murtha
Official Photograph

It Ain't So Joe: In a 2008 interview with NBC's Katie Couric, Democratic Vice Presidential nominee Joe Biden stated: **"When the stock market crashed, Franklin Roosevelt got on the television and didn't just talk about the princes of greed. He said, 'Look, here's what happened."** Actually, Herbert Hoover, not Franklin D. Roosevelt, was President when the Stock Market crashed in 1929. In addition, television was an experimental medium at the time and very few Americans had access to it.

Joe Biden
U.S. Congress Photograph

Dukakis Agrees With Bush and Dole: In a speech prior to the Iowa caucuses in 1988, Democratic Presidential candidate Michael Dukakis poked fun of Republican candidates George H.W. Bush and Bob Dole. Dukakis told a crowd in Cedar Rapids, Iowa, **"Vice President Bush and Senator Dole have been saying some rather nasty things about each other. Senator Dole says the Vice President is not much of a leader and the Vice President says Senator Dole is not much of a leader. I don't ordinarily agree with those guys but in this case I agree with both of them. Neither of them is much of a leader."**

Michael Dukakis on the Cover of
Time Magazine

Harsh Words Indeed for Presidential Candidate: In 1992, actor and Democratic Presidential candidate Tom Laughlin (of *Billy Jack* film fame) told High School students at Iowa City West High School that one of his opponents, U.S. Senator Tom Harkin (D-IA), **"doesn't care for anybody but Harkin. I think he's a sleazebag. I despise him."**

Tom Laughlin for President Pin, Using His Movie Character Billy Jack

Presidential Campaigns

Obama Inhales: During a town hall meeting in Audubon, Iowa in 2007, Democratic Presidential candidate Barack Obama was asked his views on the legalization of marijuana. He answered: **"I'm concerned about how folks will grow their own and say it's for medicinal purposes. That's kind of a slippery slope."** Obama then said with a laugh: **"There I was feeling a little intense, so I needed a joint."** Obama was then asked if he inhaled. Former President Bill Clinton had said he did not inhale during the 1992 Presidential campaign. Obama candidly said: **"I did. It's not something I'm proud of. It was a mistake as a young man. But I never understood that line. "The point was to inhale. That was the point."**

Barack Obama
Official Photograph

Former Future: In 1948, Republican Presidential nominee Thomas E. Dewey was the favorite to win the election. Members of the media were already speculating on his Presidential cabinet. Many thought John Foster Dulles would become U.S. Secretary of State. However, Democratic President Harry S. Truman upset Dewey. The next day, Dulles told a reporter: **"I'm the former future [U.S.] Secretary of State."**

John Foster Dulles
Official Photograph

A Bullet Will Not Stop a Bull Moose: In 1912, before a campaign stop in Milwaukee, former President Theodore Roosevelt (the nominee of the Progressive Party a.k.a. the Bull Moose Party), was shot in the chest by tavern operator John Schrank, a manic-depressive. While aides urged Roosevelt to go immediately to the hospital, he insisted on first delivering his scheduled speech. Roosevelt was not coughing blood, and the bullet had not penetrated his lungs. However, blood was dripping from his chest. Despite this situation, he gave a ninety-minute oration, opening by telling the crowd: **"I have just been shot; but it takes more than that to kill a Bull Moose."** That was the last campaign event he made, spending the rest of the election season recovering from the wound. The bullet was never dislodged from Roosevelt's chest due to the fact that the doctors believed the process of removing the bullet could be fatal.

Theodore Roosevelt
Library of Congress

Presidential Campaigns

Regan Compares Kennedy to Marx: In 1960, actor Ronald Regan wrote a letter to the Republican Presidential nominee, Richard M. Nixon suggesting that Nixon not 'out liberal' Democratic nominee John F. Kennedy. Reagan suggested Nixon should run as a fiscal conservative, and wrote: **"Shouldn't someone tag Mr. Kennedy's bold new imaginative program with its proper age? Under the tousled boyish haircut is still old Karl Marx - first launched a century ago."**

Karl Marx
Library of Congress

Stepping Stone to the Presidency? U.S. Representative Morris Udall (D-AZ) unsuccessfully sought the Democratic Presidential nomination in 1976. He was fond of saying: **"If you are a United States Senator and are not under indictment or in detoxification, you automatically consider yourself as a potential candidate for the Presidency."**

Pin From Morris Udall's 1976 Presidential Campaign

Fine! I Endorse John McCain: U.S. Senator Thad Cochran (R-MS), a member of the Senate Appropriations Committee, had a strained relationships with his Senate colleague John McCain (R-AZ). McCain was an opponent of earmarks, which Cochran supported. The relationship turned personal. Cochran told *The Boston Globe:* **"The thought of his being President sends a cold chill down my spine. He is erratic. He is hotheaded. He loses his temper and he worries me."** Once McCain secured the Republican Presidential nomination in 2008, Cochran endorsed McCain.

Thad Cochran
Official Photograph

Let Bygones be Bygones: In 1936, Republican Vice Presidential nominee Frank Knox ridiculed President Franklin D. Roosevelt calling him **"a blundering visionary and fanatic,"** and said that the New Deal contained **"something of Karl Marx equally as much as Groucho Marx."** (Karl Marx was the author of *The Communist Manifesto.* Groucho Marx was a comedian). Knox later became U.S. Secretary of the Navy under Roosevelt.

Frank Knox
Official Photograph

Presidential Campaigns

Who's the Dunce Now? For much of Franklin D. Roosevelt's Second term, there was speculation that he would run for an unprecedented third term. Roosevelt was circumspect in not revealing his decision. He would craftily brush off the question. He would sometimes get annoyed. At a 1937 press conference, White House Correspondent Robert Post of *The New York Times* asked Roosevelt if he would seek a third term. An irritated Roosevelt responded: **"Bob, go put on the dunce cap and stand in the corner."** In 1940, when Roosevelt accepted the Democratic Party nomination for a third term, Mr. Post wrote him a letter reading: **"Who's the dunce now?"**

Franklin D. Roosevelt
Franklin D. Roosevelt Presidential
Library and Museum

Straight Whiskey and Politics: At the 1904 Republican National Convention, the Chairman, U.S. House Speaker Joe Cannon (R-IL), introduced former Kentucky Governor William O'Connell, who seconded the nomination of President Theodore Roosevelt, as coming from a state: **"where Republicans take politics, like whisky, straight."**

William O'Connell Bradley
Sketch by M.H. Thatcher

Playing The Confederate Card: During the 1960 Presidential campaign, John F. Kennedy appeared in Phoenix, Arizona and poked fun at the state's Junior U.S. Senator, the staunch conservative Barry Goldwater. **"I came down here because I thought it was very unfair of Dick Nixon to take Governor Rockefeller, Henry Cabot Lodge, and the President to New York without taking Barry Goldwater. If they can just get Barry out of that Confederate uniform that he has been traveling in through the South - he has been traveling all over the South - and get him up North, they could see him up there."**

Barry Goldwater (L)
John F. Kennedy (R)
John F. Kennedy Presidential
Library and Museum

Vote for Me or Don't: In 1940, Republican Presidential nominee Wendell Willkie told a crowd in Kansas City, Missouri: **"I'm the cockiest fellow you ever met. If you want to vote for me, fine. If you don't, go jump in the lake."**

Wendell Willkie
Library of Congress

Presidential Campaigns

What's In A Name? In Politics? More Than One Might Think: In 2008, one of the four finalists to be Barack Obama's Vice Presidential runningmate was U.S. Representative Chet Edwards (D-TX). On paper, he was a redoubtable contender. Edwards exhibited widespread bipartisan appeal representing a conservative Congressional District in Texas, where George W. Bush garnered 70% of the vote in 2004. Edwards was charismatic and made a name for himself in Congress as a champion of veteran's issues. He could have brought the ticket gravitas with veterans, blue-collar voters, and Southerners. There was one problem however. His last name is Edwards. The Democratic Party had recently been embarrassed when it was revealed that former Presidential Candidate and U.S. Senator John Edwards (D-NC) had had an extramarital affair with film producer and campaign staffer Rielle Hunter, while Edwards' wife, Elizabeth Edwards, was suffering from breast cancer. The Obama campaign chose U.S. Senator Joe Biden (D-DE) instead. Chet Edwards later admitted to reporters that his last name was a major factor in his not being selected as Obama's runningmate, averring: **"I would have to think that a bumper sticker that said 'Obama/The Other Edwards' would be difficult."**

Chet Edwards
Official Photograph

Wrong Information: On Election night in 1948, Herbert Brownell, the campaign manager for Republican Presidential nominee Thomas E. Dewey, announced to a cheering crowd at Dewey headquarters: **"We now know that Governor Dewey will carry New York by at least 50,000 votes and that he will be the next President of the United States."** While Dewey did in fact win New York, he lost the election to President Harry S. Truman. Brownell was not the only one to get the election wrong. The *Chicago Dailey Tribune* prematurely published the blazing headline: **"Dewey Defeats Truman."** Truman stunned political prognosticators by defeating Dewey handily, garnering 114 more electoral votes than Dewey.

Harry S. Truman Holds Up False Headline
Chicago Tribune

Likability Factor: 2008 Democratic Presidential candidate Hillary Clinton was asked in a debate why some voters like her opponent Barack Obama more than her. Clinton replied: **"Well that hurts my feelings but I'll try to go on." He's very likable. I don't think I'm that bad."** Obama interjected: **"Your likable enough Hillary, don't worry about it."**

Hillary Clinton
William J. Clinton Presidential
Library and Museum

Presidential Campaigns

Headache Time: In a 1975 interview with the CBS program *60 Minutes,* First Lady Betty Ford suggested that it would be **"perfectly normal"** if her 18-year old daughter Susan was having a premarital affair. Immediately after the interview, President Gerald R. Ford said to her: **"Honey, there goes twenty million votes, but we'll get over it."**

Gerald R. Ford (L), Betty Ford (R) with Dog Liberty Ford
Gerald R. Ford Presidential Library and Museum

Corn Cobs and Ukuleles: While campaigning for the Democratic Presidential nomination in 1960, Hubert Humphrey told a crowd in La Croix, Wisconsin, *"Time, Look and Life* [Popular magazines at that time] **don't give a damn about dairy prices. They don't know the difference between a corn cob and a ukulele."**

Hubert Humphrey
West Virginia State Archives
Harry Brawley Collection

I Guess He is Not That Important After all: In 1976, Jimmy Carter ran for the Democratic Presidential nomination as a grassroots candidate and did not make an effort to get to know the Democratic Party high command and major benefactors. Averill Harriman, Former New York Governor and U.S. Secretary of Commerce, was one such Democratic Party elite. In 1975 he commented about Carter: **"He can't win the Presidency. I don't even know him."** To Harriman's surprise, Carter's anti-politics message struck a resonant chord with the Democratic electorate. Carter won the nomination and the Presidency."

Averill Harriman
Official Photograph

Not The Hollywood Candidate: In 1976, Democratic Presidential nominee Jimmy Carter attended a Hollywood fundraiser with supporters from the entertainment industry. Comedian Tony Randall said to Carter: **"You've probably never met with people of this level."** Carter answered: **"No. That's how I got the nomination."**

Jimmy Carter
Jimmy Carter Library and Museum

Presidential Campaigns

Lyndon B. Johnson Disses Electoral Prowess of George McGovern in Texas: Bill Clinton was the Co-Chairman of 1972 Democratic Presidential nominee George McGovern's Texas campaign. Many Texas Democrats endorsed Republican President Richard M. Nixon. Former President Lyndon B. Johnson offered a tepid endorsement of McGovern but did not campaign with him. He told former aide Bobby Baker: **"George McGovern? Why, he couldn't carry Texas even if they caught Dick Nixon fu*** ng a Fort Worth sow."** McGovern lost Texas, garnering just 33.24% of the vote in the state.

George McGovern
Official Photograph

Doing the Electoral Spadework Herself: During the 1976 campaign for the Democratic Presidential nomination, Rosalyn Carter, wife of candidate Jimmy Carter, would literally go to television and radio stations unannounced and say: **"I'm Mrs. Jimmy Carter and I thought you might want to interview me."** Mrs. Carter came to be a regular on the campaign trail campaigning in 41 states on behalf of her husband.

Rosalynn Carter
Jimmy Carter Library & Museum

"Granting" his Vote to Buchanan: Prior to running for the Presidency, Republican Ulysses S. Grant was apolitical. His fist vote was in 1856, just 12 years before running for the Presidency. Grant voted for Democrat James Buchanan over Republican John C. Freemont. Grant had served with Freemont in the military and viewed him as an egotist. Grant said: **"I voted for Buchanan because I didn't known him and voted against Freemont because I did know him."**

Ulysses S. Grant
Library of Congress

Comparing Truman to a Jackass: Speaking against the election of Harry S. Truman to a full term as President in 1948, U.S. Representative Cliff Clevenger (R-OH) called Truman: **"A nasty little gamin"** and **"A Missouri Jackass."**

Cliff Clevenger
Official Photograph

Presidential Campaigns

Helms Takes on Hippies and George McGovern: In 1972, Vice President Spiro Agnew campaigned for re-election as part of the Nixon/Agnew-ticket in Charlotte, NC. At one campaign event there were longhaired protestors outside the arena, visible from the stage where Agnew introduced Republicans running for office in North Carolina. Jesse Helms, the party's Senate nominee in the Tar Heel state was jeered by the protestors when introduced. He got up to the podium and pointed to a group of young singers on the stage. Helms said: **"Isn't it nice that the majority of young people are represented by them instead of that** [pointing to the protestors]. Helms then exclaimed: **"And that one with the real long hair, that's George McGovern."** McGovern was the Democratic Presidential nominee. The Republican crowd erupted in pandemonium.

Jesse Helms
Official Photograph

Landslide Landon: In 1936, Republican Presidential nominee Alfred Landon adopted the campaign slogan: **"Let's make it a Landon-slide."** Instead, the election resulted in a landslide for Democrat Franklin D. Roosevelt. In fact, Landon won just two states, Maine and Vermont, with a collective eight electoral votes.

Alfred Landon
Official Photograph

Audience "Eggs on" President Truman: Campaigning for President on a whistle-stop tour in Spokane, Washington in 1948, a supporter said he should throw eggs at his chief U.S. Senate critic Robert Taft (R-OH). Truman retorted: **"I wouldn't throw fresh eggs at Taft. You've got the worst Congress you've ever had. If you** [referring to the audience] **send another Republican Congress to Washington, you're a bigger bunch of suckers than I think you are."** Truman won the election, and the Democrats took control of both chambers of the U.S. Congress.

Harry S. Truman During His 1948 Whistle-Stop Campaign Tour
Harry S. Truman Library and Museum

Democrat Switches to Republican Party: 1940 Republican Presidential nominee Wendell Willkie was a Democrat who became a Republican the year he sought the party's nomination. He would often refer to Republicans as: **"You Republicans,"** and appeared uncomfortable in the Republican Party. One of his rivals for the nomination, Thomas E. Dewey, opined: **"Wendell Willkie was a Democrat all his life until 1940 and never got over it."**

Wendell Willkie
Library of Congress

Presidential Campaigns

Governor Judas: In 2008, New Mexico Governor Bill Richardson dropped out of the Presidential sweepstakes and endorsed Barack Obama over Hillary Clinton for President. Hillary's husband Bill had nominated Richardson to the posts of U.S. Ambassador to the U.N. and to the position of U.S. Secretary of Energy. Political Consultant James Carville, a supporter of Hillary, observed: **"Mr. Richardson's endorsement came right around the anniversary of the day when Judas sold out for 30 pieces of silver, so I think the timing is appropriate, if ironic."**

Bill Richardson
Official Photograph

Old Soldiers Never Die: They Just Appear in Political Commercials: In 1952, Republican Presidential nominee Dwight D. Eisenhower participated in the first ever Television campaign commercials for a Presidential candidate. When he finished, Eisenhower (a former 5-Star Army General) turned to the advertisement's creator Rosser Reaves and said: **"To think that an old soldier should ever come to this."**

General Dwight D. Eisenhower
Dwight D. Eisenhower Presidential
Library and Museum

Piling On Willkie: On the last day of the 1940 Presidential campaign, New York City Mayor Fiorello La Guardia, who was campaigning for Franklin D Roosevelt in his attempt at winning a third term in Office, turned to a photographer as his picture was being taken and said: **"Go away, I did not come here to have my picture taken. He then told the crowd: "He thinks I'm Wendell Willkie.** Willkie was the Republican Presidential nominee known to like his picture taken. Responding to the uproarious laughter, La Guardia continued: **"Some men have their hair mussed because their brains are working, others because the photographers are working."**

Fiorello La Guardia (L)
Franklin D. Roosevelt (R)
National Archives
and Records Administration

"Cox and Cocktails:" In 1920, Republican Presidential nominee Warren G. Harding adopted the slogan: **"Cox and Cocktails."** Harding supported prohibition and in an effort to cultivate support in the prohibition community, Harding implied that if Democratic nominee James Cox were elected President, the Eighteenth Amendment to the U.S. Constitution, instituting Prohibition, would be repealed. Hypocritically, Harding consumed alcohol in private. Harding won the election in a landslide victory.

James Cox
Official Photograph

Presidential Campaigns

The Barefoot Boy From Wall Street: 1940 Presidential candidate Wendell Willkie spoke often about his humble roots, growing up in Longwood, Indiana, but managing to become a corporate lawyer and top Utilities executive. He managed to develop many ties to Wall Street. Joking about Willkie's humble beginnings story, U.S. Interior Secretary Harold Ickies dubbed him: **"The barefoot boy from Wall Street."** Furthering this joke, Alice Roosevelt Longworth, the daughter of Theodore Roosevelt, said Willkie has: **"grassroots in every country club in America."**

Wendell Willkie
Library of Congress

The Pure Wit of George W. Bush: In a 2004 fundraiser for the Republican Governors Association, George W. Bush mocked the Democrats vying for their party's Presidential nomination. Bush mused: **"The candidates are an interesting group, with diverse opinions -- for tax cuts and against them, for NAFTA and against NAFTA, for the Patriot Act and against the Patriot Act, in favor of liberating Iraq and opposed to it. And that's just one senator from Massachusetts."** (John Kerry)

George W. Bush
White House Photograph by Eric Draper

Hughes Loses Presidency While Sleeping: In 1916, Republican Presidential nominee Charles Evan Hughes went to bed believing he had been elected President. However, while Hughes slept, Democratic President Woodrow Wilson won California and the election. When a reporter called Hughes in the early morning to ask for a reaction to Wilson's comeback victory, the butler answered the phone saying: **"The President is asleep."** The reporter responded: **"When he wakes up, tell him he isn't the President."**

Charles Evans Hughes
Library of Congress

The Past is Over: After a bitter primary fight for the 2000 Republican Presidential nomination, in which George W. Bush defeated John McCain, Bush told *The Dallas Morning News*: **"The past is over."**

John McCain (L) with George W. Bush (R)
White House Photograph by Joyce N. Boghosian

Presidential Campaigns

Great Way to Kick Off a Campaign: In 2011, Michele Bachmann returned to Waterloo, Iowa where she was born to announce her bid for the Republican Presidential nomination. In an interview at the event with *Fox News*, Bachmann said: **"What I want them to know, just like John Wayne was from Waterloo, Iowa, that's the kind of spirit that I have too."** Actually, John Wayne the tough guy actor was not from Waterloo, Iowa, but from Winterset Iowa. However, serial killer John Wayne Gacy did live in Waterloo, Iowa during his twenties.

John Wayne Gacy (R) Pictured With Frist Lady Roslyn Carter (L)
White House Photograph

Presidential Candidate Forgets Her College Major: In a 2003 interview, Democratic Presidential candidate Carol Mosley Braun was asked by a news reporter what her major was in College. Braun responded: **"I don't remember what I majored in in college. . . . I hate to guess. I'm gonna guess it was Political Science, but I'm not sure. It might have been history. I'll check. I hadn't thought of that one."** Braun did in fact major in Political Science at the University of Illinois.

Carol Mosley Braun
Official Photograph

Shark Attack: In a 2012 interview with Ben Howe of the Iowa Republican TV Channel, 2008 Republican Presidential candidate Tom Tancredo shared a story from his campaign. **"We were at the University of New Hampshire and we were all going to a debate and there are all [Republican Presidential candidate] Ron Paul people and they're very excited and there's a guy standing there in a shark suit and one of my staff goes up and says 'Oh hi, are you with the Ron Paul people?' and the guy goes, Oh No! They're all nuts. I just wear a shark suit."**

Tom Tancredo
Official Photograph

I'm Running Against Whom? In 1844, a deadlocked Democratic National Convention chose a darkhorse, former Tennessee Governor James K. Polk, as their Presidential nominee. The Whig nominee, Henry Clay, mused: **"Who is James K. Polk?"** Polk went on the defeat Clay.

James K. Polk
Photograph by Mathew Brady

138

Chapter V

U.S. House of Representatives

U.S. House of Representatives

The Conservative Message of Gangsta Rap: In a 2013 interview with *Now This is News*, U.S. Representative Trey Radal (R-FL) revealed his admiration for Gangsta Rap and its conservative message. He was asked which song represents his conservative ideology. Radal said: **"The first that I would have to refer to would be 'Fight the Power,' by Public Enemy. This is a song that... if you really get down to it, reflects the conservative message of having a heavy-handed federal government. . . . Chuck D of Public Enemy and I may disagree on certain philosophies of government, but I think at the end of the day — and this is where I take my love of hip hop music — where there have been issues and problems with either heavy-handed law enforcement . . . or heavy-handed government itself."**

Trey Radel
Official Photograph

Cure For Inflation: U.S. Representative Morris Udall (D-AZ 1961-1991), a member of the U.S. House Committee on the Post Office and Civil Service, often joked: **"Let's turn inflation over to the Post Office. That'll slow it down."**

Morris Udall
Official Photograph

It's Howdy Doody Time: During a budget debate in 1995, U.S. Representative Marion Berry (D-AR) referred to his 30-year-old Republican colleague, U.S. Representative Adam Putnam (R-FL), as a: **"Howdy Doody looking nimrod."** Berry was incensed that Putnam and some Republican colleagues attacked the conservative Blue Dog Democrats, saying they were not true fiscal conservatives. He blasted Putnam for saying the Blue Dogs were increasing spending. Putnam responded, saying: **"that was quite a performance, and I respect the gentleman's passion; but I do not respect the fact that he chose to personalize the debate, an important debate about the future of our Nation."**

Adam Putnam
Official Photograph

Comparing Republicans to the Taliban: At a 2009 rally for Democrats running for Executive offices in Virginia, U.S. Representative Jim Moran (D-VA) said: **"If the Republicans were running in Afghanistan, they'd be running on the Taliban ticket as far as I can see."**

Jim Moran
Official Photograph

U.S. House of Representatives

No Skinny-Dipping in the Sea of Galilee: In 2011, U.S. Representative Kevin Yoder (R-KS), who was part of a group of House members to go on a trip to Israel sponsored by the American Israel Educational Foundation, illegally jumped into the Sea of Galilee nude (where many Christians believe Jesus Christ walked on water). A year later when the story was revealed, Yoder did a mea culpa, telling *The Kansas City Star*: **"Part of the reason I made that decision at that moment was there was really nobody in the vicinity who could see me. I dove in, hopped right back out, put my clothes on and, regardless, that was still not the behavior people expected out of their Congressman."**

Kevin Yoder
Official Photograph

Road Kill? In Arkansas, it is a tradition that politicians visit the town of Gillett to kick off the campaign season. The main food entrée is raccoon. In 2014, U.S. Representative Rick Crawford (R-AR) told *Roll call:* **"It doesn't taste like chicken."**

Rick Crawford
Official Photograph

Republicans are Not "Meanies" In 2014, U.S. Representative Luke Messer (R-IN) told *The Hill Magazine* that the Republican Party sometimes comes off as mean-spirited. He said: **"I think a large part of our challenges with single-mother constituencies is that we sound like meanies when we talk. At times our words don't match our intentions."**

Luke Messer
Official Photograph

Imagine a World Without Balloons: During a debate about the restructuring of the sale of helium from the nation's helium reserves, U.S. Representative Hank Johnson (D-GA) said on the House Floor: **"Imagine, Mr. Speaker, a world without balloons. How can we make sure that the injustice of there being no helium for comedians to get that high-pitched voice that we all hold near and dear to our hearts."**

Hank Johnson
Official Photograph

U.S. House of Representatives

Is Honesty Really the Best Policy? In 2010, U.S. Representative Paul Kanjorski (D-PA) told a local radio station that he would supplant traditional town hall meetings with teleconferences. Kanjorski asserted: **"We're going to do everything we can to get opinions from people, to meet with people, but I'm not going to set myself up for, you know, nuts to hit me with a camera and ask stupid questions."**

Paul Kanjorski
Official Photograph

Solution to Healthcare --- Die Quickly: In 2009, on the U.S. House Floor, U.S. Representative Allan Grayson (D-FL) lambasted the Republican Party on Healthcare Reform: **"If you get sick in America, the Republican health care plan is this: Die quickly. That's right, the Republicans want you to die quickly if you get sick."**

Alan Grayson
Official Photograph

Representative Calls MIT Economist "A Nut:" In referring to MIT Economist John Reilly's claim that instituting a cap-and-trade program for carbon admissions would cost only a fourth of what Congressional Republicans claim (based on a 2007 MIT study), U.S. Representative Louis Gohmert (R-TX) countered: **"Anyone who thinks you can pay $3,100 to the federal government and thinks you can get that money back completely in services -- like I said--he may go to M-I-T but he is an N-U-T."**

Louis Gohmert
Official Photograph

OK, That Clears It Up: In 2010, U.S. Representative Eric Massa (D-NY) resigned amid an investigation by the House Ethics Committee. He allegedly sexually harassed his aides. During an interview with Radio Talk Show Host Glenn Beck, Massa defended himself, saying: **"Now they're saying I groped a male staffer. Yes, I did. Not only did I grope him, I tickled him until he couldn't breathe and four guys jumped on top of me. It was my 50th birthday."**

Eric Massa
Official Photograph

U.S. House of Representatives

A Politician who does Not Mince Words: In 2010, after the organization "Americans for Tax Reform" alleged that U.S. Representative Gene Taylor (D-MS 1989-2011) had changed his position on Health Insurance Reform, Taylor issued a press release chastising the organization. It read: **"Americans for Tax Reform are lying sacks of scum, and anyone who knowingly repeats this false information is also a liar."** Taylor was a member of the conservative Blue Dog caucus.

Gene Taylor
Official Photograph

Today's Letter 'B': In 1942, former Republican Presidential nominee Wendell Willkie comparing the Neutrality Act to giving aid to German Chancellor Adolph Hitler. In response, U.S. Representative Dewey Short (R-MO) went to the House Floor to call Willkie: **"a Bellowing--Blatant---Bellicose---Belligerent---Blow-hard."**

Dewey Short
Official Portrait

Sometiimes Politics Can Get Ugly: U.S. Representative Peter Stark (D-CA) was badgered about the national debt during a 2009 interview with TV documentarian Jan Helfield. At the end of the interview, Stark said to Helfield: **"Get the f--k out of here or I'll throw you out the window."** Helfield complied with the order.

Peter Stark
Official Photograph

Eating Tasty Pork: U.S. Representative Jack Brooks (D-TX) was asked by *The New York Times* if his effort to add an earmark to the 1994 Violent Crime Control and Law Enforcement Act, which would construct a criminal justice center at Lamar University located in Brook's Congressional District, was pork. Brooks responded: **"If it's Pork, it'll be tasty."**

Jack Brooks
Official Photograph

U.S. House of Representatives

Double-crossed in the Caucus: U.S. Representative Morris Udall (D-AZ) ran for chairman of the House Democratic Caucus. A majority of the caucus told him they would vote for him. However, the vote was a secret ballot, and Udall lost. He said: **"I have learned the difference between a cactus and a caucus. On a cactus, the pricks are on the outside."**

Morris Udall
Official Photograph

A Case of Mistaken Identity: U.S. House Minority Leader Richard Gephardt (D-MO 1995-2003) was once approached by two ladies in an airport who were debating who he was. One lady asked Gephardt "**Are you [Former Vice President] Dan Quayle or the Weatherman on CNN?"**

Richard Gephardt
Official Photograph

GOBBLEDYGOOK! The funny term "gobbledygook" was coined by former U.S. Representative Maury Maverick (D-TX 1935-1939). Maverick was serving as the head of the United States Smaller War Plants Corporation during WWII. Maverick had little forbearance for technocratic jargon that he could not understand. Accordingly, Maverick wrote a memorandum to his employees stating: **"Stay off the gobbledygook language. It only fouls people up. For Lord's sake, be short and say what you're talking about ... anyone using the words 'activation' or 'implementation' will be shot."** The word "gobbledygook" was the brainchild of Maverick, imitating the noise a turkey makes.

Maury Maverick
Library of Congress

The Apocalypse is Near: In 2013, when the U.S. Supreme Court struck down the Defense of Marriage Act (which had barred same-sex married couples from being recognized as "spouses" for purposes of federal laws), U.S. Representative Tim Walberg (R-MI) said at a press conference: **"Society itself is at risk and cannot continue."**

Tim Walberg
Official Photograph

U.S. House of Representatives

Huey, Dewey, Louie, and Gun Control: In Response to Bill Clinton's 1994 State of the Union Address, in which he called for a Federal Assault Weapons ban, U.S. Representative Robert K. Dornan (R-CA) said on the House Floor: **"The Second Amendment is not for killing little ducks and leaving Huey and Dewey and Louie without an aunt and uncle. It's for hunting politicians, like in Grozny, and in the colonies in 1776, or when they take your independence away."**

Huey, Dewey, and Louie

I am in the Constitution: U.S. House Minority Whip Tom Delay (R-TX) said on the CNN program *Talk Back Live* in 1994: **"I am not a federal employee. I am a constitutional officer. My job is the Constitution of the United States; I am not a government employee. I am in the Constitution."**

Tom Delay on the Cover of *NewsMax*

Great Comeback: In 1972, during a hearing on Home Rule for the District of Columbia, U.S. Representative John Rarick (D-LA) testified against Home Rule for the District, calling it: **"a sinkhole, rat infested . . . the laughing stock of the free and Communist world."** U.S. Representative Charles Diggs (D-MI) disagreed and retorted: **"We are stretching the First Amendment even to permit 'you' to speak before this committee."**

John Rarick
Official Photograph

Weird Analogy: In 2013, U.S. Representative Steve Stockman (R-TX) tweeted: **"About 110,000 people contract Chlamydia each month, more than signed up for Obamacare. Stated another way, Obamacare is less popular than Chlamydia."** Chlamydia is a Sexually Transmitted Disease.

Steve Stockman
Official Photograph

U.S. House of Representatives

The Rot in Washington: At a 1906 Banquet at the W.L. Club in Springfield, Massachusetts, former U.S. Representative John R. Thayer (D-MA) remarked that when he was beginning his career in the U.S. Congress: **"A United States Senator said to me: Thayer, it is so rotten in Washington that when the roll is called in Congress I don't know whether to say "present" or "not guilty."**

John T. Thayer
Official Portrait

Welcome to the Twilight Zone: During a 2009 interview with *Pajamas TV*, U.S. Representative Michele Bachmann (R-MN) observed: **"I find it interesting that it was back in the 1970s that the swine flu broke out under another, then under another Democrat president, Jimmy Carter. I'm not blaming this on President Obama, I just think it's an interesting coincidence."** Actually, the last swine flu break occurred in 1976, when Gerald R. Ford was President.

Michele Bachmann
Official Photograph

Smoked Everything But the Bong Water: While many politicians hedge when it comes to the question of whether they had ever smoked marijuana, in 1988, shortly after being elected to the U.S. Congress, Dana Rohrabacher of California said he did: **"Everything but the bong water."** (The fluid used in a water pipe)

Dana Rohrabacher
Official Photograph

Term Limits and Colonel Sanders: In 1995, U.S. Representative Bob Ingles (R-SC), a vociferous exponent of term limits for members of the U.S. Congress, admitted that it is unrealistic for his colleagues to support term limits. He said: **"Asking an incumbent member of Congress to vote for term limits is a bit like asking a chicken to vote for Colonel Sanders."**

Bob Ingles
Official Photograph

U.S. House of Representatives

I am Not An Insurance Salesman: U.S. Representative Dennis Kucinich (D-OH 1997-2013) was a vociferous exponent of universal healthcare in America. Because he sometimes sounded like an insurance salesman, he joked: **"Everyone should have health insurance? I say everyone should have health care. I'm not selling insurance."**

Dennis Kucinich
Official Photograph

Let the Party Begin: When Jimmy Carter cancelled the B1 Bomber in 1977, U.S. Representative Robert K. Dornan (R-CA) opined: **"They're breaking out Vodka bottles in Moscow."**

B1 Bomber
U.S. Air Force

A Super Duper Power: In a 2002 *Fox News* interview, U.S. House Majority Whip Tom Delay (R-TX) said: **"We're no longer a superpower. We're a super-duper power"** Delay said this to make the case for why America must topple Iraqi President Saddam Hussein.

Tom Delay
Official Photograph

No Friend of Bill: U.S. Representative Robert K. Dornan (R-CA) refused to watch the Inauguration of President Bill Clinton in 1993. He told *The Los Angeles Times*: **"As much as I love history, I could not physically watch a decorated Navy combat carrier attack pilot** [George H. W. Bush] **passing on the torch to a draft dodger."**

Inauguration of Bill Clinton
National Archives

U.S. House of Representatives

The Smartest Guy in the Room: During a Congressional hearing of the Government Oversight and Reform Committee of the U.S. House of Representatives, Trey Goudy (R-SC) questioned Todd Park, the White House Chief Technology advisor, and asked him if there was a law requiring the Affordable Care Act to launch on October 1, 2013. Park responded that he did not know. Gowdy then said, **"You're the smartest guy in this room."** After Park denied that gratuitous comment, Gowdy retorted: **"Don't short yourself. You're the smartest one in this room. Trust me I've been in this room for a while."**

Trey Gowdy
Official Photograph

Congress Drugged Most of the Time: In her 1970 book, *Unbought and Unbossed,* U.S. Representative Shirley Chisholm (D-NY) observed: **"Congress seems drugged and inert most of the time. The idea of meeting a problem is to hold hearings or, in the extreme case, to appointing a commission."**

Shirley Chisholm
Liberty of Congress

Probably Not a Charter Member of the Dick Cheney Fan Club: In a 2005 interview with *NY1*, U.S. Representative Charley Rangel (D-NY) said of Vice President Dick Cheney: **"He's a sick man you know.... He's got heart disease, but the disease is not restricted to that part of his body. He grunts a lot, so you never really know what he's thinking. Why do you think people are spending so much time praying for President Bush's health? If he ever leaves and Cheney's in charge, there's not very much else to pull together for the rest of our nation. This is a sad state of affairs."** Rangel also said in the interview: **"I would like to believe he's sick rather than just mean and evil."** Cheney responded in an interview with Conservative Radio Talk Show Host Rush Limbaugh by saying: **"Charlie is losing it, I guess."**

Charlie Rangel
Official Photograph

Shame on You: During a 2009 address on the U.S House Floor, U.S. Representative Virginia Fox (R-NC) said: **"Fool me once, shame on you. Fool me twice, shame on you."**

Virginia Fox
Official Photograph

U.S. House of Representatives

When the Democrats Get in Your Way, Line Them Up and Shoot Them: In 1992, freshman U.S. Representative Randy "Duke" Cunningham (R-CA) told the *Blade-Citizen* of Ocean Side, California that Democrats who were stifling Republican legislation **"ought to be lined up and shot. I'm talking about the liberal leadership."**

Randy "Duke" Cunningham
Official Photograph

Nixon's Revenge: U.S. Representative Bella Abzug (D-NY 1971-1977), one of the most liberal members of Congress and a constant thorn in the sided of the Nixon and Ford administrations, observed: **"Richard Nixon impeached himself. He gave us Gerald Ford as his revenge."**

Bella Abzug
Library of Congress

Gerald R. Ford, a Master of Alliteration: During the 1967 Republican Response to Democratic President Lyndon B. Johnson's State of the Union Address, U.S. House Minority Leader Gerald R. Ford (R-MI) stated: **"The years have slipped by and now Americans in 1967 see the decade that dawned in hope fading into frustration and failure, bafflement and boredom."**

Gerald R. Ford
Lyndon Baines Johnson Library and Museum

He calls the President a 'Scumbag:' In 1998, U.S. Representative Dan Burton (R-IN), the Chairman of the U.S. House Government and Oversight Committee (which was investing alleged campaign finance violations by President Bill Clinton). told *The Indianapolis Star* Editorial Board: **"If I could prove 10 percent of what I believe happened, he'd [Clinton] be gone. This guy's a 'scumbag.' That's why I'm after him."**

Dan Burton
Official Photograph

U.S. House of Representatives

Congressman Suggests Shooting Vietnam War Protesters: In 1992, U.S. Representative Randy "Duke" Cunningham (R-CA) said of those who protested U.S. involvement in the Vietnam War: **"I would have no hesitation about lining them up and shooting them."**

Vietnam War Protestors
Lyndon Baines Johnson Library and Museum

The Difference Between the House and the Senate: In a 1959 interview, U.S. Representative Louis C. Rabaut (D-MI) delineated the difference between the U.S. House and the U.S. Senate. **"Why, we're the guinea pigs of the country. We have to go back to the country every two years and face the people. The senators can stay down here and do what they want for four years, and then get awful nice the last two years and rely on the short memory of the people."** Representative Rabaut is best known for drafting the legislation which added the words "under God" to the Pledge of Allegiance.

Louis C. Rabaut
Official Photograph

Comparing Congress to Junior High School: U.S. Representative Patrick McHenry (R-NC) compared the U.S. Congress to Junior High school, exclaiming: **"This place is a much more sophisticated junior high school. There are the nice guys that everybody likes, the jocks, the geeks, the bullies? They're all here. It's a representative democracy."**

Patrick McHenry
Official Photograph

Justified Homicide? In 1998, during the Monica Lewinsky episode, U.S. House Majority Leader Dick Armey (R-TX) was asked what he would do if he ever found himself in a similar situation. Armey replied: **"If I were, I would be looking up from a pool of blood and hearing** [my wife ask] **'How do I reload this thing?'"**

Dick Armey
Official Photograph

U.S. House of Representatives

Rectal Procedure: In 1998, U.S. Representative Randy "Duke" Cunningham (R-CA), a prostate cancer survivor, said on the House Floor that a rectal procedure he had undergone was **"just not natural, unless maybe you're** [U.S. Representative] **Barney Frank** (D-MA)." Barney Frank (Who is openly gay) responded: **"He seems to be more interested in discussing homosexuality than most homosexuals."**

Barney Frank
Official Photograph

Friends With Convictions: After Arkansas Governor Jim Guy Tucker and two of Bill Clinton's former business partners (James and Susan McDougal) were convicted on Whitewater related charges, U.S. House Minority Leader Dick Armey (R-TX) averred: **"Say what you want about the President, but we know his friends have convictions."**

Jim Guy Tucker (L), Bill Clinton (R)
National Archives and
Records Administration

The History of The Modern Bra: During One Minute Speeches in 2001, U.S. Representative James Traficant (D-OH) told his colleagues: **"Madam Speaker, it started with the training bra and then it came to the push-up bra; the support bra, the Wonder bra, the super bra. There is even a Smart Bra. Now, if that is not enough to prop up your curiosity, there is now a new bra. It is called the holster bra, the gun bra. That is right, a brassiere to conceal a hidden handgun. Unbelievable. What is next? A maxi-girdle to conceal a stinger missile? Beam me up. I advise all men in America against taking women to drive-in movies who may end up getting shot in a passionate embrace. I yield back all those plain old Maiden form brassieres and chain link pantyhose."**

James Traficant
Official Photograph

Having it Both Ways: U.S. Representative Walter P. Brownlow (R-TN 1897-1910) observed: **"The best legislator is the one who votes for all appropriations and against all taxes."**

Walter P. Brownlow
Official Photograph

152

U.S. House of Representatives

They Ran Like Rats: In 1992, U.S. Reprehensive Joseph Early (D-MA) was one of 22 U.S. House members named by the House Ethics Committee in the House Check-Writing Banking Scandal. Early was inflamed that the Committee had not asked for his explanation. He was accused of bouncing 124 House checks. Angered by the committee members ignoring him, Early declared: **"They ran like rats! What's wrong with going eyeball to eyeball when you're not afraid?"**

Joseph Early
Official Photograph

Environmental Disaster: In 1994, U.S. Representative Don Young (R-AK), the incoming Chairman of the U.S. Natural Resources Committee, was highly critical of the environmental movement, stating: **"Environmentalists: the self-centered bunch, the waffle-stomping, Harvard-graduating, intellectual idiots that don't understand that they're leading this country into environmental disaster."**

Don Young
Official Photograph

Just a Tad Supercilious: In 2006, U.S. House Majority Leader Tom Delay (R-TX) was told to put out a cigar he was smoking at the Ruth Chris Steak House in Washington, D.C. He was informed that a federal government regulation disallows individuals from smoking in public restaurants, Delay replied: **"I am the Federal Government."**

Ruth Chris Steak House Official Logo

The Spiraling Federal Deficit: In a statement released after George W. Bush delivered his 2004 State of the Union Address, U.S. Representative Brad Sherman (D-CA) stated: **"The President forgot to mention the Moon, Mars, and the federal deficit - all of which are sky-high."**

Brad Sherman
Official Photograph

153

U.S. House of Representatives

Give The Decision To 12 Honest Men, Not To The Congress: Vice President Spiro Agnew contemplated being tried by the U.S. Congress rather than in a court of law for accepting bribes and falsifying tax returns. When U.S. Representative Charles Vanik (D-OH) was apprised of this, he deadpanned: **"He's trying to take the decision out of the hands of twelve honest men and give it to 435 Congressmen."** Agnew eventually pleaded *nolocontendre* to the lesser charge of falsifying tax returns in Federal Court and did not face a trial on the condition that he resign his office.

Charles Vanik
Official Photograph

The Sad Truth of the Matter: In his private papers, U.S. Representative Sam Steiger (R-AZ) observed: **"Being a member of Congress is 90 percent form – you get attention, you view with alarm, you offer no solutions."**

Sam Steiger
Official Photograph

Who Cares? In 2012, the U.S. Supreme Court ruled that the Defense of Marriage Act (DOMA) was unconstitutional. The Act, signed by President Bill Clinton in 1996 in conjunction with other statutes, had barred same-sex married couples from being recognized as 'spouse' for purposes of federal laws, effectively barring them from receiving federal marriage benefits. However, DOMA's passage did not prevent individual states from recognizing same-sex marriage, but it imposed constraints on the benefits received by all legally married gay couples. U.S. Representative Michele Bachmann (R-MN) released a statement excoriating the decision. When a reporter asked U.S. House Minority Leader Nancy Pelosi (D-CA) to comment on Bachmann's statement, she responded: **"Who cares?"**

Nancy Pelosi
Official Photograph

Singer Goes Off To Congress: When renowned singer Sonny Bono (R-CA) was sworn into the U.S. Congress in 1997, he looked around at his new colleagues and observed: **"I feel like the black sheep, but here I am."**

Sonny Bono
Official Photograph

154

U.S. House of Representatives

Keeping It Classy: In 2002, U.S. House Minority Leader Richard Gephardt (D-MO) said that U.S. Representative James Traficant (D-OH) should resign from office after he was convicted of filing false tax returns, taking bribes, racketeering, and forcing his Congressional aides to do chores on his Ohio farm and on his houseboat. When a reporter asked Traficant to respond to Gephardt's request, Traficant responded: **"Gephardt has no balls and he can go f--k himself."** Later when he defended himself before the House prior to being expelled, Traficant said: **"Mr. Gephardt, if you're here, I apologize for my comments; it was in the heat of battle. If you had been there, I probably would have hit you too. But I apologize for these words."**

James Traficant
Official Photograph

A Racist Tax: At a Town Hall Meeting, U.S. Representative Ted Yoho (R-FL) told his constituents that he recently told U.S. House Speaker John Boehner (R-OH) that the 10% surcharge on tanning booths as part of the Affordable Care Act, a.k.a. Obamacare, is: **"a racist tax."**

Ted Yoho
Official Photograph

Grimm Situation: In 2014, NY1-TV Reporter Michael Scotto interviewed U.S. Representative Michael Grimm (R-NY) about President Barack Obama's State of the Union Address. During the interview, Scotto asked Grimm about an investigation into the illegal donations given to Grimm's 2010 campaign for Congress. Grimm refused to answer and walked off the set. After Scotto signed off, Grimm, not knowing the camera was still rolling, confronted Scotto and said: **"Let me be clear to you, you ever do that to me again I'll throw you off this f------g balcony."** Grimm later apologized, but contends the question was: **"a cheap shot."**

Michael Grimm
Official Photograph

Down on FEMA: In 1989, the Federal Emergency Management Agency (FEMA) was criticized for its poor handling of a hurricane in the Southeast and an earthquake in Northern California. U.S. Representative Norman Mineta (D-CA) concluded that the agency **"could screw up a two-car parade."**

Norman Mineta
Official Photograph

U.S. House of Representatives

Congressman Asks Constituent What Planet she Spends Most of her Time on: At a town hall meeting with constituents in Dartmouth, Massachusetts, U.S. Representative Barney Frank (D-MA) was asked by constituent Rachel Brown (who came to the meeting holding a sign depicting Barack Obama with an Adolf Hitler-style mustache): **"Why do you continue supporting the Nazi** [Heath Care] **policy as Obama has expressly supported this policy? Why are you supporting it?** Frank Responded: **"When you ask me that question I am gonna revert to my ethnic heritage and answer your question with a question: On what planet do you spend most of your time? As you stand there with a picture of the President defaced to look like** [Adolph] **Hitler and compare the effort to increase health care to the Nazis, my answer to you is, as I said before, it is a tribute to the First Amendment that this kind of vile, contemptible nonsense is so freely propagated. Ma'am, trying to have a conversation with you would be like arguing with a dining room table: I have no interest in doing it."**

Barney Frank
Official Photograph

Goal: To Be a Nicer Son of a Bitch: In 1974, some reform-minded House Democratic caucus members wanted to oust U.S. Representative Wayne Hayes (D-OH), the longtime House Administrative Committee Chairman. Hayes survived in part because of his fundraising prowess in his role as Chairman of the Democratic Congressional Campaigning Committee (DCCC). Hayes was liked by few colleagues because of his short temper and vindictive personality. After surviving the attempt to dislodge him, Hayes told the Democratic Caucus: **"Obviously from everything that has been said in the newspapers, and quite a few things said publicly, I am a 'son of a bitch.' I will try to be a nicer 'son of a bitch.'"**

Wayne Hayes
Official Photograph

Who Let The Dogs Out? In a speech to the U.S. Chamber of Commerce in 1999, U.S. Representative Bill Thomas (R-CA) said: **"How many crossbreeds between a Great Dane and a Chihuahua have you seen? Likewise there is great difficulty with a House -- Senate conference."**

Bill Thomas
Official Photograph

U.S. House of Representatives

Obama's Heart: At a 2012 political fundraiser in Colorado for the re-election campaign of U.S. Representative Mike Coffman (R-CO), Coffman told attendees: **"I don't know whether Barack Obama was born in the United States of America. I don't know that. But I do know this --- that in his heart, he's not an American. He's just not an American."** Coffman later apologized for making the remark.

Mike Coffman
Official Photograph

Outburst: In 2009, when Barack Obama was addressing a joint session of the U.S. Congress regarding Healthcare Reform, the President said: **"The reforms I'm proposing would not apply to those who are here illegally."** U.S. Representative Joe Wilson (R-SC) shouted: **"You Lie."** Wilson later apologized to the President for his obvious **"lack of civility."**

Joe Wilson
Official Photograph

The Incoming Intelligence Committee Chairman Needs Better Intelligence. In 2006, Jeff Stein of the *Congressional Quarterly* asked Silvestre Reyes (D-TX), the incoming Chairman of the House of Representatives Permanent Select Committee on Intelligence, if al-Qaeda members were Sunni or Shia. Reyes incorrectly answered: **"They are probably both, Predominantly Shiite."** In actuality, Al Qaeda members are Sunni and they view Shia as heretics. Stein then asked Reyes to define Hezbollah. Not knowing the answer, Reyes' response to the question was: **"Why do you ask me these questions at five o'clock."**

Sylvester Reyes
Official Photograph

The Ongoing Asparagus Feud: During a 2013 U.S. Judiciary Committee meeting, a confrontation broke out between U.S. Attorney General Eric Holder and U.S. Representative Louie Gohmert (R-TX) about the FBI's investigation of the alleged Boston bomber Tamerlan Tsarnaeev. Gohmert said: **"The Attorney General will not cast aspersions on my asparagus."** During another hearing almost a year later, the two once again clashed, and Holder, remembering Gohmert's previous malapropism, said in a sarcastic tone to Gohmert: **"Good luck with you asparagus."**

Louie Gohmert
Official Photograph

U.S. House of Representatives

Governmental Official Needs to Enroll in 'Firearms 101: U.S. Representative Dianne DeGette (D-CO), speaking at a 2013 gun control forum in her Denver-based Congressional District, talked of her support for outlawing high-capacity magazines. She said: **"If you ban them in the future, the number of these high-capacity magazines is going to decrease dramatically over time because the bullets will have been shot and there won't be any more available."** She does not seem to realize that the magazines can be refilled.

Dianne DeGette
Official Photograph

Too Big to Fail: In 1984, after the federal government bailed out the Continental Illinois Bank just before it went into default, U.S. Representative Stewart B. McKinney (R-CT) stated: **"We have a new kind of bank. It is called 'Too Big to Fail:' TBTF, and it is a wonderful bank."** The term gained notoriety during the Bank bailout of 2009, when the federal government bailed out the nation's banks.

Stewart B. McKinney
Official Photograph

What if Guam Capsizes: During a hearing of the U.S. House Committee on Armed Services, which was meeting to deal with a planned buildup of U.S. military personnel at a military installation in Guam, U.S. Representative Hank Johnson (D-GA) said to the Commander of the U.S. Pacific Command, Robert F. Willard: **"My fear is that the whole island will become so overly populated that it will tip over and capsize."** Willard responded: **"We don't anticipate that."** After the exchange went viral, Johnson later said he was trying to be **"humorous."**

Hank Johnson
Official Photograph

Creative Criticism: During an 1866 debate on the U.S. House Floor, U.S. Representative James G. Blaine (R-ME) excoriated his colleague U.S. Representative Roscoe Conklin (R-NY) for **"haughty disdain, his grandiloquent swell, his majestic, supereminint overpowering, turkey-gobbler strut."**

James G. Blaine
Library of Congress

U.S. House of Representatives

Scary Stuff Here: In the 1976 book *Introduction to the Rockefeller Files* by Gary Allen, U.S. Representative Larry McDonald (D-GA) warned: **"The drive of the Rockefellers and their allies is to create a one-world government, combining Super-Capitalism and Communism under the same tent, all under their control ... Do I mean conspiracy? Yes I do. I am convinced there is such a plot, international in scope, generations old in planning, and incredibly evil in intent."**

Larry McDonald
Official Photograph

Green Bananas: U.S. Representative Claude Pepper (D-LA) died in 1989 at the age of 88 years old. At that time he was the oldest member of the U.S. Congress. Pepper once joked in his later years: **"A stockbroker urged me to buy a stock that would triple its value every year. I told him, 'At my age, I don't even buy green bananas.'"**

Claude Pepper
Official Photograph

Making a Difference Wearing a Bag Over One's Head: In 1992, U.S. Representative Jim Nussle (R-IA) placed a bag over his head on the House Floor to exhibit his embarrassment to be a part of the Body during the House Check-writing Banking scandal. The ploy made the 32-year-old freshman lawmaker a national figure. He told students at a vocational school in his Congressional District: **"One person can put a bag on his head and make a difference."**

Jim Nussle
Official Photograph

The Funny Farm: In a 2006 address to the Agribusiness Club of Washington, U.S. House Minority Leader Nancy Pelosi (D-CA) stated: **"As many of you know, I come from San Francisco. We don't have a lot of farms there. Well, we do have one—it's a mushroom farm, so you know what that means."**

Nancy Pelosi
Official Photograph

U.S. House of Representatives

The Burro Massacre: In 1975, U.S, Representative Steve Steiger (R-AZ) received a call that 14 escaped burros were garrisoned along the highway in his Congressional District. Steiger went to investigate and landed up shooting them dead. He claimed it was in self-defense because they allegedly charged him. To Steiger's chagrin, the incident made national news, and he was broadly excoriated by the public for shooting the animals. Twenty years later, a frustrated Steiger told *The Associated Press*: **"I could find a cure for cancer and they'd remember me as the guy who shot the burros."**

Burros
Photograph by Eciphr

Better to Keep Congress on the Links: In 2005, U.S. Representative Chet Edwards (D-TX), referring to golfing, told *The Hill* that **"Congress would be better if we played more rather than less."**

Chet Edwards
Official Photograph

The Inmate Runs the Asylum: In 2011, four members of the Nuclear Regulatory Commissions testified at a U.S. House Committee on Oversight and Government Reform that Chairman Gregory B. Jackzo withheld information from them and berated staff members. U.S. Representative Trey Gowdy (R-SC), a former federal prosecutor, said at the hearing: **"When you have four eyewitnesses that testify to someone under oath, you know what they call a defendant after that? An inmate."**

Gregory B. Jackzo
Official Photograph

Don't Tax the Dead! In a 2003 debate about the elimination of the estate tax, U.S. Representative Tom Feeney (R-FL) stated: **"No taxation without respiration."**

Tom Feeney
Official Photograph

U.S. House of Representatives

The "Show Me" State: In 1899, U.S. Representative William Duncan Vandiver (D-MO), in a speech at the Five O' Clock Club in Pennsylvania, remarked: **"I come from a state that raises corn and cotton, and cockleburs, and Democrats, and frothy eloquence neither convinces nor satisfies me. I am from Missouri. You have got to show me."** The phrase "show me" had became synonymous with Missouri, and the Vandiver address solidified it. Consequently, the state's unofficial nickname became: "The Show Me State."

William Duncan Vandiver
Official Photograph

Gangsta Rap: In 1988, U.S. Representative Mario Biaggi (D-NY) was convicted for taking illegal gratuities while in office. During his trial, Assistant U.S. Attorney Edward J. Little called Biaggi: **"A thug in a Congressman's Suit."**

Mario Biaggi
Official Photograph

Edward Snowden v. Jeffrey Dahmer: Speaking at the 2014 Breitbart National Security Action Summit, U.S. Representative Steve King (R-IA) drew a comparison between former NSA employee Edward Snowden and serial rapist and murderer Jeffrey Dahmer: **"Snowden has done more damage to America than anybody I can think of in history. I would take it so far as to say that probably Jeffrey Dahmer . . . didn't do nearly as much damage as Snowden did."**

Steve King
Official Photograph

The Dead Will Never be the Same Again: In 1989, after an earthquake battered San Francisco, U.S. Representative Barbara Boxer (D-CA) exclaimed: **"Those who survived the San Francisco earthquake said, 'Thank God, I'm still alive.' But, of course, those who died, their lives will never be the same again."**

Barbara Boxer
Official Photograph

U.S. House of Representatives

Political Theater: In 1983, Chicago Mayor Jane Byrne asked U.S. Representative Dan Rostenkowski (D-IL), the Chairman of the House Ways and Means Committee, to help the City procure an Urban Development Action Grant (UDAG) to preserve the Chicago Theater from being demolished. Rostenkowski called Vice President George H. W. Bush and told him: **"Tell the President,** [Ronald Reagan] **if he can't give me this piddly UDAG to save the Chicago Theatre, he'll have one pissed off chairman during the next round of tax reforms."** Housing and Urban Development Secretary Samuel Peirce telephoned Rostenkowski, asking if he could come to his office and visit him. Rostenkowski responded: **"Sure, just bring the papers for the theater project."** Knowing the immense power Rostenkowski possessed, The UDAG was granted and the theater remains in use today.

Dan Rostenkowski
Official Photograph

Playing the Lemmings Card: On the eve of the partial shutdown of the Federal Government in 2013 (Resulting from the Affordable Care Act, A.K.A. ObamaCare), U.S. Representative Devin Nunes (R-CA) called out his fellow Republican members of Congress, branding them: **"Lemmings with suicide vests."**

Devin Nunes
Official Photograph

Not in a New York State of Mind: In 1834, U.S. Representative David "Davy" Crocket (Whig-TN) visited New York City for the first time. He told S.D. Jackson: **"I would rather risk myself in an Indian fight than venture among these creatures after night. God deliver me from such constituents or from a party supported by such."**

David "Davy" Crockett
Library of Congress

U.S. House of Representatives

Political Candidates Should be Required to Leave the Country: In 1940, U.S. Representative George Tinkham (R-MA) told *Life Magazine* that all candidates for political office should be forced to leave the country the months preceding an election. He said: **"It would spare everyone a great deal of pain: Those who are running and those who are listening."**

George Tinkham
Official Photograph

Heroin Here: New York Mayor John Lindsey was considering experimenting with legalizing heroin in parts of New York City for addicted adults. U.S. Representative Charlie Rangel (D-NY), who represents Harlem, joked to Lindsey: **"Well, we got plenty of heroin in my district. We don't need any more. So I suggest you try it in Queens and Staten Island. They don't have very much there."**

Charlie Rangel
Official Photograph

Still Two Vietnams? In a 2010 speech on the House Floor, U.S. Representative Shelia Jackson Lee (D-TX) exclaimed: **"Today, we have two Vietnams, side by side, North and South, exchanging and working."** After the conservative intelligencia ridiculed Lee for making this remark, she issued a statement saying she **"misspoke."** There is only "one" Vietnam.

Shelia Jackson Lee
Official Photograph

He is No Gentleman: In 1995, during a fiery debate on the elimination of an exemption for nuclear carriers and submarines under the Clean Water Act, Democratic Socialist Representative Bernie Sanders (I-VT) asked his colleague Randy Duke Cunningham (R-CA) to yield. Rather than yield, Cunningham responded: **"Sit down, you Socialist."** U.S. Representative Patricia Schroeder (D-CO) responded: **"Mr. Chairman, do we have to call the gentleman 'The gentleman' as he is not one?"**

Patricia Schroeder
Official Photograph

U.S. House of Representatives

U.S. Representative Tells Constituent to 'Go to Hell:' U.S. Representative John Steven McGroarty (D-CA 1935-1939) once wrote back to a constituent who sent him a critical letter saying he had not kept a campaign promise. McGroarty wrote: **"One of the countless drawbacks of being in Congress is that I am compelled to receive impertinent letters from a jackass like you in which you say I promised to have the Sierra Madre mountains reforested and I have been in Congress two months and haven't done it. Will you please take two running jumps and go to Hell?"**

John Steven McGroarty
Official Photograph

But He's Still Alive: In 1998, U.S. Representative Bob Stump (R-AZ) announced on the House Floor: **"It is with sadness I announce that** [Comedian] **Bob Hope is dead."** The problem is that Hope was alive. *The Associated Press* mistakenly posted on its Web site that he had died. U.S. House Majority Leader Dick Armey (R-TX) saw it, and gave the article to Stump and asked him to announce his death. When *Reuters* reported that Hope was alive, Armey went to the House Floor to apologize. Hope lived for another five years.

Bob Hope
Library of Congress

Another Case of Live Microphone: U.S. Representative Martin R. Hoke (R-OH) was about to be interviewed jointly with U.S. Representative Eric Fingerhut (D-OH) after President Bill Clinton's 1994 State of the Union Address. A female television producer asked Hoke to unbutton his jacket, Hoke responded: **"You can ask me to do anything you want."** Hoke then said to Fingerhut: **"She's got ze beega breasts."** The incident was taped, though not broadcast live. The tape was soon played on Cleveland television stations, prompting Hoke to publically apologize and declare: **"I need a 2-by-4 to the head."**

Martin R. Hoke
Official Photograph

He Just Doesn't Get It: During a 2011 appearance on MSNBC, U.S. Representative John Fleming (R-LA) blasted a proposal by President Barack Obama to increase taxes on the wealthy. Fleming told host Chris Jansing: **"The amount that I have to invest in my business and feed my family is more like $600,000 of that $6.3 million** [his Gross Income]. **So by the time I feed my family I have, maybe, $400,000 left over to invest in new locations, upgrade my locations, buy more equipment."** This statement resulted in Fleming being characterized by liberal commentators as an elitist.

John Fleming
Official Photograph

Chapter VI

Speakers of the U.S. House of Representatives

Speakers of the U.S. House of Representatives

Kooks, Commies, and Egghead Professors: In 1966, future U.S. House Speaker Tip O'Neill (D-MA) addressed a rally at the Massachusetts State House in support of U.S. involvement in the Vietnam War. In his speech, O'Neil took aim at those who opposed the war, including many in academia who were his Cambridge constituents. O'Neill said: **"I believe in Academic Freedom, but not as it is expounded by kooks, commies, and egghead professors."** A year later, O'Neill became an opponent of the war.

Tip O'Neill
Official Photograph

Tell Them How You Really Feel Mr. Speaker: U.S. House Speaker Thomas Bracket Reed (R-ME 1889-1891 and 1895-1899) did not speak very highly of his House colleagues. He said: **"They never open their mouths without subtracting from the sum of human knowledge."**

Thomas Bracket Reed
Library of Congress

Boehner and Wiener: In an address to the New York and Puerto Rican delegations to the 2012 Republican National Convention in Tampa, Florida, U.S House Speaker John Boehner (R-OH) joked about his last name and compared it to former U.S. Representative Anthony Weiner (D-NY): Boehner quipped: **"People have trouble with my name. Is it Bainer? Bonner? Boner? At least it's not Weiner."**

John Boehner
Official Photograph

Bragging About the Dirt in His Congressional District: In a 1900 Column written for *The Saturday Evening Post*, future U.S. House Speaker Champ Clarke (D-MO) referred to his Congressional District as:

"The rich Mesopotamian Country of the Western World." He was comparing the fertile lands of Missouri with the fertile lands of ancient Mesopotamia, a country between two rivers.

Champ Clarke
Library of Congress

Speakers of the U.S. House of Representatives

Bipartisan Friendship: Although they were political rivals, Sam Rayburn (D-TX) and Joe Martin (R-MA) were close personal friends. Both served as Speaker of the U.S. House of Representatives and as House Minority Leader (depending on which party was in power). Some Democratic members of the U.S. Congress wanted Rayburn to campaign against Martin in his Massachusetts Congressional District. Sam Rayburn responded: **"Speak against Joe? Hell, if I lived up there, I'd vote for him."**

Sam Rayburn (L) and Joe Martin (R)
Library of Congress

Speaker References 'The Three Stooges': U.S. Representatives Newt Gingrich (R-GA), Robert Walker (R-PA), and Vin Webber (R-MN) often used Special Orders (Speaking in an empty House Chamber after the House has adjourned) to bash the Democratic Congressional Leadership. They often rankled U.S. House Speaker Tip O'Neill (D-MA). When a reporter asked O'Neill if he listened to this criticism, he replied: **"What are the names of the Three Stooges? I think I'll let Larry, Moe, and Curley talk to themselves."**

Tip O'Neill
Official Photograph

Newt Slams Ronald Reagan: In 1985, after it was announced that President Ronald Reagan would meet with Soviet General Secretary Mikhail Gorbachev, future U.S. House Speaker Newt Gingrich (R-GA) warned that the meeting would be **"The most dangerous summit for the West since Adolf Hitler met with Chamberlain** [British Prime Minister Neville Chamberlain, 1937-1940] **in 1938 in Munich."**

Ronald Reagan (L), Mikhail Gorbachev (R)
Ronald Reagan Presidential
Foundation and Library

Words To Live By: U.S. House Speaker Joe Martin (R-MA 1947-1949 and 1951-1953) believed that the best approach for members of the House was to keep their head down and say very little. His advice to all U.S. House members: **"A closed mouth gathers no feet."**

Joe Martin
Official Portrait

Speakers of the U.S. House of Representatives

Friendly Partisan Banter: In 1977, when U.S. Representative Tip O'Neill (D-MA) was sworn in as Speaker of the House, he was introduced by U.S. House Minority Leader John Rhodes (R-AZ) as: **"The greatest one-term Speaker in the History of the House."** O'Neill retorted: **"I understand you have your eye on the Speaker's seat. I'm sure that's all you'll have on it."** O'Neill would go on to serve as Speaker for ten years before retiring in 1987.

Tip O'Neill
Official Portrait

GOP Feud: In 1984, U.S. Senator Bob Dole (R-KS) suggested that a tax increase might be necessary to reduce the proliferating federal budget deficit. Future U.S. House Speaker Newt Gingrich (R-GA) dubbed Dole: **"The tax collector of the Welfare State."**

Newt Gingrich
Official Photograph

Republican Cat Fight: President Theodore Roosevelt, who hailed from the progressive bloodline of the Republican Party, often clashed with U.S. House Speaker Joseph Cannon (R-IL). Cannon worked actively to stymie Roosevelt's domestic program, which was titled: "The Square Deal." Cannon hailed from the conservative bloodline of the Party. Cannon said of Roosevelt: **"He has no more use for the Constitution than a tomcat has for a marriage license."** Cannon also said of Roosevelt: **"That fellow at the other end of the Avenue wants everything from the birth of Christ to the death of the devil."** Roosevelt supported conserving federal land. Cannon was no conservationist, declaring: **"Not One Cent for Scenery."**

Joseph Cannon
Library of Congress

The Cobra and the Mongoose: U.S. House Speaker Joe Martin (R-MA) described his relationship with Democratic President Harry S. Truman in the following way: **"like a cobra and a mongoose."**

Joe Martin
Official Photograph

Speakers of the U.S. House of Representatives

LBJ: A Hog on Ice: U.S. House Speaker Sam Rayburn (D-TX) served as a mentor to a fellow member of the Texas Congressional Delegation, U.S. Representative Lyndon B. Johnson (D-TX). Rayburn witnessed Johnson's independent streak when Johnson was the only member of the Texas Congressional Delegation who refused to sign a letter supporting fellow Texan and Vice President John Nance Garner against charges of being anti-labor and a whisky drinker. After Rayburn failed to secure Johnson's vote, Rayburn called him: **"A damn independent boy; independent as a hog on ice."**

Sam Rayburn (L) Gets Kissed by his Protégé Lyndon B. Johnson (R)
From the Sam Rayburn Papers at the Dolph Briscoe Center for American History

The Real Story Comes Out Nearly a Century Later: In 1902, just two weeks before the mid-term Congressional election, U.S. House Speaker David B. Henderson (R-IN) announced that he would not seek re-election to the House. His public reason was that while he, like most Republicans at the time, supported high protective tariffs, his Indiana constituents did not. Accordingly, Henderson said he could not represent his constituents' views in the U.S. Congress. Henderson's announcement came out of the blue. The real reason for the abrupt move was unearthed by Forest Maltzman and Eric Lawrence of George Washington University in 1997. They found a letter written by House Clerk Henry H. Smith to Henderson's successor as Speaker, Joseph Cannon (R-IL). In the letter, Smith claims: **"There can be but one explanation of the reason for his action . . . they relate not alone to poker playing, but to his alleged intimacy with a certain `lobbyess' who is reported to have some written evidence that would greatly embarrass the Speaker. . . . He seemed to have lost all control of himself and become reckless. . . . This is not mere guesswork at all but private and reliable information which I am sure you will recognize when I tell you the name."**

David B. Henderson
Official Portrait

Speakers of the U.S. House of Representatives

He's Got Ice-Water for Blood: Though he shared an Irish heritage with Ronald Reagan and they shared a cordial personal relationship, U.S. House Speaker Tip O'Neill (D-MA) publicly held President Ronald Reagan in very low regard. He said of Reagan: **"The evil is in the White House at the present time. And that evil is a man who has no care and no concern for the working class of America and the future generations of America, and who likes to ride a horse. He's cold. He's mean. He's got ice water for blood."**

Ronald Reagan (L), Tip O'Neill (R)
Ronald Reagan Presidential
Foundation and Library

Passive Speaker: U.S. House Speaker Fredrick Gillett (R-MA 1919-1925) had a passive personality. A reporter once said: **"He did not drink coffee in the morning for fear it would keep him awake all day."**

Frederick Gillett
Official Photograph

Real Political Experience Counts: In 1961, Vice President Lyndon B. Johnson was mesmerized by the intelligence of members of the administration of John F. Kennedy. After a meeting, he told U.S. House Speaker Sam Rayburn (D-TX) about their sterling educations, credentials, and intelligence. Rayburn responded: **"Well, Lyndon, everything you say may be true, but I'd feel a whole lot better if one of them had ever run for sheriff."**

**Lyndon B. Johnson Stands Beside
a Statue of Sam Rayburn**
Lyndon Baines Johnson Library and Museum

The Trouble With Taft: U.S. House Speaker Joseph Cannon (R-IL) made the following observation about his fellow Republican, President William Howard Taft, who was a Unitarian and who many thought had unorthodox religious views: **"The trouble with Taft is that if he were Pope, he would think it necessary to appoint a few Protestant cardinals."**

Joseph Cannon
Official Photograph

Speakers of the U.S. House of Representatives

Just Shut Up! U.S. House Speaker Sam Rayburn (D-TX) often reminded his colleagues: **"No one has a finer command of language than the person who keeps his mouth shut."**

Sam Rayburn
Official Photograph

The Czar of The House: U.S. House Speaker Joseph Cannon (R-IL) was near omnipotent in the House. U.S. Representative George Norris (R-NE) mused that the national government: **"is divided into the Senate, the President, and the Speaker."**

Joseph Cannon
Library of Congress

Good Humor Partisanship: During a 2007 farewell ceremony for U.S. House Speaker Dennis Hastert (R-IL), his Democratic Successor as Speaker, Nancy Pelosi (D-CA), said: **"I rise to salute Speaker Dennis Hastert, the longest-serving Republican Speaker in history. And long may that record stand."** Hastert served as U.S. House Speaker for eight consecutive years.

Dennis Hastert
Official Photograph

Pelosi's Mistake: In a 2009 speech to the National Association of Counties in Washington D.C., U.S. House Speaker Nancy Pelosi (D-CA) said of the Affordable Care Act, a.k.a. Obamacare: **"We have to pass the bill so that you can find out what is in it, away from the fog of controversy."** Pelosi Spokesman Brendan Day suggested the remark was taken out of context. **"She meant there was so much talk about process (in Congress) that people have lost sight of what's actually in the bill. Once it's passed, we can remind them of all the good things that are in it."** However, Republicans had a field day with the original comment.

Nancy Pelosi
Official Photograph

Chapter VII

U.S. House of Representatives Campaigns

U.S. House of Representatives Campaigns

An Angry Davy Crocket---King of the Wild Frontier---Leaves Tennessee for Texas in a Huff: After losing a re-election bid in 1834, U.S. Representative Davy Crocket (Whig-TN) exclaimed: **"I told the people of my district that I would serve them as faithfully as I had done; but if not ... you may all go to hell, and I will go to Texas."** He did go to Texas and died at the Battle of the Alamo on March 6, 1836.

Davy Crockett
Library of Congress

U.S. House Member Heading for Walmart? After failing to garner the requisite 50.1% of the vote to avoid a Republican runoff, U.S. Representative Ralph Hall (R-TX), at 90 years old the oldest man ever to serve in the House, was asked by Fox News if he will win the runoff. Hall's Response: **"If not, I'll go to work at Walmart. I've got to have a job."**

Ralph Hall
Official Photograph

If Babies Had Guns: U.S. Representative Steve Stockman (R-TX) returned to the U.S. House of Representatives in 2012 after a 16-year hiatus. He had been defeated in 1996. Stockman, a staunch conservative, was elected by voters in the conservative Thirty-Sixth Congressional District of Texas, located in the conservative southeast area of the state. His campaign bumper stickers read: **"If babies had guns, they wouldn't be aborted."**

Bumper Sticker from the Steve Stockman for Congress Campaign

Boating Can Be Dangerous: John F. Kennedy served in WWII as a Commander of a Patrol boat. In 1943, Kennedy's boat, the PT-109, was cut in half by a Japanese destroyer while out on patrol. He received a commendation for saving the life of a badly wounded crew-member and leading the rest of his crew to safety. In 1946, while a candidate for U.S. Congress in the Eleventh Congressional District of Massachusetts, a child asked John F. Kennedy how he became a hero in WWII. Rather than exploit the situation, Kennedy deadpanned: **"It was easy. They cut my boat in half."**

John F. Kennedy on the PT-109
John F. Kennedy Presidential Library and Museum

U.S. House of Representatives Campaigns

The Choice Between Going To Congress or Going to Hell: In 1846, Abraham Lincoln was running for a seat in the U.S. House of Representatives against Democrat Peter Cartwright, a Methodist minister. At an event where both candidates were present, Cartwright, said: **"All those who do not wish to go to hell will stand."** Lincoln was the only person to remain seated. Cartwright said: **"May I inquire of you Mr. Lincoln, where are you going?** Lincoln responded: **"Brother Cartwright asks me directly where I am going. Well, I am going to Congress."** Lincoln won the election and Cartwright went back to his preaching at the pulpit.

Peter Cartwright
A Youth's History of Kentucky for School and General Reading by Ed Porter Thompson (1897)

Not a Good Party Man: When former conservative Democrat U.S. Representative Gene Taylor of Mississippi became a Republican in 2013 and announced he would run to try to regain his old seat, he said: **"I was never a good Democrat. So I could be just as bad a Republican."**

Gene Taylor
Official Photograph

Charles Darwin Runs for U.S. House in Georgia and Loses to Creationist: Plant biologist Jim Lebanese-Mack of the University of Georgia orchestrated a write-in campaign for the late English geologist Charles Darwin after his U.S. Representative, Paul Broun (R-GA), said at the Sportsman's Banquet at the Liberty Baptist Church in Hartwell, Georgia, that **"God's word is true. I've come to understand that. All that stuff I was taught about evolution and embryology and the big bang theory, all that is lies straight from the pit of Hell. It's lies to try to keep me and all the folks who were taught that from understanding that they need a savior. You see, there are a lot of scientific data that I've found out as a scientist that actually show that this is really a young Earth. I don't believe that the Earth's but about 9,000 years old. I believe it was created in six days as we know them. That's what the Bible says."** Broun, a Republican, was safely re-elected with 209,917 votes. Darwin garnered just 4,000 votes. There was no Democratic challenger on the ballot.

Paul Broun
Official Photograph

U.S. House of Representatives Campaigns

Disparaging a Unitarian Candidate: In 1942, Former Massachusetts Governor James Michael Curley defeated U.S. Representative Thomas H. Elliot (D-MA) in the Democratic Primary. Curley exploited Elliot's religious background, which was Unitarian (Elliot was the son of a Unitarian minister). In campaign speeches in the State's urban ethnic Eleventh Congressional District, Curley exclaimed to the crowd: **"My young opponent is a Unitarian. Do you know what a Unitarian is? A Unitarian is a person who believes that our Lord and Savior is a funny little man with a beard who runs around in his underclothes."**

James Michael Curley
Library of Congress

Look at it as a Favor: In his 2014 bid for re-nomination, a reporter asked U.S. Representative Ralph Hall (R-TX) about his runoff opponent John Ratcliffe. Hall said: **"Well, I'm going to do something for him. Rockwell [Texas] needs good men. I'm gonna leave him right here in Rockwell where they can have him."** Unfortunately for Hall, Ratcliffe went on to defeat Him.

John Ratcliffe
Official Photograph

Long Time Resident of Hanoi Runs For Office in Arizona: In John McCain's first political race for the U.S. House of Representatives in Arizona, a voter labeled him a carpetbagger because he had only lived in the Grand Canyon state for less than a year. McCain responded: **"Listen, pal. I spent 22 years in the Navy. My grandfather was in the Navy. We in the military service tend to move a lot. We have to live in all parts of the country, all parts of the world. I wish I could have had the luxury, like you, of growing up and living and spending my entire life in a nice place like the First District of Arizona, but I was doing other things. As a matter of fact, when I think about it now, the place I lived longest in my life was Hanoi."** McCain won the race.

Campaign Button for John McCain in his First Run for the U.S. House of Representatives

Let's Make a Deal: In 2006, U.S. Representative Christopher Shays (R-CT) heard that Rahm Emanuel (D-IL), the chairman of the Democratic Congressional Campaign Committee, was planning on appropriating $3 million to defeat him in his re-election bid. Upon crossing paths with Emanuel, Shays joked to Emanuel: **"Just give me $3 million, and I'll retire voluntarily."**

Christopher Shays
Official Photograph

Chapter VIII

U.S. Senate

U.S. Senate

Taking the Term 'Son of a Bitch' Literally: When told the Imperial Wizard of the Ku Klux Klan was going to come to Louisiana, U.S. Senator Huey Long (D-LA) said: **"You tell that imperial bastard in Mississippi to keep out of Louisiana. Tell that son of a bitch that I am not just using an expression; I am referring to the circumstances of his birth."**

Huey Long
Library of Congress

It's Like Teenage Sex: After the Persian Gulf War had concluded, U.S. Senator Tom Harkin (D-IA) told the *Independent of London:* **"The Gulf War was like teenage sex. We got in too soon and out too soon."**

Tom Harkin
Official Photograph

Cigarettes are 'Kind to the Throat:' In 1927, U.S. Senate Majority Leader Charles Curtis (R-KS) appeared in a magazine advertisement for Lucky Strike Cigarettes. Curtis writes: **"Lucky Strikes do not affect the voice. I notice that most of my colleagues in the Senate now use them. They do so, not only because they know that they are kind to the throat, but also they give the greatest enjoyment."**

Charles Curtis
The Kansas State Historical Society

A Different World: After being elected to the U.S. Senate, Republican Fred Thompson of Tennessee quipped: **"I've still got a lot to learn about Washington. Thursday, I accidentally spent some of my own money."**

Fred Thompson
Official Photograph

181

A Zebra Cannot Change It's Stripes: In 1990, while Blasting President George H.W. Bush's environmental record on the Senate Floor, U.S. Senator Al Gore (D-TN) exclaimed: **"Anyone who sees George Bush as the environmental President at the Grand Canyon ought to look closely for Elvis, alive and well, rafting by on the Colorado River. A zebra cannot change its stripes by standing on a busy street corner in a city."**

Al Gore
Official Photograph

Standing Strong with the NRA: Speaking to a National Rifle Association Convention in 1994, U.S. Senator Phil Gramm (R-TX) garnered applause by saying: **"I own more shotguns than I need, but not as many as I want."**

National Rifle Association Logo

A Witty Rejoinder: A constituent asked her U.S. Senator Margaret Chase Smith (R-ME 1949-1973): **"What would you do if you woke up one morning and found yourself in the White House?"** Smith deadpanned: **"I would go to the President's wife and apologize, and then leave at once."**

Margaret Chase Smith
Official Photograph

Oxymoron? Pat Roberts served as the Chairman of the U.S. Senate Select Committee on Intelligence. He joked: **"I have the privilege of being Chairman of the Senate Intelligence Committee. It is not an oxymoron I assure you."**

Pat Roberts
Official Photograph

U.S. Senate

Hard to Argue With: In 1984, U.S. Senator Paul Tsongas (D-MA) announced he would not seek re-election after being diagnosed with non-Hodgkin Lymphoma. He said: **"No one on his deathbed ever said, I wish I had spent more time on my business."**

Paul Tsongas
Official Photograph

Not a Monolith: In 1990, noting the ideological diversity of the Democratic Party at the time, U.S. Senator Patrick Leahy (D-VT) observed: **"You get fifteen democrats in a room, and you get twenty opinions."**

Patrick Leahy
Official Photograph

Graveyard of Good Ideas: U.S. Senator Tom Udall (D-NM) came to the Senate in 2009 and made the following observation: **"The Senate is a graveyard for good ideas. Gridlock, hyper partisanship, delay, obstruction – it adds up to one thing: broken."**

Tom Udall
Official Photograph

Kiss Ass Job: In 1989, when asked about the powers he would employ upon assuming the office of U.S. Senate Majority Leader, George Mitchell (D-ME) replied: **"You have to kiss 99 asses."**

George Mitchell
Official Photograph

183

U.S. Senate

Its About Sex: During the closing arguments on the impeachment of President Bill Clinton before the U.S. Senate, former U.S. Senator Dale Bumpers (D-AR), arguing for the defense, told his former Senate colleagues: **"H. L. Mencken [Essayist] said one time, 'When you hear somebody say: This is not about money' – it's about money.' And when you hear somebody say: 'This is not about sex' – it's about sex."**

Dale Bumpers
Official Photograph

Wayne's World: In 1953, U.S. Senator Wayne Morse of Oregon left the Republican Party believing that the party had moved too far to the right. He declared himself an Independent. The Republican Party no longer afforded him a seat on the Senate Floor. Accordingly, Morse brought his own chair to the Senate Floor from home. He said: **"Since I haven't been given any seat in the Senate, I've decided to bring my own."** Two years later, Morse became a Democrat and received a chair on the Democratic side of the aisle.

Wayne Morse
Lyndon Baines Johnson Library and Museum

Not Nice: U.S. Senator Jesse Helms (R-NC), a vociferous critic of President Bill Clinton, told *The Raleigh News and Observer* in 1995: **"Mr. Clinton better watch out if he comes down here. He'd better have a bodyguard."** He was referring to Clinton's unpopularity throughout military bases in North Carolina. Helms later said it was: **"an offhand remark."**

Jesse Helms
Official Photograph

Delivering a Press Release Rather Than a Speech: At a dinner, U.S. Senator Joseph Montoya (D-NM 1964-1977) inadvertently picked up a press release rather than a speech written for him by aides. Montoya said to the crowd: **"Ladies and Gentlemen, it is a great pleasure to be with you today. For immediate release today."**

Joseph Montoya
Official Photograph

184

U.S. Senate

Culinary Diplomacy: U.S. Senator Mike Enzi (R-WY) was a member of the Gang of Six, who negotiated Health Care Reform. Enzi opposed the Democrats' Healthcare Plan. Speaking to his constituents at a Wyoming town hall meeting, Enzi insisted that he was trying to negotiate concessions. Enzi defended his negotiations with the Democrats, by saying: **"If you're not at the table, you're on the menu."**

Mike Enzi
Official Photograph

A Drone Exception: In 2013, U.S. Senator Rand Paul (R-KY) filibustered for 13 hours to get the administration of Barack Obama to say they would not kill non-combatants in America. Though Paul has become identified as a critic of drones, when he found out that drones are being used for beer delivery at an outdoor music festival in South Africa, Paul tweeted: **"Perhaps I am not against all drones."**

Rand Paul
Official Photograph

Lewinsky and Enron: In 2002, Kenneth Lay, the former Chairman of the collapsed Energy Corporation named Enron, cancelled testimony before a U.S. Senate Committee. Ernest "Fritz" Hollings (D-SC), a member of the Committee, compared the relationship between Lay and President George W. Bush with that of Bill Clinton and Monica Lewinski. Clinton had said: **"I did not have sexual relations with that woman, Ms. Lewinsky."** Hollings, imitating Bush, quipped: **"I did not have political relations with that man, Mr. Lay."**

Kenneth Lay
Official Mug Shot, Taken by
U.S. Marshalls Service

He'll Be Here All Night: In 2014, During a 21-hour and 19 minute speech in the U.S. Senate in opposition to funding The Affordable Care Act, a.k.a. Obama Care, U.S. Senator Ted Cruz (R-TX) exclaimed: **"I'll talk until I can't stand anymore. Don't worry, I have government-run health insurance. I'll be fine."** This was the fourth longest speech in U.S. Senate history. Cruz did however yield time to his like-minded colleagues.

Ted Cruz
Official Photograph

U.S. Senate

Strutting his Stuff: U.S. Senator Warren G. Magnuson (D-WA) said of Admiral Lewis Strauss (a rejected nominee to the serve on the Atomic Energy Commission): **"He is the only guy I know that could strut sitting down."**

Lewis Strauss
U.S. Department of Commerce

Hey! I'm that Son of a Bitch: When future U.S. Senator Fred Harris (D-OK) was running for "re-election" to the Oklahoma State Senate in 1958, he entered a bar and greeted a patron, and said: **"I'm Fred Harris and I'm running for 're-election' to the State Senate and I would appreciate your help."** The patron responded: **"All right kid, I'll help you. Anybody who can beat that Son of a Bitch that's up there now."**

Fred Harris
Official Portrait

McConnell Chides the First Duffer: During his address to the Republican National Convention in 2012, U.S. Senate Minority Leader Mitch McConnell (R-KY) received laughter when he joked that: **"For years, Barack Obama has been running from the nation's problems. He hasn't been working to earn re-election. He's been working to earn a spot on the PGA** [Professional Golf Association] **Tour."** Obama was often criticized for spending too much time on the links.

Mitch McConnell
Official Photograph

No Political Pandering Here: U.S. Senator Stephen M. Young (D-OH 1959-1971) was known for his blunt and sometimes sarcastic responses to constituents who challenged his views. One letter-writer ended his letter by saying: **"I would welcome the opportunity to have intercourse with you."** Senator Young responded: **"You sir, can have intercourse with yourself."**

Stephen M. Young
Official Photograph

U.S. Senate

Republican Gangsta Rap Enthusiast: U.S. Senator Marco Rubio (R-FL) told *GQ Magazine* that the rapper Pit Bull's songs are **"all party songs. There's no message for him, compared to like an Eminem. But look, there's always been a role for that in American music. There's always been a party person, but he's a young guy. You know, maybe as he gets older, he'll reflect in his music more as time goes on. I mean he's not Tupac. He's not gonna be writing poetry."**

Marco Rubio
Official Photograph

Words Taken Back: In 2005, at an event at Del Sol High School in Las Vegas, U.S. Senate Minority Leader Harry Reid (D-NV) said of George W. Bush: **"This man's father was a wonderful human being. I think this guy is a loser."** Reed later apologized to Deputy Chief of Staff Karl Rove for making this remark.

Harry Reid
Official Photograph

Definitive Statement: After *Roll Call* reported that U.S. Senator Larry Craig (R-ID) had been arrested on suspicion of lewd conduct in a men's restroom at the Minneapolis-St Paul International Airport, Craig announced: **"I am not Gay and never have been gay."**

Larry Craig
Official Photograph

False Positive: In 2006, U.S. Senator Orrin Hatch (R-UT) told a group of Utah Politicians: **"Nobody denies that [Saddam Hussein] was supporting al-Qaeda. Well, I shouldn't say nobody. Nobody with brains."**

Orrin Hatch
Official Photograph

U.S. Senate

A Bird of a Different Feather: On matters of foreign policy, U.S. Senator Henry "Scoop" Jackson (D-WA) was considered by many as a hawk during the Cold War. Jackson rejected that characterization, saying: **"I'm not a hawk nor a dove, I just don't want my country to be a pigeon."**

Henry "Scoop" Jackson
Official Photograph

Pragmatic Idealism: U.S. Senate Minority Leader Everett Dirksen (R-IL 1959-1969) was known for his ability to compromise. He said: **"I am a man of fixed and unbending principles, the first of which is to be flexible at all times."**

Everett Dirksen
Library of Congress

Liking the Spotlight: U.S. Senator Ernest "Fritz Hollings" (D-SC) was a sponsor of the 1983 Gramm Rudman Hollings Deficit Reduction Act with Warren Rudman (R-NH) and Phil Gramm (R-TX). Hollings remarked on Gramm's tendency to enjoy the limelight. **"If you want a lesson in political anonymity, sponsor a bill with Phil Gramm."**

Ernest "Fritz" Hollings
Official Photograph

A Horse-whipping Senator: During a debate on proposed legislation to combat Aids in 1991, U.S. Senator Jesse Helms (R-NC) said: **"I'm so old-fashioned, I believe in horse-whipping."** (Horse-whipping is the act of whipping a horse to control it.)

Jesse Helms
Official Photograph

U.S. Senate

No Love for the East Coast: In 1961, Western conservative U.S. Senator Barry Goldwater (R-AZ) joked at a press conference: **"Sometimes I think this country would be better off if we could just saw off the Eastern Seaboard and let it float out to sea."**

Barry Goldwater
Library of Congress

Theological Humor: Edward Everett Hale, who held the position of Chaplin of the U.S. Senate from 1903-1909, was once asked: **"Do you Pray for the Senators?"** Everett responded: **"No, I look at the Senators and I pray for the country."**

Edward Everett Hale
The Critic: An Illustrated Monthly Review of Literature, Art and Life

Trash Talking Senators: U.S. Senators Daniel Webster (Whig-MA) and Henry Clay (Whig-KY.) witnessed a pack of mules walking by. Webster commented: **"There goes a number of your Kentucky constituents."** Clay retorted: **"Yes, they must be on their way to Massachusetts to teach school."**

Henry Clay
Official Photograph

Arlen Specter's Bikini Analogy: During an interview with Gwenn Ifell on *The News Hour* on PBS in 2005, U.S. Senate Judiciary Committee Chairman Arlen Specter (R-PA) discussed his meeting with Judge John Roberts, President George W. Bush's nominee to serve on the U.S. Supreme Court. Specter said: **"I don't like labels. I think they conceal more than they reveal, sort of like a bikini."** Roberts won Specter's vote and was confirmed by the U.S. Senate.

Arlen Specter
Official Photograph

U.S. Senate

American Idle Material? On the Senate Floor in 1994, U.S. Senator Alfonse D'Amato (R-NY) performed a rendition of the popular nursery rhyme *Old Macdonald Had a Farm* in opposition to the proposed crime bill supported by President Bill Clinton. While standing next to a drawing of a pink pig, D'Amato sang: **"President Clinton had a bill, E-I-E-I-O. And in that bill was lots of pork, E-I-E-I-O. New pork here, old pork there, here pork, there pork, everywhere pork, pork."**

Alfonse D'Amato
Official Photograph

Humming Bird Flies to Mars with Washington Monument: In 1933, the Twenty-first Amendment to the U.S. Constitution was ratified. The Amendment repealed the Eighteenth Amendment, which prohibited: "the manufacture, sale, or transportation of intoxicating liquors." The author of the Eighteenth Amendment, U.S. Senator Morris Sheppard (D-TX), predicted just three years before the repeal: **"There's as much chance of repealing the 18th Amendment as there is for a humming bird to fly to Mars with the Washington Monument tied to its tail."**

Morris Sheppard
Official Portrait

Ahhh --- Now I Understand What the Internet is: In 2006, while arguing against an amendment to disallow Internet service providers from changing to a tiered Internet structure, U.S. Senator Ted Stevens (R-AK) said: **"The Internet is not a big truck. It's a series of tubes."**

Ted Stevens
Official Photograph

Dole Calls Nixon "Evil": Upon seeing Presidents Jimmy Carter, Gerald R. Ford and Richard M. Nixon standing together at the 1978 funeral of Vice President Hubert Humphrey, U.S. Senator Bob Dole (R-KS) remarked: **"See no evil, hear no evil — and evil."**

Richard M. Nixon (L), Bob Dole (R)
Robert J. Dole Archive and Special Collections

U.S. Senate

Get your Own Damn Dam: U.S. Senator Frank Church (D-ID 1957-1981), a stalwart supporter of President Lyndon B. Johnson on most issues, broke from the President on his handling of the Vietnam War. He told the President he was persuaded by nationally syndicated columnist Walter Lippmann that the U.S. should negotiate with the North Vietnamese Government. Johnson responded: **"The next time you want a dam in Idaho, go talk to Walter Lippmann."**

Frank Church
Official Photograph

The Benefits of Mis-Quoting: U.S. Senate Minority Leader Everett Dirksen (R-IL) is often credited with the quote: **"A billion here, a billion there, pretty soon you're talking real money."** A passenger on an airplane once asked him about the quote, and Dirksen replied: **"Oh, I never said that. A newspaper fella misquoted me once, and I thought it sounded so good that I never bothered to deny it."**

Everett Dirksen
Official Photograph

Just Horsing Around: U.S. Senator William Borah (R-ID) was known as an independent-minded legislator. When President Grover Cleveland was told that Borah had taken up horseback riding, he replied: **"Its hard to imagine Senator Borah going in the same direction of the horse."**

William Borah
Library of Congress

Holding a Press Conference to Announce He Will Make a Decision, But Not Now: In 2007, U.S. Senator Chuck Hagel (R-NE), who had not decided if he would 1) seek re-election to the Senate, 2) run for President, or 3) retire from politics all together, called a press conference to announce his political future. Television networks in the state carried the announcement live. Hagel told the assembled audience: **"I'm here today to announce that my family and I will make a decision on my political future later this year."**

Chuck Hagel
Official Photograph

U.S. Senate

Upon Leaving the U.S. Senate: Good Bye and Good Riddance: Speaking at his retirement dinner in 1923, which was hosted by the Mississippi Society of Washington D.C., U.S. Senator John Williams (D-MS) was blunt about not wanting to stay for another term in the Senate. He told the crowd: **"I may have grown cynical from long service, but this is a tendency I do not like, and I sometimes think I'd rather be a dog and bark at the moon than stay in the Senate another six years and listen to it."**

John Sharpe Williams
Library of Congress

Words of Wisdom from a Retired Senator: In his 2004 book, *Parting Shots from MY Brittle Bow,* former U.S. Senator Eugene McCarthy (D-MN) observed: **"It's dangerous for a candidate to say things that people might remember."**

Eugene McCarthy
Official Photograph

All in the Family: U.S. Senator Mike Lee (R-UT) is the son of Rex Lee, who served as U.S. Solicitor General under President Ronald Reagan. Mile Lee became steeped in Constitutional Law. Mike Lee told CBS News in 2011: **"I think I was about 30 before I realized that not every family talks about the Presentment Clause on a regular basis."** (The Presentment Clause is Article I, Section 7, Clauses 2 and 3 of the United States Constitution. It defines how legislation passed by the U.S. Congress must be "presented" to the President of the United States.)

Mike Lee
Official Photograph

Republican takes on Viagra: In an appearance on CNN's *Larry King Live*, former U.S. Senator Bob Dole (R-KS) said that he is a test subject for Viagra. He joked: **"I wish I had bought stock in it. Only a Republican would think the best part of Viagra is the fact that you could make money off of it."**

Bob Dole
Robert J. Dole Archives and
Special Collections

U.S. Senate

No Defense for Nepotism: When Alaska Governor Frank Murkowski was elected to the U.S. Senate in 2002, he appointed his daughter, Lisa Murkowski to fill out the remaining two years of his senate term. In response to charges of nepotism, Lisa Murkowski responded: **"I have never once asked Alaskans to like how I got this job."**

Lisa Murkowski
Official Photograph

Hollywood, the Epitome of Sincerity: U.S. Senator Fred Thompson (R-TN), a former actor, joked: **"After two years in Washington, I often long for the realism and sincerity of Hollywood."**

Fred Thompson
Official Photograph

Not in my Back Yard: As reported in the 2007 book: *Cape Wind*: M*oney, Celebrity, Class, Politics, and the Battle for Our Energy Future on Nantucket Sound* by Wendy Williams and Robert Whitcomb, Jim Liedell, a retired utility executive, asked U.S. Senator Ted Kennedy (D-MA), a usual supporter of alternative Energy, if he would support the Cape Wind Project (an offshore wind farm in Nantucket Sound). Kennedy replied: **"But don't you realize that's where I sail?"**

Ted Kennedy
U.S. National Archives & Records Administration

The Most Dangerous Place in Washington: In 1995, U.S. Senate Minority Leader Bob Dole (R-KS) commented on U.S. Representative Charles Schumer (D-NY) and his many on-air appearances. Dole said: **"The most dangerous place in Washington is between Charles Schumer and a television camera."**

Charles Schumer
Official Photograph

U.S. Senate

Deep Thoughts with Roman Hruska: During the confirmation hearings for Richard M. Nixon's failed U.S. Supreme Court nominee Harold Carswell, U.S. Senator Roman Hruska (R-NE) defended allegations that Carswell was of mediocre intelligence by stating: **"Even if he were mediocre, there are a lot of mediocre judges and people and lawyers. They are entitled to a little representation, aren't they, and a little chance? We can't have all Brandeis's, Frankfurters and Cardozo's."**

Roman Hruska
Library of Congress

Ouch: In a conference call with Iowa reporters, U.S. Senator Tom Harkin (D-IA), the Chairman of the Senate Agricultural Committee, said: **"The farm bill is like giving birth to a porcupine. It's very painful."**

Tom Harkin
Official Photograph

Goldwater Recommends that all Good Christians Should Kick Preacher's Ass: Reverend Jerry Falwell was a vociferous opponent of Ronald Reagan's nomination of Sandra Day O'Connor to the U.S. Supreme Court. Falwell thought her views on social issues were too liberal. He urged **"All Good Christians to oppose the nomination of Sandra Day O'Connor to the U.S. Supreme Court."** In response to Falwell's statement, U.S. Senator Barry Goldwater (R-AZ), a Libertarian-oriented conservative who virulently opposed social conservative inroads in the Republican Party, quipped: **"All good Christians should kick Jerry Falwell's ass."**

Barry Goldwater
Official Photograph

Love and Marriage: In 2008, former U.S. Senator Rick Santorum (R-PA) authored a column for *The Philadelphia Inquirer* criticizing same-sex Marriage. In the column, Santorum asserts: **"Is anyone saying same-sex couples can't love each other? I love my children. I love my friends, my brother. Heck, I even love my mother-in-law. Should we call these relationships marriage, too?"**

Rick Santorum
Official Photograph

U.S. Senate

Political One-upmanship: When Lyndon B. Johnson served as U.S. Senate Majority Leader, he had a teasing, friendly relationship with his Republican political foe U.S. Senate Minority Leader Everett Dirksen (R-IL). Johnson was thrilled when he was the first in Washington to have a car phone. Dirksen, to keep up with Johnson, wanted one too. One day when Johnson was riding around in his limousine, he got a call from Dirksen, who proudly informed him that he was calling him from his new car phone. Without skipping a beat, Johnson replied, **"Hold on a minute, my other phone is ringing."**

Lyndon B. Johnson (L), Everett Dirksen (R)
Lyndon Baines Johnson Presidential
Library and Museum

Tax The Fellow Behind The Tree: In 1973, U.S. Senate Finance Committee Chairman Russell B. Long (D-LA) told *Money Magazine*: **"Most people have the same philosophy about taxes: Don't tax you, don't tax me, tax that fellow behind the tree."**

Russell B. Long
Official Photograph

Euphemistic License: In an address to the U.S. Senate in 1960, Minority Leader Everett Dirksen (R-IL) joked: **"I like euphemistic terms. I am reminded of the lady who was having her family tree examined. Unfortunately they found one brother who had occupied the electric chair in Sing Sing. The genealogist who was doing the work did not particularly want to state that fact. He hunted for something which would get around that fact and still tell the truth. At long last, at that part in the genealogical tree, he wrote: 'There was one brother who occupied the chair of applied electricity in a large public institution.'"**

Everett Dirksen on the Cover of
Time Magazine

One Box or Another: U.S. Senator Claiborne Pell (D-RI) served for six terms. He finally retired in 1997 after 36 years in the Senate. Pell observed: **"People who leave Washington do so by way of the box, ballet or coffin."**

Claiborne Pell
Official Photograph

195

U.S. Senate

Political Trash-Talking: In 1919, U.S. Senate Majority Leader Henry Cabot Lodge Sr. (R-MA) called Democratic President Woodrow Wilson, who he had feuded with over the ratification of the Treaty of Versailles, **"the most sinister figure that ever crossed the country's path."**

Henry Cabot Lodge Sr.
Library of Congress

Sexual One-upmanship: U.S. Senate Majority Leader Lyndon B. Johnson (D-TX) and U.S. Senator John F. Kennedy (D-MA) were both known as playboys by their colleagues. Johnson sometimes got jealous when he heard about Kennedy's affairs. He would tell his colleagues: **"I had more women by accident than Kennedy ever had on purpose."** The playboy proclivities of the two continued when each became President.

John F. Kennedy (L), Lyndon B. Johnson (R)
Lyndon B. Johnson Presidential
Library and Museum

Now Starting for the Green Bay Packers: Tight End Ted Kennedy: U.S. Senator Ted Kennedy (D-MA) played tight end for the Harvard University Crimson Football Team and was recruited by Green Bay Packers coach Lisle Blackbourn. Kennedy turned down the offer, informing Blackbourn that he: **"intended to go into another contact sport, politics."**

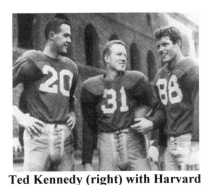

Ted Kennedy (right) with Harvard Crimson Teammates
John F. Kennedy Presidential Library and Museum

Joe Lieberman is Too Sexy for His Shirt: In an exit interview with Mark Liebovich of *The New York Times* in 2012, U.S. Senator Joe Lieberman (I-CT) was asked: **"Are you puzzled that more attention was not paid to your physique?"** Lieberman responded: **"I am. Because beneath this shirt, there is really a lot to behold that would give voters a sense of confidence about my capacity for balanced leadership."**

Joe Lieberman
Official Photograph

U.S. Senate

Counting Tanks the Bulgarian Way: During a hearing of the U.S. Senate Foreign Relations Committee, U.S. Senator Wayne Morse (I-OR) asked Defense Secretary Robert McNamara how many tanks there were in Latin America. He responded: **"964 and that is 60% as many tanks as the single country of Bulgaria has."** Fellow committee member U.S. Senator Eugene McCarthy (D-MN) drew laughter from his colleagues when he asked: **"Why Bulgaria? Do you count tanks relative to Bulgaria? Is there a Bulgarian absolute relative to tanks?"** McNamara responded: **"If there were, I would tell you about it."**

Eugene McCarthy
Official Photograph

A Dog Lover and Democrat to the End: Before his 2007 death, former U.S. Senator Thomas Eagleton (D-MO) wrote a letter of Farwell to friends and family to be released at his funeral. He ended the address by writing: **"So go forth in love and peace – be kind to dogs – and vote Democratic."**

Thomas Eagleton
Official Photograph

U.S. Senator Advocates for Colored Handkerchiefs: In 1994, U.S. Senator Howell Heflin (D-AL) was feasting with reporters on Capital Hill when he pulled out a pair of panties from his pocket. Heflin issued a Press Release to explain what happened: **"I mistakenly picked up a pair of my wife's white panties and put them in my pocket while I was rushing out the door to go to work. Rather than take a chance on being embarrassed again, I'm going to start buying colored handkerchiefs."**

Howell Heflin
Official Photograph

To the Victor Goes the Spoils: The term "Spoils System" (referring to political patronage) was originated by a statement from U.S. Senator William Marcy (D-NY) in 1832. He was defending President Andrew Jackson's nomination of former Secretary of State Martin Van Buren (a Jackson political supporter) as the Ambassador to the Court of St. James (England) by saying: **"To the victor goes the spoils."**

William Marcy
Library of Congress

U.S. Senate

Truman Tries to Reenlist in the Army: When U.S. Senator Harry S. Truman (D-MO) was serving on the Military Affairs Committee in 1942, he approached General George Marshall and said: **"I'd like to go on active duty. I'm a colonel in the field artillery."** Marshall asked Truman: **"How old are you Senator?"** Truman responded: "Fifty-six." Marshall told Truman: **"Why, you're too old, Senator."** Truman replied: **"Why, I'm not as old as you are by three years, General."** Marshall then replied: **"Yes, but I'm a general and I'm in and you're a colonel and you're not in."**

Harry S. Truman (L), General George Marshall (R)
Harry S. Truman Library and Museum

Dating Games: As Bill Clinton's job approval rating increased in 1997, U.S. Senator Ernest "Fritz" Hollings (D-SC) quipped: **"If they reach 60 percent, then he can start dating again."**

Ernest "Fritz" Hollings
University Library South Carolina
Political Collections

No Spring Break in Siberia for McCain: In 2014, the U.S. placed sanctions on Russia and certain Russian officials for Russia's invasion and annexation of the Crimean Peninsula, In retaliation, Russia imposed sanctions on some U.S. government officials, including U.S. Senator John McCain (R-AZ). In response, McCain tweeted: **"I guess this means my Spring Break in Siberia is off, my Gazprom stock is lost, and my secret bank account in Moscow is frozen."**

John McCain
Official Photograph

What A Head of Hair: From the Senate Floor, U.S. Senate Majority Leader Harry Reid (D-NV) paid tribute to his colleague U.S. Senator Ben Nelson (D-NE), stating: **"I mean that is a mop of real hair. It's often that people call his office---email his office. They believe he has a toupee. It's his hair! He'll pull it for you any time just to show you that it's real. It is his real hair. I mean he has hair like a 15-year-old."**

Ben Nelson
Official Photograph

U.S. Senate

Was He Naked or Nekkid? In 2014, former U.S. Senator Alan Simpson (R-WY) was called by Jennifer Jacobs of *The Des Moines Register* reporter for an interview. Simpson first asked the reporter to hold on because he is: **"stark nekkid."** After putting his clothes on, Simpson said to the reporter: **"Do you know the difference between naked and nekkid. If you're naked, you don't have any clothes on, but if you're nekkid you don't have any clothes on but you're up to something."**

Alan Simpson
Official Photograph

Congenital Biased: President Lyndon B. Johnson said of U.S. Senator James Eastland (D-MS 1943-1978), an ardent segregationist and anti-communist: **"Jim Eastland could be standing right in the middle of the worst Mississippi flood ever known and blame it on the negroes helped by the communists."**

James Eastland (L)
Lyndon B. Johnson (R)
Lyndon Baines Johnson Library and Museum

In Defense of Junk Mail: In a 2012 defense of the United States Postal Service, U.S. Senate Majority Leader Harry Reid (D-NV) stated on the U.S. Senate Floor: **"I'll come home tonight here to my home in Washington and there'll be some mail there. A lot of it is what some people refer to as junk mail, but for the people who are sending that mail, it's very important, and when talking about seniors, seniors love getting junk mail. It's sometimes their only way of communicating or feeling like they're part of the real world."**

Harry Reid
Official Photograph

Cure For Inflation: Eat Less Meat: In 1947, after U.S. Senator Robert A. Taft (R-OH) mentioned that the proliferating demand for food was responsible for inflation, a reporter asked him if inflation could be moderated if Americans eat less. Taft responded: **"Yes, eat less meat and eat less extravagantly."** This comment made Taft appear insensitive to the plight of the poor and as a tribune of the elite. During many of his speeches, opponents held up signs reading: **"Taft says: 'tighten your belt – eat less meat.'"**

Robert A. Taft
Official Photograph

U.S. Senate

Polyging v. Monoging: In 1902, the Utah State Legislature elected Mormon apostle Reed Smoot to serve in the U.S. Senate. Many in the Senate believed Smoot should be expelled because of reports that his church still allowed polygamy. Although the Mormon Church had renounced polygamy in 1890, and Smoot was married to just one woman, Protestant groups pressured the Senate to expel Smoot. In 1904, the Senate held hearings on expelling Smoot. The hearings lasted three years. In 1907, a majority of the Senate voted to expel Smoot, but they did not reach the constitutionally-required 2/3 vote for expulsion and Smoot kept his seat. U.S. Senator Boies Penrose (R-PA) defended his colleague, telling one Senator known to be a philanderer: **"As for me, I would rather have seated beside me in this chamber a polygamist who doesn't polyg than a monogamist who doesn't monog."** Smoot went on the serve in the Senate for 30 years. He was the co-sponsor of the Smoot-Hawley Tariff of 1930, which raised U.S. import tariffs on over 20,000 items.

Reed Smoot
Official Photograph

Human By Default: U.S. Senator Thomas Gore (D-OK 1907-1921) was one of the few politicians who did not like people. At a 1994 address in front of the National Press Club, Gore's grandson, the esteemed historian and playwright, disclosed that his Grandfather told him: **"If there was any other race other than the human race, I'd go join it."**

Thomas Gore
Library of Congress

Should Be The Other Way Around: U.S. Senator Paul Simon (D-IL 1985-1997) authored 21 books. Most of these books deal with serious subjects like world hunger, the American dollar, and the coming water crises. Simon quipped: **"I write the type of books that people can't pick up after they have put them down."**

The Culture of Pandering by Paul Simon

U.S. Senate

Is that Supposed to be a Compliment? Observing the actions of Freshman U.S. Senator Huey Long in 1933 Senate veteran U.S. Senator Alben Barkley (D-KY) said to Huey Long (D-LA), **"You are the smartest lunatic I have ever seen in my whole life."**

Huey Long
Official Photograph

When Backbone Exceeds Intelligence: During an appearance on *Firing Line* with host William F. Buckley, U.S. Senator Sam Ervin (D-NC) suggested public officials should have more **"backbone."** Buckley then asked Ervin about Watergate burglar G. Gordon Liddy, to which Ervin responded: **"Well, [G.] Gordon Liddy has a little too much backbone. I'll have to admit that I have a sort of sneaking admiration for a fellow like Gordon Liddy that does have an excess of backbone. His backbone exceeds his intelligence, really."**

Sam Ervin
Official Photograph

The Byrd and the Peckerwoods: U.S. Senator Robert C. Byrd (D-WV) was often chastised by fiscal conservative groups like Citizens against Government Waste for his propensity to allocate money to his home state of West Virginia. Byrd had little patience for these critics, believing that he was bringing needed resources to his home state. In 1995, Byrd told *ABC News,* **"What these peckerwoods call pork is infrastructure."**

Robert C. Byrd
U.S. Department of Transportation
Photograph

Money, Money, Money: In the 1992 book, *Who Will Tell The People,* U.S. Senator Dale Bumpers (D-AR) explains: **"If you're on the Banking or the Finance Committee, you don't even have to open your mouth. They'll throw money at you over the transom."**

Dale Bumpers
Official Photograph

U.S. Senate

Senator Plays Saxophone at Topless Bar: Before being elected to the U.S. Senate in 1972, U.S. Senator Jesse Helms (R-NC) was a well-known commentator on WRAL in Raleigh, NC. After being elected to the Senate, he once told a story of a man who came up to him and said, **"Hey, ain't you Jesse Helms? And I said 'Ya,' I couldn't deny that. He said 'I haven't seen you on television for a few nights. Have you quit?' I said this guy is pulling my leg. Here I've been in the United States Senate for a few months, been through a campaign. I said 'well as a matter of fact I have.' He said, 'what are you doing now?' I said 'I got a new job up in Washington.' He said, 'what are you doing up there?' I said 'I got a job as a saxophone player at a topless bar.' He said 'some fool told me you got elected to the United States Senate and I knew that couldn't be so.'"**

Jesse Helms
Official Photograph

Regarding Congressional Benefits: U.S. Senator Paul Douglas (D-IL 1949-1967) claimed that anything goes when members of the U.S. Congress attend luncheons with lobbyists. Regarding what was allowed, he said: **"Anything you can eat, drink, or fornicate in one afternoon."**

Paul Douglas
Official Photograph

Hey! At Least He Was Being Honest: When U.S. Senator Huey Long (D-LA) asked his colleague, Harry S. Truman (D-MO), who was presiding over the Senate, what he thought of his fiery populist speech, Truman answered: **"I had to listen to you because I was in the chair and couldn't walk out."** Long was furious, and the two senators never spoke to each other again.

Harry S. Truman
Harry S. Truman Library and Museum

Better Stupid Than Evil: U.S. Senator Allen Simpson (R-WY 1979-1997) explains the two major political parties this way: **"We have two political parties, the Stupid Party and the Evil Party. I belong to the Stupid Party."**

Allen Simpson
Official Photograph

U.S. Senate

Jesse Helms Attends U2 Concert: In 2001, 79-year-old U.S. Senator Jesse Helms (R-NC) became friends with U2 front-man Bono. Helms even attended a U2 Concert. The conservative Senator told *The Charlotte News & Observer:* **"It was the noisiest thing I ever heard. I turned my hearing aids all the way down and kept my hands over my ears much of the time."**

U2 in Concert
Photograph by Wikpedia Brown

The Anatomy of Guilt: U.S. Senator Joe Lieberman (I-CT), who happens to be Jewish, told *The New York Times* in 2012 about a conversation he had with his colleague Susan Collins (R-ME) who happens to be Roman Catholic. Collins told Lieberman: **"Your people invented guilt, but my people perfected it."**

Susan Collins
Official Photograph

Loses Election By Just a Single Vote: U.S. Senator Byron "Pat" Harrison (D-MS) refused to speak to his home state colleague, fellow Democrat Theodore Bilbo, who was a vociferous segregationist. The two Senators had a heated rivalry over the New Deal, which Harrison largely supported and Bilbo largely opposed. They also clashed on how federal largess should be distributed in the state. In 1937, Harrison and U.S. Senator Alben Barkley (D-KY) were tied in the race for U.S. Senate Majority Leader. The only Democrat who had not decided who to vote for was Bilbo. He told Harrison's campaign manager that he would vote for him as Majority Leader if he would meet with him and personally ask for his vote. Harrison subsequently told his campaign manager: **"Tell the son of a bitch I wouldn't speak with him even if it meant the Presidency of the United States."** Accordingly, Bilbo voted for Barkley, who won the race by just one vote.

Byron "Pat" Harrison
Official Photograph

U.S. Senate

A Lady Lover Even at 100: At a 2002 100th birthday celebration for U.S. Senator Strom Thurmond (R-SC), Thurmond told the crowd: **"I love all of you men, but you women even more."** Thurmond was known as a ladies' man. When he was 66 years old, he married Nancy Moore, the 22-year-old Miss South Carolina.

Strom Thurmond receives a cake for his 100th birthday from Army Chief of Staff Eric Shinseki
U.S. Army Photograph by Jerome Howard

IRS Code Exemption and Preferences: U.S. Senator Warren Magnuson (D-WA 1944-1981) would often say: **"The first 9 pages of the Internal Revenue Code define income; the remaining 1,100 pages spin the web of exceptions and preferences."**

Warren Magnuson
University of Washington Special Collections

Biden: Obviously, I Don't Know What the Hell I'm Talking About: In 1977, U.S. Senator Joe Biden (D-DE) offered an amendment to the U.S. Criminal Code. He began reading the amendment and discovered that his staff had changed the wording of the amendment. Biden then admitted to his colleagues: **"Obviously I don't know what the hell I'm talking about. I thought I had a two-for-one provision there. The staff, in its wisdom, rewrote it, so I guess I did not want that after all."**

Joe Biden
Official Photograph

Paying Off a Debt: In 2001, U.S. Senator Jim Jeffords (R-VT) left the Republican Party, becoming an Independent who caucuses with the Democrats. This threw the divided Chamber into Democratic hands. U.S. Senate Minority Leader Tom Daschle (D-SD) was credited for his role in persuading Jeffords to make the move. Daschle joked in a speech to the Democratic Leadership Council: **"I've got to leave a bit early. I've got to mow Jim Jeffords lawn this afternoon."**

Tom Daschle
Official Photograph

U.S. Senate

The Senate Animal Farm: During a 1978 debate on the U.S. Senate Floor about restructuring the Committee System, U.S. Senator Lawton Chiles (D-FL) observed: **"The Senate is a little like [George] Orwell's Animal Farm. All pigs are equal, but some are more equal than others."**

Lawton Chiles
Official Photograph

Name Calling: As a U.S. Senator, Harry S. Truman knew his colleagues were no angels. He often told friends that some were: **"liars, trimmers, and pussy-footers."**

Harry S, Truman
Harry S. Truman Library and Museum

Flat Hairy Insult: In an 1894 letter to his son, Theodore Roosevelt Jr., future President Theodore Roosevelt, then a New York City Police Commissioner, called U.S. Senator William A. Peffer (People's Party-KS) **"a well-meaning, pin-headed, anarchistic crank, of hirsute** [Covered with facial hair] **and slab-sided** [Having Flat sides] **aspect."**

William A. Peffer
Official Photograph

U.S. Senator gets into Eisenhower's Skull: U.S. Senator Thomas W. Bricker (R-OH) proposed a Federal Constitutional Amendment to limit the treaty making power of the President. President Dwight D. Eisenhower put out a full court press to defeat it. He became annoyed at the time it was taking out of his Presidency to fight it. The amendment failed to be ratified by the U.S. Senate by just one vote. Eisenhower commented: **"If it's true that when you die the things that bothered you most are engraved on your skull, I am sure that I'll have there in the mud and dirt of France during the invasion and the name of Senator Bricker."**

Thomas W. Bricker
Official Photograph

205

Chapter IX

U.S. Senate Campaigns

U.S. Senate Campaigns

Kennedy Country: When Robert F. Kennedy was considering running for a Senate seat from New York in 1964, a state where he did not reside and was not even eligible to vote in, *Life Magazine* Publisher Clare Booth Luce commented: **"What the Kennedys want, the Kennedys get."**

Clare Booth Luce
Library of Congress

Psychiatric Reason to Vote for Markey: In 2013, Vice President Joe Biden spoke at a fundraiser for Massachusetts Democratic U.S. Senate nominee Ed Markey. Biden gave the crowd an atypical reason to support Markey. He said: **"Folks, Ed Markey has a distinct advantage over the rest of us: He has a psychiatrist for a wife. It's not often noted, but it is very important. I can think of at least a half a dozen people who I wished [they] had a psychiatrist for a wife."** Markey is married to Rear Admiral Susan J. Blumenthal, M.D.

Ed Markey
Official Photograph

Checkmate: After Republican Senate nominee Harry McMaster challenged his opponent, U.S. Senator Ernest "Fritz" Hollings (D-SC), to take a drug test, Hollings responded: **"I'll take a drug test if you take an IQ test."**

Ernest "Fritz" Hollings
Official Photograph

Voters give it a lot of Thought: In 1952, U.S. Senator Kenneth Mackellar (D-TN) ran for re-election on the slogan: **"Thinking Feller? Vote McKellar."** His Democratic primary opponent, U.S. Representative Albert Gore Sr. (D-TN), replied with the slogan: **"Think Some More – Vote for Gore."** Gore won.

Kenneth McKellar
Official Photograph

U.S. Senate Campaigns

John F. Kennedy's Unlikely Friend: Anti-Communist U.S. Senator Joseph McCarthy (R-WI) had a close personal relationship with U.S. Senator John F. Kennedy (D-MA). In 1952, at the high watermark of his political popularity, McCarthy barnstormed the country supporting Republican U.S. Senate candidates. The only Republican he would not campaign for was U.S. Senator Henry Cabot Lodge, Jr. (R-MA) (Kennedy's political opponent). In support of McCarthy, Kennedy stormed out of a Harvard Reunion Dinner when a speaker extolled the fact that alleged American Communist Alger Hiss and Joseph McCarthy had never graduated from Harvard. Kennedy bellowed: **"How dare you couple the name of a great American patriot with that of a traitor!"**

Joseph McCarthy
Library of Congress

Whatever: During a 2014 campaign stop at the Red Arrow Diner in Manchester, New Hampshire, U.S. Senate candidate Scott Brown responded to *The Associated Press:* **"Do I have the best credentials? Probably not, cause, you know, 'whatever.' But I have long and strong ties to this state."**

Scott Brown
Official Photograph

Warner v. Warner: In the 1996 U.S. Senate race in Virginia, the Democrats nominated Mark Warner to challenge Republican U.S. Senator John Warner. Mark Warner's slogan was **"Mark not John."** Mark Warner had the bumper-sticker on his car and a passerby once asked him: **"Is that a Biblical Reference?"** Despite Mark Warner's creative slogan, he lost the election to John Warner.

Mark Warner
Official Photograph

In a State of Ambivalence: During a U.S Senate debate on NBC's *Meet the Press* in 2006, Democratic Nominee Claire McCaskill was asked by moderator Tim Russert: **"Bill Clinton raised money for you. Do you think Bill Clinton was a Great President?"** McCaskill responded: **"I think he's been a great leader but I don't want my daughter near him."** McCaskill later apologized to Clinton for the comments.

Claire McCaskill
Official Photograph

U.S. Senate Campaigns

Trust Me, The Others are Not all that Impressive. Following his election to the United States Senate in 1934, where he dislodged incumbent U.S. Senator Roscoe C. Patterson (R-MO), a friend advised Harry S. Truman: **"Harry, don't you go to the Senate with an inferiority complex. You'll sit there about six months, and wonder how you got there. But after that you'll wonder how the rest of them got there."**

Harry S. Truman
Harry S. Truman Library and Museum

Naked Politics: During the 2012 U.S. Senate campaign, challenger Elizabeth Warren was asked how she made money to get through college. She joked: **"I kept my clothes on."** She was joking about her opponent, U.S. Senator Scott Brown (R-MA), who had modeled nude to pay for college. During an appearance on WZLX *Radio* in Boston, Brown responded to Warren's dig by stating: **"Thank God!"**

Scott Brown in *Cosmopolitan Magazine*

Don't Take Rank-and-File Voters for Granted: In her 2010 campaign for U.S. Senate, Massachusetts Attorney General Martha Coakley spent an inordinate amount of time courting activists and elected officials and raising money for her campaign at the expense of retail politicking. When David Filpov of *The Boston Globe* asked her about this, her response was: **"As opposed to standing outside Fenway Park in the cold shaking hands."** Her Republican opponent, State Senator Scott Brown, had in fact stood out in front of Fenway Park in the cold shaking hands the day before. Brown won the election.

Martha Coakley
Official Photograph

No Fan of Boxer: Speaking at a campaign rally for California's 2010 Republican Senate nominee Carly Fiorina, U.S. Senator John McCain chastised her opponent, U.S Senator Barbara Boxer (D-CA). He said: **"Barbara Boxer is the most bitterly partisan, most anti-defense senator in the United States Senate today. I know that because I've had the unpleasant experience of having to serve with her."**

Barbara Boxer
Official Photograph

211

U.S. Senate Campaigns

The "Byrd" is the Word: After being re-elected with 77.75% of the vote in 2000, U.S. Senator Robert C. Byrd (D-WV) told supporters: **"West Virginia has always had four friends, God Almighty, Sears Roebuck, Carter's Liver Pills, and Robert C. Byrd."**

Robert C. Byrd
Official Photograph

Abe Lincoln Behind the Bar: Abraham Lincoln was a licensed bartender. He once co-owned a bar in his hometown of Springfield, Illinois. During a 1858 debate for the U.S. Senate, his opponent, Stephen A. Douglas (D-IL), mentioned that he first met Lincoln as a customer at his bar. Lincoln deadpanned: **"I have left my side of the counter. But, Mr. Douglas still sticks as tenaciously as ever, to his."**

Abraham Lincoln
Library of Congress

That's "Not" What I Said: It was reported first by *Time Magazine* that U.S. Representative George Smathers (D-FL) made the following charge about U.S. Senator Claude Pepper (D-FL) while campaigning to defeat him in the 1950 Democratic Primary: **"Are you aware that the candidate is known all over Washington as a shameless extrovert? Not only that, but this man is reliably reported to have practiced nepotism with his sister-in-law and he has a sister who was once a wicked thespian in New York. He matriculated with co-eds at the University, and it is an established fact that before his marriage he habitually practiced celibacy."** Smathers denied making the quote and offered $10,000 to anyone who could prove he made it. No one could prove it. Smathers won the election.

George Smathers
Library of Congress

We Stole it Fair and Square: During his successful 1976 campaign for a U.S. Senate Seat in California, Republican Samuel Ichlye Hayakawa exclaimed: **"We should keep the Panama Canal. After all we stole it fair and square."**

Samuel Ichlye Hayakawa
Official Photograph

U.S. Senate Campaigns

Chock Full of Nuts: The Democratic nominee for the U.S. Senate in Wyoming in 2012 was Tim Chestnut. He had an inimical campaign slogan: **"Chestnut, the best nut for Senate."** Cowboy State Voters strongly disagreed, giving him just 22% of the vote. Chestnut currently serves as a County Commissioner in his hometown of Albany, Wyoming.

Tim Chestnut
Official photograph

Appealing to the Little People: U.S. Senator Ralph Yarborough (D-TX, 1957-1971), who represented the liberal bloodline of the Texas Democratic Party, when running against more conservative candidates in the primary, tried to buttress his populist appeal with the inimical campaign slogan: **"Let's put the jam on the lower shelf so the little people can reach it."**

Ralph Yarborough
Official Photograph

Lincoln Displays his Self-Deprecating Humor: During a 1858 U.S. Senate debate between incumbent Stephen Douglas and challenger Abraham Lincoln, Douglas said that Lincoln was **"two-faced."** Lincoln retorted: **"I leave it to my audience. If I had another face, do you think I would wear this one?"**

1958 U.S. Postage Stamp Commemorating the 100th Anniversary of the Lincoln-Douglas Debates
U.S. Postal Service

No Letting Bygones be Bygones: After losing to Democrat Barack Obama in a race for an open U.S. Senate Seat in Illinois in 2004, Republican nominee Allan Keyes refused to call Obama and concede the election, claiming it would be a **"false gesture."** Keyes said that Obama stands for **"a culture evil enough to destroy the very soul and heart of my country."**

Bumpersticker: Allan Keyes for U.S. Senate

213

U.S. Senate Campaigns

A Blistering Denunciation of the "Wall Street Kitchen:" In 1932, U.S. Senator Huey Long (D-LA) toured his neighboring state of Arkansas, campaigning for U.S. Senator Hattie Caraway (D-AR), in her bid to serve a full term. Long railed against both the Democratic and Republican Parties. He exclaimed: **"They've got a set of Republican waiters on one side and a set of Democratic waiters on the other side, but no matter which set of waiters brings you the dish, the legislative grub is all prepared in the same Wall Street kitchen."**

Huey Long
Library of Congress

I am NOT a Carpetbagger! In 1964, the Democrats nominated Robert Kennedy for U.S. Senate. Kennedy moved to New York to run for the seat and was labeled a "carpetbagger." The Republican nominee, U.S. Senator Kenneth Keating (R-NY) began a press conference by joking: **"Well, ladies and gentlemen, we all know what we're here for. And I want to announce at the outset that I will not be a candidate for the United States Senate from Massachusetts."**

Kenneth Keating
Official Photograph

The Physical "Anatomy" of an Election: In 1992, Claire Sargent, the Democratic nominee for U.S. Senate in Arizona, gave the following reason to make her the first female Senator from the Grand Canyon State: **"I think it's about time we voted for Senators with breasts. After all, we've been voting for boobs long enough."** She lost.

Claire Sargent for U.S. Senate Pin

Senator Pays Political Price for Not Toeing the Party Line: In 1918, President Woodrow Wilson endorsed Pat Harrison in the Democratic U.S. Senate Primary against the incumbent Democrat James K. Vardaman (D-MS). Wilson was inflamed that Vardaman had voted against the Congressional Declaration of War with Germany. Vardaman did not take Wilson's endorsement of Harrison in stride. He called Wilson: **"The coldest blooded, most selfish ruler beneath the stars today."**

James K. Vardaman
Library of Congress

U.S. Senate Campaigns

Why Doesn't He Tell Him How He Really Feels: In the 1994 Virginia U.S. Senate race, Democratic incumbent Chuck Robb was challenged by Republican Oliver North who had been implicated in the Iran-Contra scandal during the Presidential Administration of Ronald Reagan. Senator Robb brought out the heavy rhetorical artillery, telling an audience in Alexander, VA that his Senate opponent: **"is a document-shredding, Constitution-trashing, Commander in Chief-bashing, Congress-thrashing, uniform-shaming, Ayatollah-loving, arms-dealing, criminal-protecting, résumé-enhancing, Noriega-coddling, Social Security-threatening, public school-denigrating, Swiss-banking-law-breaking, letter-faking, self-serving, election-losing, snake-oil salesman who can't tell the difference between the truth and a lie."** The next day, Robb won the Senate election.

Chuck Robb
Official Photograph

I am Not a Witch: When it was revealed that Christine O'Donnell, a U.S. Senate Republican candidate from Delaware, had **"dabbled in witchcraft"** when she was younger, O'Donnell appeared in a television advertisement declaring: **"I am not a witch."**

Christine O'Donnell
Photograph by Greg Skidmore

Tea Anyone: In 1952, U.S. Representative John F. Kennedy (D-MA) upset incumbent U.S. Senator Henry Cabot Lodge Jr. (R-MA) in his race for re-election. Polly Fitzgerald, who was married to Kennedy Cousin Edward J. Fitzgerald, organized tea parties with wealthy women voters in ornate homes, where Kennedy would meet the attendees. Lodge Jr. later said: **"It was those damn tea parties that did me in."**

Henry Cabot Lodge Jr.
Library of Congress

Who Woulda Thunk It? In 1964, Robert F. Kennedy easily won the Democratic New York U.S. Senate Primary. U.S. Representative Samuel S. Stratton (D-NY) had been the favorite before Kennedy moved to the state solely to run for the seat. After the election, Stratton joked: **"When Bobby Kennedy decided he was a New Yorker, that was the end of my campaign."**

Samuel S. Stratton
Official Photograph

215

U.S. Senate Campaigns

Republican Calls Birthers "Dumb Asses:" At a 2010 campaign event in Pueblo Colorado, Republican U.S. Senate candidate Ken Buck (Who enjoyed the support of many exponents of the Tea Party Movement) ignored a question about the birth certificate of President Barack Obama. At another event later that day, Buck saw a Democratic campaign tracker, who unbeknownst to Buck had a tape recorder in his pocket. Buck stated: **"Will you tell those dumbasses at the Tea Party to stop asking questions about birth certificates while I'm on the camera?"** After the remark became public, Buck's campaign apologized. Despite this incident, Buck won the Republican Primary. However, he lost in the General Election to incumbent Democratic U.S. Senator Michael Bennett.

Ken Buck
Photograph by Ken Buck

Making Washington Squeal: after starting her career castrating pigs, Joni Ernst won the 2014 Republican nomination for an open U.S. Senate seat in Iowa. In a campaign advertisement Ernst exclaimed: **"I grew up castrating pigs on an Iowa farm. So, when I get to Washington, I'll know how to cut pork. Let's make 'em squeal."**

Joni Ernst
Official Photograph

Bartering for Health Care: In 2010, Nevada Republican U.S. Senate Candidate Sue Lowden said during an appearance on *Nevada Newsmakers:* **"I'm telling you that this works. You know, before we all started having health care, in the olden days, our grandparents, they would bring a chicken to the doctor. They would say, 'I'll paint your house.' I mean, that's the old days of what people would do to get health care with your doctors. Doctors are very sympathetic people. I'm not backing down from that system."** Lowden lost the nomination to Sharron Angle.

Bumper sticker:
Sue Lowden for U.S. Senate

Work is Not All It's Cracked Up to Be: When Ted Kennedy was running for a U.S. Senate seat in Massachusetts in 1962, John McCormick, his primary opponent, implied that the 30-year-old had not worked a day in his life. One day, Kennedy was greeting voters at a factory and one worker came up to him and said: **"Mr. Kennedy, I understand that you have never worked a day in your life. Let me tell you, you haven't missed a thing."**

Ted Kennedy in 1962
John F. Kennedy Library and Museum

U.S. Senate Campaigns

Republican Ignorant of Tea Party: In 2014, U.S. Senator Thad Cochran, who was running for re-election against Chris McDaniel, a well-funded Tea Party supported opponent, told *WAPT NBC News* in Jackson *Mississippi* **"The Tea Party is something I don't know a lot about."** When asked about these comments in an interview with *WXXV-TV* in Gulfport, Mississippi, Cochran again professed ignorance of the movement. **"I said I didn't know much about the Tea Party, and I didn't. I heard...I read newspaper articles about them, and that's about all I knew. It's kind of like [Political Humorist] Will Rogers, you know. He said he knew what was in the papers."** McDaniel exploited Cochran's ignorance on his campaign web site.

Thad Cochran
Official Photograph

Put Your Man Pants On: In the 2010 Republican primary for an open U.S. Senate seat in Delaware, a consulting firm aired a video on the Internet intimating that Republican candidate Mike Castle was a homosexual. His opponent, Christine O'Donnell, distanced herself from the advertisement, but told Radio talk show host Mark Levin: **"This is not a bake-off, put your man-pants on."**

Mike Castle
Official Photograph

If Caribou Could Vote: Speaking at a fundraiser for U.S. Senator Frank Murkowski (R-AK), George H.W. Bush said**: "You know, the critics said years ago when the debate was on the pipeline up there, the Alaska pipeline, that caribou would be extinct because of this. Well, there's so many caribou they're rubbing up against the pipeline, they're breeding like mad. They're having a great time. And it is a sound environment up there. . . . Listen to the President who says we, our national security, our own national interest depends upon our having an energy program that makes us less dependent on foreign oil. And I'm never going to change my view on that. If caribou could vote, Murkowski would be in by a landslide."**

Frank Murkowski
Official Photograph

Curt Schilling is No Yankee Fan: In a 2010 interview with Dan Rae of WBZ-radio, Massachusetts Democratic U.S. Senate nomine Martha Coakley was asked about the endorsement of former Red Sox World Series hero Curt Schilling of her Republican opponent, Scott Brown. Apparently not knowing who Schilling was, Coakley replied: **"Curt Schilling is a Yankee fan."**

Martha Coakley
Official Photograph

U.S. Senate Campaigns

An Exercise in Sarcasm: In 1999, when New York Mayor Rudy Giuliani was considering running for an open U.S. Senate seat in New York, he poked fun at the presumptive Democratic nominee for the seat, Hillary Clinton who had purchased a home in New York to run for the seat. Giuliani decided to make a campaign visit to Clinton's former home state of Arkansas where he quipped: **"I've never lived here, I've never worked here, I've never gone to school here, it's the first time I've been here. I guess it would be cool to run for the Senate."** Ultimately, Giuliani did not run due to his messy divorce and diagnosis of prostate cancer. U.S. Representative Rick Lazio (R-NY) supplanted him as the nominee, losing to Clinton in the General Election.

Rudy Giuliani
Official Photograph

Secret Code Phrase: Sharron Angle, the Republican U.S. Senate nominee from Nevada in 2010, had a hostile relationship with the media. In fact, she often avoided the media. Her staff used a code phrase whenever a member of the media entered the campaign headquarters. It was: **"It's time to water the plants."**

Sharron Angle
Official Photograph

No Modesty Here: After being crushed in the 2010 U.S. Senate Election to U.S. Senator Jim DeMint (R-SC), Democratic nominee Alvin Greene hinted he might run for President in 2012. He told *The Columbia Free Times*: **"I'm the next president. I'll be 35 ... just before November, so I was born to be president. I'm the man. I'm the man. I'm the man. Greene's the man. I'm the man. I'm the greatest person ever. I was born to be president. I'm the man, I'm the greatest individual ever."**

Alvin Greene
Official Photograph

Humans v. Entities: In 2010, U.S. Senate Candidate Chris Coons (D-DE) said of the U.S. Supreme Court ruling in *Citizens United, v, Federal Elections Commission* (which ruled that the Federal Government can not ban labor unions or corporations from spending money to support or oppose candidates during election season): **"In terms of political contributions, the free speech rights of corporations I don't think deserve the same protections as the free speech rights of real living, breathing, voting humans."**

Chris Coons
Official Photograph

U.S. Senate Campaigns

Perfect Response: In a 2012 debate for an open U.S. Senate seat in North Dakota, Republican Rick Berg tried to tether his Democratic opponent, Heidi Heitkamp, to President Barack Obama and U.S. Senate Majority Leader Harry Reid, both unpopular in North Dakota. Heitkamp responded: **"Congressman Berg will repeatedly talk about Harry Reid and Barack Obama, and I find it interesting because this morning when I woke up and brushed my teeth, I looked in the mirror and I did not see a tall, African-American, skinny man."**

Heidi Heitkamp
Official Photograph

Meat Ax v. The Scalpel: In the 1976 election for an open U.S. Senate seat in Arizona, Republican candidate John Bertrand Conlan said of his primary opponent Sam Steiger: **"We are both conservatives, but our style is different. He uses a meat ax and I use a scalpel."** Steiger retorted: **"John thinks of himself as a scalpel. I prefer to think of him as a Roto-Rooter."** Conlan Steiger won the primary but lost in the General Election to Democrat Dennis Deconcini.

John Bertrand Conlan
Official Photograph

A Voice For The Next Century -- Not the Last One: In 1996, 43-year old Democratic U.S. Senate nominee Elliot Close ran against U.S. Senator Strom Thurmond (R-SC), who was 94-years old and had been in office since 1954. In an advertisement, Close said: **"This election is about the next century, not the last one."** Thurmond won the election.

Strom Thurmond
Official Photograph

Predictions are in --- Warner Will Win: During the 1996 U.S. Senate Campaign, Democrat Mark Warner challenged Republican John Warner. At the end of a debate hosted by the Virginia Bar Association, the group's President, Douglas Rucker, quipped: **"The Virginia Bar Association doesn't take political stands, but speaking for myself personally, I'll be voting for Warner and I encourage you to do the same."** John Warner won the race. Mark Warner was elected Governor of the state in 2001.

A Pin Produced by the Mark Warner Campagin reading: Mark Not John

U.S. Senate Campaigns

The Cuttlefish Analogy: During one of the Lincoln-Douglas U.S. Senate debates in 1858, Republican Abraham Lincoln said of his opponent, Democrat Stephen Douglas, who he believed was evading the issues: **"Judge Douglas is playing cuttlefish — a small species of fish that has no mode of defending himself when pursued except by throwing out a black fluid which makes the water so dark the enemy cannot see it, and thus it escapes."**

Cuttlefish
Photograph by Borazont

Message: Voters Don't Want Governor to Leave: In his 1996 concession speech, after losing a hotly-contested U.S. Senate race to incumbent John Kerry, Massachusetts Governor Bill Weld announced: **"I'm not stupid. I got the message. The message is I'm a real good governor, and I should stick to that."**

Bill Weld
Official Portrait

Time To Return to the Pigs: In 1998, when Democrat John Edwards defeated Republican U.S. Senator Lauch Faircloth (R-NC), in his re-election bid. Washington D.C. Mayor Marian Berry rejoiced. Faircloth by profession was a hog farmer. Berry had had a rocky relationship with Faricloth, who chaired the U.S. Senate Appropriations subcommittee for the District of Columbia. Speaking at a victory rally for Anthony Williams, who won the election to succeed Berry as Mayor, Berry told the crowd: **"Senator Faircloth has lost, lost, lost. Gone. Dead and buried . . . . He's so busy picking on me and the residents of the District of Columbia that he neglected his constituents in North Carolina. Now he can go back and deal with the pigs. Goodbye, Faircloth."**

Lauch Faircloth
Official Photograph

An Odd Comparison: In his 2004 re-election bid, U.S. Senator Jim Bunning (R-KY) faced a firestorm of criticism for saying that his Democratic opponent, Daniel Monglaro, **"looks like one of Saddam Hussein's sons. . . . I mean before they were dead, of course . . . . I really mean that he looks like one of Saddam's sons, and he even dresses like them, too."**

Jim Bunning
Official Photograph

U.S. Senate Campaigns

Give My Brother Teddy a Job: When he first ran for a seat in the U.S. Senate in 1962, Ted Kennedy had held only one job since graduating from the University of Virginia Law School. He had been an Assistant District Attorney for Suffolk County in Massachusetts. His brother, President John F. Kennedy, would often quip: **"Give Teddy a job, elect him to the Senate."**

John F. Kennedy (L) with Ted Kennedy (R)
John F. Kennedy Presidential Library and Museum

Good Thinking! In 1926, the two leading Democratic candidates for an open U.S. Senate seat, John Bankhead and Thomas E. Kilby, respectively agreed to a string of debates. They did not invite the other three candidates to the debates. Accordingly, one of those candidates, Hugo Black, orchestrated a mule-drawn dray (wagon) to march in front of the debate site carrying a sign reading: **"Bankhead says Kilby won't do. Kilby says Bankhead won't do. Both are right. Vote for Hugo Black."** The escapade struck a resonant chord with Alabama voters. Black won the primary and the election.

Hugo Black
Official Photograph

I Did it the Old Fashioned Way: In 2010, Paul Raese, the Republican nominee for a U.S. Senate seat in West Virginia, told Talk Show Hot Matt Lewis: **"I made my money the old-fashioned way, I inherited it. I think that's a great thing to do. I hope more people in this country have that opportunity as soon as we abolish inheritance tax in this country, which is a key part of my program."** Raese is the legatee of Greer Industries, which produces many products, including steel and limestone. Raese lost the race.

Punch Card For John Raese for U.S. Senate

No Beltway Turtles in Texas: In his unsuccessful run to wrest the Republican nomination from U.S. Senator John Cornyn (R-TX) Dwayne Stovall blasted Cornyn for supporting U.S. Senate Minority Leader Mitch McConnell (R-KY). In the advertisement, Stovall states: **"As a U.S. Senator from Texas, you vote for Texas. You don't stab her in the back for voting for cloture** (Ending a Filibuster) **on Obamacare. You don't enslave its children with unconstitutional laws and overwhelming debt and you sure don't do this to please some guy that looks and fights like a turtle. I'm a Texan. We don't need a beltway turtle telling us what to do."**

Image used in Dwayne Stovall Advertisement

U.S. Senate Campaigns

What Have You Done For Me Lately? In 1944, When U.S. Senator Alben Barkley (D-KY) was running for re-election, he encountered a voter he had personally helped. The voter said he was undecided on whether to re-elect him. An astonished Barkley recounted that he had helped him to build an access road to his farm, helped him secure an early honorable discharge from the U.S. Navy, and even got his wife a job at the Post Office. Barkley told the man: **"You remember all these things I have done for you?"** The constituent replied: **"I remember, but what have you done for me lately?"**

Alben Barkley
Harry S. Truman Library and Museum

Way Too Much Information: In 2014, U.S. Senator Thad Cochran (R-MS), was running for re-election. He told a crowd about how as a kid he visited his father's family farm in Richton, Mississippi. He mused that he did **"all kinds of indecent things to animals."**

Thad Cochran
Official Photograph

I Said "Failing": During a 1994 U.S. Senate debate between challenger Mitt Romney and incumbent U.S. Senator Ted Kennedy (D-MA), Romney was asked by Sally Jacobs of *The Boston Globe* to name his greatest personal failing. Romney answered: **"One of the challenges in this society today is the burden of occupation and I've been very busy in my work. I have a wonderful family I'm very busy there. But you grow too far apart from the people you care about and that's, after all, how we're judged in this life what we've done for other people. And so I've spent two and a half years early in my life living with the poor and serving with the poor. And when we came here to Massachusetts, we decided that one day each week I would give in-service to people less fortunate than myself. I have spent hours and hours, hundreds of hours in hospitals from Worcester to Boston, working with sick people, consoling them**. Moderator Ken Body then interjected: **"Can I interrupt you. This was a question about your greatest personal failing. You have thirty seconds to get to that part of the answer."** Romney then said: **"My greatest personal failing then Ken is my inability to fulfill what I think is a God-given obligation to do more, and I do what I can one day a week, but I don't do as much as I think we all can do."**

Mitt Romney Campaigning for the U.S. Senate in 1994
Photograph by Joeff Davis

222

Chapter X

U.S. Supreme Court Justices

U.S. Supreme Court Justices

Supreme Court Justice was No Dopehead: During the 2011 Federalist Society Gala, U.S. Supreme Court Justice Clarence Thomas was interviewed on stage by Diane S. Sykes of the U.S. Court of Appeals for the 7th Circuit. She asked him about his days as a campus radical while a student at the College of the Holy Cross in Worcester, Massachusetts. Thomas responded: **"Yeah, but I was no dopehead. The sixties were different."**

Clarence Thomas
Official Photograph

Recipe for Making Perfect Children: Supreme Court Justice Antonin Scalia has nine children. He joked: **"In a big family the first child is kind of like the first pancake. If it's not perfect, that's okay there are a lot more coming along."**

Antonin Scalia
Official Photograph

Hard to Define: In the U.S. Supreme Court ruling in: *Jacobellis v. Ohio 378 U.S. 184 (1964),* regarding possible obscenity in the movie *The Lovers,* Justice Porter Stewart remarked: **"I shall not today attempt further to define the kinds of material I understand to be embraced within that shorthand description** [pornography]; **and perhaps I could never succeed in intelligibly doing so. But I know it when I see it, and the motion picture involved in this case is not that."**

Potter Stewart
Official Photograph

God Presides Over the U.S. Supreme Court: Chief Justice of the United States Charles Evans Hughes (1930-1941) sported a deep voice and a white beard, prompting U.S. Solicitor General Robert Jackson to remark: **"He looks like God and talks like God."**

Charles Evans Hughes
Official Photograph

U.S. Supreme Court Justices

"Three Generations of Imbeciles is Enough:" In 1927, the U.S. Supreme Court ruled in *Buck v. Bell* that states are permitted to pass laws to forbid: **"feebleminded and socially inadequate"** individuals from procreating using compulsory sterilization. Justice Oliver Wendell Holmes Jr., in writing for the Majority, declared: **"Three Generations of imbeciles is enough."** This ruling remains on the books today.

Oliver Wendell Holmes Jr.
Library of Congress

Conservative Jurist Discusses Orgies: During a question and answer session after a 2004 address at Harvard University, U.S. Supreme Court Justice Antonin Scalia was asked about sexual morality. The Justice stunned the crowd by telling them: **"I even accept for the sake of argument that sexual orgies eliminate social tensions and ought to be encouraged."**

Antonin Scalia
Official Photograph

Worthy Ambitions: When he was nominated by President Lyndon B. Johnson to serve on the U.S. Supreme Court, Thurgood Marshall remarked: **"I have a lifetime appointment and I intend to serve it. I expect to die at 110, shot by a jealous husband."** In fact, Justice Marshall died in 1993 at the age of 84, and did not die at the hands of a jealous husband --- he died from heart failure.

Thurgood Marshall (L),Lyndon B. Johnson (R)
Lyndon Baines Johnson Presidential
Library and Museum

Constitutional Versus Unconstitutional: U.S. Supreme Court Justice Hugo Black (1937-1971) was fond of exclaiming: **"The layman's constitutional view is that what he likes is constitutional and that which he doesn't like is unconstitutional."**

Hugo Black
Official Photograph

U.S. Supreme Court Justices

Not the President's Marionette: In 1902, President Theodore Roosevelt nominated Massachusetts Justice Oliver Wendell Holmes Jr. to serve on the U.S. Supreme Court. Holmes was confirmed by the U.S. Senate. Justice Holmes proved that he was not Roosevelt's puppet. After Holmes was the deciding vote against Roosevelt's position in the case of *Northern Security Co. v. United States*, an inflamed President exclaimed: **"I could carve out a banana judge with more backbone than that."**

Oliver Wendell Holmes Jr.
Library of Congress

The Term 'Numbskull' Enters The Judicial Lexicon: Writing for the majority in the 2014 U.S. Supreme Court Case of *Abramski v. United States*, which ruled that the 1968 prohibition of the straw purchase of guns is constitutional, U.S. Supreme Court Justice Elena Kagan wrote: **"Putting true numbskulls to one side, anyone purchasing a gun for criminal purposes would avoid leaving a paper trail by the simple expedient of hiring a straw."**

Elena Kagan
Official Photograph

Don't Believe Everything You Hear: U.S. Supreme Court Justice Samuel Alito told an assembly of lawyers that he once watched television and heard a commentator mendaciously state that the High Court had a pro-business bias, in part because Justice Alito and Chief Justice John Roberts had been members of the Chamber of Commerce, which neither had. Justice Alito responded: **"I almost fell off my treadmill. I wondered if I was suffering from amnesia and thought I'd better check my resume. The only employers I've ever had has been the Department of Justice and the Supreme Court. I've never earned an honest living."**

Samuel Alito
Official Photograph

Do We Have to Do All this Work? During the legal case of *National Meat Association v. Harris,* U.S. Supreme Court Justice Steven Breyer asked if the Court had to **"write an 11-part opinion"** on each provision of a state law to determine if it was superseded by federal law. Justice Breyer deadpanned: **"I'm not trying to get out of work. I just want to know."** His colleague, Justice Antonin Scalia, responded: **"I'd like to get out of work, to tell you the truth."**

Stephen Breyer
Official Photograph

U.S. Supreme Court Justices

Burn Baby Burn: John Jay, the first Chief Justice of the United States, was unpopular because of his role in negotiating The Treaty of London in 1794 (a.k.a. The Jay Treaty). The treaty ended British control of posts located in the Western territory of the country and established America's claim for damages that were the result of British seizures of colonial boats. The U.S. also gained a limited right to trade within the West Indies. He once commented: **"I can walk the length of the country at night only guided by the light of my effigies burning."**

John Jay
Official Portrait by Gilbert Stuart

Just One More Justice To Go: In a 2011 speech in Cooperstown, NY, U.S. Supreme Court Justice Ruth Bader Ginsberg noted that four of the nine Justices hail from one of the five boroughs of New York City. The only borough not represented by a Supreme Court Justice is Staten Island. Accordingly, Ginsburg averred: **"Staten Island Jurists should stay close to their phones."**

Ruth Bader Ginsberg
Official Photograph

Divine Intervention? When Chief Justice of The United States Fred M. Vinson died in 1953, Justice Felix Frankfurter, a jurisprudential opponent of Vinson, told an aid: **"This is the first indication I have ever had that there is a God."** The death came before re-argument of the landmark case of *Brown v. Board of Education*. With Vinson at the helm, the Court likely would have split on upholding the racial doctrine from *Plessey v. Ferguson* that affirmed the segregationist doctrine of Separate but Equal. With Vinson's successor, Earl Warren, at the helm, the Court unanimously ruled that "Separate but Equal is inherently unequal."

Felix Frankfurter
Official Photograph

Fail: In testimony before the U.S. Senate Judiciary Committee, U.S. Supreme Court Justice Anthony Kennedy told a story about a calendar he gave to the Chinese Premier, which included an event in American history for every day of the year. **"I said when was your birthday? And he said April 17th, and I said read April 17th. And the interpreter kind of hesitated . . . He said April 17th. The Supreme Court of the United States affirms United States v. Dennis, affirming five prison terms for five communist leaders in America."**

Anthony Kennedy
Official Photograph

Chapter XI

Governors

Governors

Hell has Frozen Over: When Massachusetts Republican Governor Mitt Romney signed the Commonwealth Care Act, which provided Health Insurance to most Bay State residents, he made note of the fact that U.S. Senator Ted Kennedy (D-MA) had worked with him on the legislation. At the signing ceremony, Romney joked: **"My son said that having Senator Kennedy and me together like this on this stage behind the same piece of landmark legislation will help slow global warming. That's because hell has frozen over."** Kennedy joked back: **"My son said something, too. When Kennedy and Romney support a piece of legislation, usually one of them hasn't read it."**

Mitt Romney
Photograph by Greg Skidmore

Golfing and Governing: California Governor George Deukmejian (1983-1991) observed: **"The difference in golf and government is that in golf you can't improve your lie."**

George Deukmejian
Official Photograph

Stupid Party Is - As Stupid Party Does: After losing the 2012 Presidential election, Louisiana Governor Bobby Jindal delivered a blunt assessment on how the Republican Party must recover. In his Keynote Address at the Republican National Committee's winter meeting in Charlotte, NC, Jindal proclaimed to he crowd: **"We've got to stop being the stupid party. Its time for a new Republican Party that acts like adults."**

Bobby Jindal
Official Photograph

Lobbyist Whores: At his first Press Conference after assuming the Governorship of New York in 2008, a reporter asked David Paterson: **"Have you ever patronized a prostitute?"** (His predecessor Elliot Spitzer resigned after it came to light that he had patronized a prostitute). Paterson jokingly responded: **"Only the lobbyists."**

David Paterson
Photograph by David Shankbone

231

Governors

Wait, Isn't that Backwards? When explaining why Georgia does not need to establish a consumer protection agency, the state's Governor, Lester Maddox, commented: **"Honest businessmen should be protected from the unscrupulous consumer."**

Lester Maddox
Official Photograph

Political Insensitivity: Arizona Governor Evan Mecham garnered heat in 1988 for telling the Downtown Phoenix Kiwanis Club: **"The Japanese like to play golf, and their eyes really light up when you say we've got over 40 golf courses in Arizona. My goodness. Golf courses. Suddenly they've got round eyes."**

Evan Mecham
Official Photograph

My Life is a Tangled Wreck of Failures: In 1996, Massachusetts Governor Bill Weld lost a bid to serve in the U.S. Senate, losing to incumbent John F. Kerry. In an interview with *The New York Times,* Weld poked fun at both his loss and his patrician pedigree. He told reporter Sara Rimer: **"It was not my first defeat. There was the Rhodes scholarship, the Marshall scholarship, Harvard Law Review. My life is a tangled wreck of failures."**

Bill Weld
Official Photograph

Governor Makes Fun of His Own State: In 2005, in his role as the Chairman of the Republican Governors Association, Massachusetts Governor Mitt Romney made fun of his home state to Republican audiences. He would say: **"Being a conservative in Massachusetts is a bit like being a cattle rancher at a vegetarian convention."**

Mitt Romney
Official Portrait

Governors

Democrat Has Nothing 'Nice' to Say About Obama: During an appearance on *Morning Joe* on *MSNBC,* former Montana Governor Brian Schweitzer was asked to cite **"a single thing President Obama has done that you consider a positive achievement?"** The Democrat answered: "My mother, God rest her soul, told me 'Brian, if you can't think of something nice to say about something change the subject.'"

Brian Schweitzer
National Resources Conservation Service

Who Wants to be a Governor? As a former U.S. Senator, Van Harke (D-IN) once visited Indiana Governor Roger Branigan. Branigan candidly told him: **"You know, I never wanted to be Governor, I just wanted to be elected Governor."**

Roger Branigan
Official Portrait

Vaseline: In 2013, Maine Governor Paul LePage became inflamed after State Senator Troy Jackson suggested that the Governor's veto threat of the State Budget was a "stunt." LePage responded: **"Jackson claims to be for the people, but he's the first one to give it to the people without providing Vaseline."**

Paul LePage
Photograph by Matt Gagnon

Political Aspirations? In a 2011 interview with *The New York Times,* Connecticut Governor Dan Malloy commented on the deleterious effects of laying off public sector workers. He suggested that his colleagues with Presidential aspirations are doing so simply to say they did it. Malloy stated: **"I'm not sure that some governors just don't want to lay off people for the sake of laying off people and being able to say they did."**

Dan Malloy
Official Photograph

Governors

Hot Microphone: In the wake of the September 11, 2001 hijackings, Acting Massachusetts Governor Jane Swift delivered an address to the Commonwealth, announcing that State Police Superintendent John DiFava would replace Joe Lawless as Airport Security Chief. With the microphone still on, Swift said: **"They work for me and they know I'm in a firing mood. Just kidding. I hope my mic wasn't on."**

Jane Swift
Official Photograph

The Kissing Governor: In 1947, South Carolina Governor Strom Thurmond crowned 19-year-old Jean Griffin as Miss South Carolina. Thurmond commented: "**She walks well, she looks good. Let's see how she kisses**." The Governor proceeded in public view to kiss her. Griffin later said she was not surprised by the gesture: **"I'd heard he might do that."**

Strom Thurmond
Official Photograph

Living in La La Land: The day before his 2008 arrest for allegedly soliciting bribes in return for an appointment to the U.S. Senator seat being vacated by President-Elect Barack Obama, Illinois Governor Rob Blagojevich told a press conference: **"I don't believe there's any cloud that hangs over me. I think there's nothing but sunshine hanging over me."**

Rob Blagojevich
Official Photograph

I Intend to Drive the Snakes out of the State House: In 2006, Massachusetts Gubernatorial candidate Deval Patrick told a capacity crowd at the St. Patrick's Day Breakfast in South Boston: **"I do identify with St. Patrick, not just in name. He drove the snakes out of Ireland. I intend to drive the snakes out of the State House."**

Deval Patrick
Official Photograph

Governors

No More Mr. Nice Guy: After beating a failed attempt by the State Legislature to impeach him on a variety of charges in 1929, Louisiana Governor Huey Long asserted: **"I used to get things done by saying please. Now I dynamite 'em out of my path."**

Huey Long
Official Photograph

It's that Simple: Whenever Montana Governor Brian Schweitzer was asked his position on gun control, the Democrat would respond: **"Gun control is 'you' control your gun and I'll control mine."**

Brian Schweitzer
Official Photograph

Be Real, It's all a Lie: In 1996, as a guest on the Program *CNN*, host Frank Sesno asked former Governor Jerry Brown what he lied about as Governor of California. Brown responded: **"You run for office and the assumption is 'Oh, I know what to do.' You don't. I didn't have a plan for California. Clinton doesn't have a plan. Bush doesn't have a plan.... You say you're going to lower taxes, you're going to put people to work, you're gonna improve the schools, you're going to stop crime ... crime is up, schools are worse, taxes are higher. I mean, be real!"**

Jerry Brown
Official Photograph

Dietary Advice for "The Body": In a 1999 interview with *Playboy Magazine,* Minnesota Governor Jesse Ventura said: **"Every fat person says it's not their fault, that they have gland trouble. You know which gland? The saliva gland. They can't push away from the table."**

Jesse Ventura
Official Portrait

Governors

The "Body" and Religion: In 1999, Minnesota Governor Jesse Ventura commented in an interview with *Playboy Magazine* **"religion is a sham and a crutch for weak-minded people."** After being labeled a bigot by Republican Presidential candidate Gary Bauer, Ventura said of the word bigot: **"I looked it up. It's someone who's intolerable of any other religion but their own. I'm the opposite. I'm tolerant of all religions ... I don't care if someone wants to go out there and worship the bark on a tree."**

Jesse Ventura
Official Photograph

Death Should Not Stop a Man from Participating in the Political Process: Louisiana Governor Earl K. Long (1939-1940), noting the corruption in his state's electoral process, quipped: **"When I die, I want to be buried in St. Martin's Parish so I can remain politically active."**

Earl Long
Official Portrait

Arkansas Governor Pardons a Rolling Stone: In 2006, Governor Mike Huckabee (R-AR) pardoned lead guitarist Keith Richards of the rock band The Rolling Stones. Richards was pulled over for reckless driving in 1975, and was assessed a $162.50 fine for the offense. When Huckabee was accused of pardoning Richards because of his celebrity status, he replied: **"Hey, if you can play guitar like Keith Richards, I'll consider pardoning you too."** The pardon was a "good will gesture" initiated by the Governor, not Keith Richards.

Keith Richards
Photograph by Machocarioca

The Wizard of North Carolina: In the winter of 2014, a snowstorm hit North Carolina. Prior to the storm, the state's Governor, Pat McCrory, told residents: **"Stay smart. Don't put your stupid hat on at this point in time."**

Pat McCrory
Official Photograph

Governors

Governor Wages a War on Soda While Praising Cold Beer: South Carolina Governor Coleman Livingston Blease had an antagonistic relationship with soda. He preached against soda in his State of the State Address in 1911, vehemently warning about: **"The evil of the habitual drinking of Coca-Cola, Pepsi-Cola, and such like mixtures, as I fully believe they are injurious. It would be better for our people if they had nice, respectable places where they could go and buy a good, pure glass of cold beer than to drink such concoctions."**

Coleman Livingston Blease
Library of Congress

Nature Gone Wild? In 1992 Alaska Governor Walter Hickel defended his state's aerial predator control operation. He told *NBC News*: **"You just can't let nature run wild."** This inflamed the environmentalists.

Walter Hickel
Official Photograph

Grammar Policeman takes over the Governorship: California Governor John Neely Johnson (1856-1858) was a very colorful figure. He did not take constructive criticism well and once twisted the nose of J.E. Lawrence, the Editor of *The Sacramento Times and Transcript* after he published a critical article about him. In addition to his impetuous personality, Johnson was a stickler for proper grammar and once vetoed an important bill that was to create Del Norte County in Northwest California. He vetoed the bill not for its content or its constitutionality but because of: **"bad spelling, improper punctuation and erasures."**

John Neely Johnson
Official Photograph

Do it NOW! In a 2011 press conference prior to Hurricane Irene reaching the New Jersey shore, the state's Governor, Chris Christie, announced to the public: **"Get the hell off the beach in Asbury Park and get out. You're done. It's 4:30 PM. You've maximized your tan. Get off the beach. Get in you cars and get out of those areas."**

Chris Christie
Official Photograph

Governors

Taking a "Somewhat" Firm Stand: June 15, 1991, after the U.S. Senate voted to authorize President George H.W. Bush to use military force to repel Iraqi forces from Kuwait, Governor Bill Clinton of Arkansas told members of the media: **"I guess I would have voted with the majority if it was a close vote. But I agree with the arguments the Minority made."**

Bill Clinton in 1991
Old State House Museum

Wait! Isn't it the Other Way Around? In 1995, former and future California Governor Jerry Brown, hosting a talk radio show on Pacifica Radio, stated: **"The conventional viewpoint says we need a jobs program and we need to cut welfare. Just the opposite! We need more welfare and fewer jobs. Jobs for every American is doomed to failure because of modern automation and production."**

Jerry Brown
Official Photograph

The Cracking of Concrete: When Ronald Reagan ran for re-election as Governor of California in 1970, he promised voters his feet were **"in concrete"** against establishing a withholding system of state income tax. As Governor, Reagan reversed course, signing a tax increase to obliterate the state's $200 million deficit. Using humor as opposed to an excuse, Reagan commented: **"I can hear the concrete cracking around my feet."**

Ronald Reagan
Ronald Reagan Presidential Library and Museum

Déjà Vu All Over Again: Walter Hickel served as Governor of Alaska from 1966-1969. He then came back and served from 1990 to 1994. During his second stint as Governor, Hickel visited the small Alaska village of Point Hope. When he arrived, one of the first official greeters of the town said: **"Welcome Governor. You're only the second governor we've ever had here. The last was a guy named Hickel back in 1967."**

Walter Hickel
Official Photograph

Governors

Governor Thinks He's Still Mayor: During his 1987 inaugural address as Governor of Maryland, William Donald Schaefer said: **"I am honored today to begin my first term as the Governor of Baltimore-that is Maryland."** Schaeffer had served two terms as the Mayor of Baltimore.

William Donald Schaefer
Photograph by Marylandstater

Democratic Governor Lashes Out at Harry Reid: When U.S. Senate Minority Leader Harry Reid (D-NV) called his fellow Democrat, Montana Governor Steve Bullock, to ask him who he would appoint to the U.S. Senate seat vacated by Democrat Max Baucus (who became U.S. Ambassador to China), Bullock responded: **"None of your damn business. You know what? Stay out of my decision-making. This is a decision I make and no one else. This is one of those decisions that voters entrusted me with."** Bullock ultimately appointed Lieutenant Governor John Walsh to the seat.

Steve Bullock
Official Photograph

Governor Calls for a 'Bloodbath': In 1969, California Governor Ronald Reagan was a steadfast critic of "The Peoples Park," which was created as a citadel for liberal activists. Reagan argued that the park belonged to the University of California at Berkeley. He sent the State Highway Patrol and National Guard to reclaim the park for the university. The troops were armed with bayonets and tear gas. A riot ensued, as about 3,000 people chanted, **"We Want the Park."** A year later, in an address to the California Council of Growers, Reagan defended his actions, stating: **"If it takes a bloodbath, let's get it over with. No more appeasement."**

Ronald Reagan as Governor of California
Ronald Reagan Presidential Library

Thank God for Mississippi: Upon becoming Governor of Arkansas in 1971, Dale Bumpers observed: **"It's not enough anymore to say 'Thank God for Mississippi.'"** (In many economic rankings, Arkansas was 49th, while Mississippi was ranked 50th in the nation.)

Dale Bumpers
Official Photograph

Governors

Governor-Elect Uses the Term Nitwit: In 1991, Governor Kirk Fordice told Mississippi legislators that he favored a jungle primary system where all candidates run in a single primary. If no candidate pockets a majority of the vote, there would then be a runoff. However, Fordice said: **"Now everything's got downsides . . . and two or three people are sitting back there saying, 'Yeah, that's what got Louisiana so close to David Duke . . . and got 'em the nitwit that they got again . . . an old crook."** Duke was a former Grand Wizard of the Ku Klux Klan. He was defeated in the runoff by former Governor Edwin Edwards (Who Fordice called a crook) whose previous term as Governor was engulfed in scandals.

Kirk Fordice
Official Photograph

The Omnipotent *Boston Globe*: *The Boston Globe* was a constant thorn in the side of Massachusetts Governor Ed King. The paper delivered a torment of criticism of the Governor for charges of cronyism, mainly hiring fellow Irish Catholics for state positions. King remarked: **"If God is with you, who can be against you, except *The Boston Globe*."**

Ed King
Official Portrait

Expanding Gubernatorial Ignorance: When Democratic Texas Agricultural Commissioner Jim Hightower was informed that Republican Governor Bill Clements was studying Spanish, Hightower deadpanned: **"Oh good. Now he'll be bi-ignorant."**

Jim Hightower
Photograph by Larry D. Moore

What's so Bad About Stealing a Few Dollars? While serving as Military Governor of New Orleans, Louisiana, Benjamin Franklin Butler requisitioned $8,000 from a local bank without accounting for where the money went. At trial, the bank's attorney asked Butler what his neighbors in Lowell, Massachusetts would think of his action, to which Butler replied: **"The people would think I was a fool for not having taken twice as much."**

Benjamin Franklin Butler
Library of Congress

Governors

It's a Small World After All: When a coterie of German editors visited his office in Providence, Rhode Island, Governor John O. Pastore (1945-1950), who stood at just 5-foot-4 inches tall stated: **"Rhode Island is the smallest state in the Union, and I am the smallest governor in the United States."**

John O. Pastore
Official Photograph

A Frank Assessment of The Duke: State Representative Barney Frank (D-MA) was a vociferous critic of Massachusetts Governor Michael Dukakis during his first term in office. Frank excoriated Dukakis for budget cuts he believed hurt the poor. A reporter asked Frank if he had a problem with Dukakis riding the subway from his Brooklyn home to his office in the State House. Frank replied: **"No, I don't object that he rides the subway. I merely object that he gets off at the State House."** When Dukakis ran for re-election in 1978, Frank supported primary challenger Barbara Ackerman, who garnered just 6.72% of the vote in the primary. Dukakis lost to the other Democratic challenger in the race, Ed King.

Michael Dukakis During His First Term as Governor
Library of Congress

The Problem of Cat Versus Bird: In 1949, Illinois Governor Adlai Stevenson vetoed legislation which would levy fines against cat owners who let their felines out alone. He issued a very thoughtful veto statement which read: **"The problem of cat versus bird is as old as time. If we attempt to resolve it by legislation, who knows but what we may be called upon to take sides as well in the age old problems of dog versus cat, bird versus bird, or even bird versus worm. In my opinion, the State of Illinois and its local governing bodies already have enough to do without trying to control feline delinquency. For these reasons, and not because I love birds the less or cats the more, I veto and withhold my approval from Senate Bill No. 93."**

Adlai Stevenson
U.S. Department of Defense Photograph

Misstatement or Clarification? During the 1996 Whitewater Trial, James McDougal, a former business partner of President Bill Clinton, was asked if he had said that Arkansas Governor Jim Guy Tucker, a lawyer, **"was a thief who would steal anything not nailed down?"** McDougal clarified his statement, insisting that he had positive feelings about Tucker, but not about lawyers. McDougal insisted: **"I think I said: like most lawyers, he would steal anything that's not nailed down."**

Jim Guy Tucker
Official Photograph

Governors

Reverse Evolution: In 1987, Arizona Governor Evan Mecham was under investigation for misuse of campaign funds, and was taking heat for voiding the Martin Luther King Jr. Holiday. His predecessor as Governor, Bruce Babbitt, told *Newsweek Magazine*: **"Evan Mecham proves that [Charles] Darwin was wrong."**

Bruce Babbitt
Official Photograph

A Mixed Marriage: Discussing his willingness to work with Democrats in the State Legislature, California Governor Arnold Schwarzenegger said on *The Charlie Rose Show* on PBS: **"I have no trouble understanding Democrats. I sleep with one every night.** He was referring to his wife, Maria Shriver.

Maria Shriver
Photograph by LIfeScript

The Story of the Eighteen Dollar Bill: In 1964, Alabama Governor George Wallace told an audience at Auburn University. Wallace said: **"I think you and I from this section of the country are going to teach those who are trying to pawn off some counterfeit movements upon us, sort of like the Northeast Alabama mountaineer treated some Washington counterfeiters who made some eighteen dollar bills by mistake. They looked so good and crisp and green that they said 'what do we do with them? We don't want to throw them away.' One of them said: 'Well, I've been reading *The Milwaukie Journal*, and the *Baltimore Sun*, and *Life Magazine* and *The Saturday Evening Post*, and if what they say is true, about them, we can pass them off in Alabama and they won't ever know the difference. So they brought the eighteen dollar bills south and they saw a northeast Alabama mountaineer sitting by a little store, and one of these Washington DC counterfeiters said 'here's a good place to pass the first one. He said you could always tell a book by its cover. And so they agreed and they went into the little store and one of them said: 'Captain, can you give us change for an eighteen dollar bill?' And the old southern northeast Alabama mountaineer said to the Washington counterfeiters: 'I sure can, do you want three sixes or two nines.'"**

George Wallace
Official Portrait

Chapter XII

Gubernatorial Campaigns

Gubernatorial Campaigns

Different Sheets: In 1991, Louisiana Democrat Edwin Edwards was asked about the similarities between himself and his Republican Gubernatorial opponent, David Duke, a former Grand Wizard of the Ku Klux Klan, His response: **"We're both wizards in the sheets."**

Edwin Edwards
Official Photograph

A Sobering Question: In 1990, when Republican Arkansas Gubernatorial candidate and former U.S. Representative Tommy Robinson (R-AR) was asked about charges that he used to imbibe a pint of whiskey daily, Robinson responded: **"I get in enough trouble when I'm sober."**

Tommy Robinson
Official Photograph

Thinking Big: In 1994, the Democratic nominee for Governor of Massachusetts was Mark Roosevelt. In an interview with *The Boston Globe*, he made the following comment about his tenure in the Massachusetts State Legislature: **"A record of accomplishment probably unsurpassed by any legislator in the 20th Century in Massachusetts."** Roosevelt later retracted the comment, stating: **"I can be sanctimonious."**

Mark Roosevelt
Official Photograph

Leave it to Beavers: During a 1990 Massachusetts Gubernatorial debate, Republican nominee Bill Weld exploited a claim by the Democratic nominee, John Silber Ph.D., that beavers created so much wetland that preserving wetlands should not be of concern. Weld quipped: **"Would you tell us doctor, what plans, if any, you have for the preservation of open spaces in Massachusetts, other than leave it to beavers?"**

William F. Weld
Photograph by Mathew W. Hutchins,
Harvard Law Review

Gubernatorial Campaigns

Going Too Far: In 1994, Texas Governor Ann Richards, on a campaign stop in Texarkana, Texas, heaped approbation on Debbie Colman who was the recipient of the city's Teacher of the Year Award Richards was inflamed that her Republican opponent, George W. Bush, had argued that the achievement scores for students were manipulated because it is an election year. Richards then asserted: **"You just work like a dog, do well, the test scores are up, the kids are looking better, the dropout rate is down. And all of a sudden, you've got some jerk who's running for public office** [George W. Bush] **telling everybody it's all a sham and it isn't real and he doesn't give you credit for doing your job. So far as he is concerned, everything in Texas is terrible."**

Ann Richards
Photograph by Kenneth C. Zirkel

The Super Bowl is Played Again: In 2003, opponents of California Governor Grey Davis gathered the requisite number of signatures to effectuate a recall election against Governor Grey Davis. Davis said: **"It's like the Oakland Raiders saying to Tampa Bay, 'We know you beat us, but we want to play the Super Bowl again.'"** Davis was recalled, losing the recall election to actor Arnold Schwarzenegger.

Grey Davis
Official Photograph

Nothing to Worry About: In 1978, Massachusetts Democratic Gubernatorial candidate Ed King promised the Massachusetts business community that he would repeal all environmental regulations implemented by his main primary opponent Governor Michael Dukakis. King was a vociferous supporter of nuclear power, despite the potential link to cancer. When he was asked about its potential dangers, King answered: **"I'm sure we'll find a cure for cancer."**

Ed King
United States Department of Transportation

Love Your Mamma: During the 1970 Florida Gubernatorial race, incumbent Republican Claude Kirk Jr. said of his Democratic opponent Reubin Askew: **"a nice, sweet-looking fellow, but being Governor is a tough job and being a mamma's boy won't get the job done."** Askew responded simply: **"I love my Mamma."** Askew won the election.

Reubin Askew
Official Photograph

Gubernatorial Campaigns

Touché: At a Louisiana Gubernatorial debate in 1983, Democrat Edwin Edwards was asked by his opponent David Treen: **"How Come you talk out of both sides of your mouth?"** Edwards replied: **"so people like you with only half a brain can understand me."**

Edwin Edwards
Official Photograph

The Comeback Kid: After losing the California Governorship to incumbent Edmund Gerald "Pat" Brown Sr. in 1962, former Vice President Richard M. Nixon told reporters: **"You won't have Nixon to kick around anymore."** Six years later he was elected President of the United States.

Richard M. Nixon
The Los Angeles Times

Political Family Feud: In 1994, Massachusetts, State Representative Mark Roosevelt, the grandson of Theodore Roosevelt Jr., was the Democratic nominee for Governor of Massachusetts. He ran against Republican Governor Bill Weld. Weld was married to Susan Roosevelt Weld, a cousin of Mark Roosevelt. This family feud was a nasty slugfest. Despite Weld's commanding lead, Weld ran up the electoral score in part by approving advertisements attacking Roosevelt. Roosevelt in turn said of Weld: **"He's indifferent, apathetic, feckless, aloof, passive and lazy. Did I say uncaring? He's uncaring."** Weld won the race with a record 71 percent of the vote.

Mark Roosevelt
Photograph by Mark Rauterkus

Baby Talk: In 1966, Georgia Democratic Gubernatorial nominee Lester Maddox called his Democratic opponent, Howard Hollis "Bo" Calloway, **"a baby in his crib reaching for his rattler."** Maddox won the election.

Howard Hollis "Bo" Callaway
Official Portrait

Gubernatorial Campaigns

Tick Tick Tick Tick: In 1983, Democrat Louisiana Gubernatorial candidate Edwin Edwards said of his Republican opponent David Treen: **"He's so slow it takes him an hour and a half to watch *60 Minutes*."**

David Treen
Official Photograph

So He's Clean: On the eve of his 1983 election as Governor of Louisiana, Edwin Edward told reporters: **"The only way I can lose this election is if I'm caught in bed with either a dead girl or a live boy."** Edwards won the election.

Edwin Edwards
Official Photograph

The Politics of Inclusion: In describing how conservative Ed King defeated Massachusetts Governor Michael Dukakis in the 1978 Democratic Primary, King aide Angelo Berlandi told supporters: **"We created a hate campaign. We put all the hate groups in one pot and let it boil."**

Campaign Button for the Ed King Gubernatorial Campaign

It's a Start: In 1978, President Jimmy Carter spoke at a fundraiser for Maryland Democratic Gubernatorial nominee Harry Hughes. The President noted that earlier in the year he had negotiated the Camp David Accords in Maryland (which ended the official state of war between Egypt and Israel). He noted that his standing with the public had been enhanced since then. Carter quipped: **"My Esteem in this country has gone up substantially since then. It's very nice now that when people wave at me, they use all their fingers."**

Jimmy Carter (C) with Egyptian President Anwar Sadat (L) and Israeli Prime Minister Menachem Begin (R) at the Signing of the Camp David Accords
National Archives and Records Administration

Gubernatorial Campaigns

This Campaign is Just Not Going Right: Republican nominee George Kariotis lost his bid for the Massachusetts Governorship in 1986 to Governor Michael Dukakis 68-31%. During his concession speech Kariotis deadpanned. **"In fairness to Mike, I should clear up something. He was criticized, I think, for giving me only one televised debate during the seventh game of the World Series** [Between the Boston Red Sox and the New York Mets]. **I should point out that that was really his second choice; his first choice was tomorrow."**

Campaign Pin for the George Kariotis for Governor Campaign

Letter Opening Event: During the 2006 Gubernatorial debate between Republican Kerry Healey, Democrat Daval Partick, Independent Chrity Mihos, and Green–Rainbow Party nominee Grace Ross, Mihos noted that the administration of Governor Mitt Romney would hold closed-door meetings to discuss the state's Health Care System. Mihos asked the candidates if they would favor open meetings. After Ross agreed, Mihos said: **"We've got one, and I know Deval you'll go anywhere --- You'll go to a letter opening."**

**Christy Mihos
CMIHOS**

Gay Marriage Should Be Between a Man and a Woman: In a 2003 interview with conservative radio talk show host Sean Hannity, California Gubernatorial candidate Arnold Schwarzenegger misspoke in trying to state his opposition to same-sex marriage. He said: **"I think that gay marriage is something that should be between a man and a woman."**

Arnold Schwarzenegger on the Cover of
Time Magazine

Not the Best Way to Cultivate the Hispanic Vote: When 1990 Republican Texas Gubernatorial nominee Clayton Williams was asked why the state's Hispanic voter should support him, he responded: **"I met Modesta** [Williams' wife] **at a Mexican restaurant."**

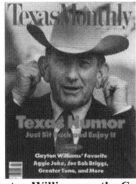

Clayton Williams on the Cover of *Texas Monthly*

Gubernatorial Campaigns

Playing the Elitist Card: Political opponents of Massachusetts Governor Endicott "Chub" Peabody (1963-1965) joked that there were three municipalities in the Bay State named after him. They were: **"Peabody, Marblehead and Athol."** They also tried to exploit classism within the electorate by pointing to Peabody's patrician background, characterizing him as an elitist. During the Democratic Primary for re-election, supporters of Peabody's opponent, Lieutenant Governor Francis X. Bellotti, distributed bumper stickers which read: **"Vote for Peabody. He's better than you."** Bellotti won the primary, but lost the General Election to former Massachusetts Republican Governor Frank Volpe in the General Election.

Endicott "Chub" Peabody"
Chicago Tribune Photograph

How Hard Can Being Governor Be? In 2005, humorist and musician Kinky Friedman ran for Governor of Texas as an Independent. His campaign slogan was: **"How hard could it be?"** Friedman lost the race to Republican Governor Rick Perry. Friedman garnered just 12.4% of the vote.

Kinky Friedman
Photograph by Larry D. Moore

A Real City Boy: During his failed 1982 run for the Democratic nomination for Governor of New York State, Mayor Ed Koch asked Peter Manso of *Playboy Magazine:* **"Have you ever lived in the suburbs? I haven't but I've talked to people who have, and it's sterile. It's nothing. It's wasting your life, and people do not wish to waste their lives once they've seen New York** [City.]**"** When Manso asked Koch why people would live in New York City, given **"lousy city services and a late subway,"** Koch again exploded on the suburbs, asserting, **"As opposed to wasting time in a car? Or out in the country, wasting time in a pickup truck? When you have to drive 20 miles to buy a gingham dress or a Sears Roebuck suit. The rural American thing – I'm telling you, it's a joke."**

Ed Koch
Official Photograph

Freeloading? During his successful 1966 campaign for the position of California Governor, Ronald Reagan told *The Sacramento Bee:* **"Unemployment insurance is a pre-paid vacation for freeloaders."**

Campaign Button for Ronald Reagan's 1966 Gubernatorial run

Gubernatorial Campaigns

Tell the President to "shove" the Endorsement! In 2010, Barack Obama broke precedent and did not endorse all Democratic nominees. Frank Caprio of Rhode Island was the Democratic nominee for Governor. President Obama did not endorsement Caprio. He did this out of deference to Lincoln Chaffee, an Independent, who had supported Obama for President in 2008. When Caprio learned Obama would not endorse him, he said in an interview with *WPRO Radio* in Providence: **"I didn't ask for President Obama's endorsement. You know, he could take his endorsement and really shove it as far as I'm concerned."**

Frank Caprio
Official Photograph

Acting Governor: In 1966, former actor Ronald Reagan, the Republican Gubernatorial nominee in California, was asked what kind of a Governor he would be. Reagan responded: **"I don't know, I've never played a Governor."**

Ronald Reagan During His Acting Days
Ronald Reagan Presidential Foundation

Silber Shockers: In 1990, one week before winning the Democratic nomination for Massachusetts Governor, John Silber was asked why he did not campaign in the inner-city Boston community of Roxbury. Silber responded: **"There's no point in my making a speech on crime control to a bunch of drug addicts."** After mustering the nomination, Silber said during a healthcare discussion: **"Shakespeare was right when he said, 'Ripeness is all.' When you've had a long life and you're ripe, then it's time to go."** The biggest "Silber blunder" came in the last week of the campaign when Silber, up by nine points at the time, was asked by Natalie Jacobson of *WCVB-TV* what his biggest weakness was. Silber snapped: **"You find a weakness. I don't have to go around telling you what's wrong with me. The media have manufactured about 16,000 nonexistent qualities that are offensive and attributed them all to me. Let them have their field day. You can pick any one of them."** With that statement, Silber's poll numbers took a nosedive and he lost the election to Republican Bill Weld by four points. His statements created a new term in the American political lexicon: **"Silber shockers."**

John Silber
Photograph by Jackhsiac

Gubernatorial Campaigns

Losing a Case With Brother on Jury: In 1999, U.S. Representative Asa Hutchinson (R-AR) was an Impeachment Manager during the U.S. Senate trial of Bill Clinton. Clinton was acquitted of perjury and obstruction of justice. One of the jurors was U.S. Senator Tim Hutchinson (R-AR), Asa's brother. In 2014, Democratic Gubernatorial candidate Mike Ross used the issue against Asa Hutchinson, who was now his Republican opponent for Arkansas Governor. Ross told *The Associated Press*: **"He may be the only lawyer in America who has conducted a trial with his brother on the jury and lost."**

Mike Ross
Official Photograph

Just Win: In 2014, former Republican Governor Charlie Crist ran for Governor of Florida as a Democrat. Crist had branded himself **"a pro-life, pro-gun, anti-tax Republican"** before becoming a Democrat. Republican political strategist Rick Wilson commented on the party's willingness to support someone like Crist. He said: **"Democrats are so desperate to win the Governors race, if Charlie Crist had a dead hooker in the trunk of his car, they'd still be, [fine] we're good. He's the guy."**

Charlie Crist
Official Photograph

Ma and Pa Governorship: In 1917, Texas Governor James Ferguson was removed from office for misappropriation of state funds, yet he remained popular in the state. In 1932, his wife Miriam Amanda. Ferguson ran for Governor. She had the nickname "Ma" because of her initials. Her husband became known as "Pa." Ma told voters they would get: **"Two Governors for the price of one."** Her campaign slogan was: **"Me for Ma, and I ain't got a thing against Pa."** Ma won the election, becoming the first female Governor of Texas in history.

Miriam Amanda "Ma" Ferguson (L) and James "Pa" Ferguson (R)
Library of Congress

A Bit Too Corny: At the end of the final 2002 Massachusetts Gubernatorial debate between Republican Mitt Romney and Democrat Shannon O'Brien, host Tim Russert said: **"Enjoy the Buffalo Bills-New England Patriots game on Sunday."** Romney replied: **"And may the best team win."**

Mitt Romney for Governor Pin

Chapter XIII

Mayors

Mayors

Mayor Calls out a Bitch: In 1990, FBI agents arrested Washington D.C. Mayor Marian Berry for possession of crack cocaine. In referring to his former girlfriend and FBI informant Hazel Diane "Rasheeda" Moore (who brought Berry to the hotel), the Mayor exclaimed: **"Bitch set me up . . . . I shouldn't have come up here . . . goddamn bitch."**

Marian Berry Smoking a Crack Pipe on FBI Surveillance Video
Federal Bureau of Investigation

Police Officers Arrests Their Boss, The Mayor: In 2013, Gordon Jenkins, the Mayor of Monticello, New York, was arrested by his city's police officers on suspicion of drinking and driving. While in custody, Jenkins said to one police officer that he had hired: **"What are you going to do? Put me in jail five years? I'll get out in five years, and I going to f***ing tell you what the f**k you did to me, and I'm going to come back to you."**

Gordon Jenkins
Official Photograph

The Emperor: The Office of Mayor in Boston is almost omnipotent in that the city has a strong Mayor system, and a weak City Council. In 1967, when Kevin White was about to assume the office, his predecessor John Collins told him: **"It's Not Mayor, It's Emperor."**

John Collins
Boston Redevelopment Authority

Don't print what he says, print what he meant: Mayor Richard J. Daley became known for his mangled syntax. His Press Secretary, Earl Bush, told reporters: **"Don't print what he says, print what he meant."**

Richard J. Daley on the Cover of
Time Magazine

255

Mayors

A Vagina-Friendly Mayor: At a 2008 press conference to announce the tenth anniversary of the Vagina Monologues V-Day Celebration, New Orleans Mayor Ray Nagin told the assembled reporters: "**I am a vagina-friendly Mayor.**"

Ray Nagin
Photograph by Jeff Schwartz

Big Difference: Reading a speech, Chicago Mayor Richard J. Daley misread the phrase "**We shall reach greater and greater plateaus of achievement.**" Instead, he said: "**We shall reach greater and greater platitudes of achievement.**"

Richard J. Daley
Official Photograph

The Curley Dictum: Boston Mayor James M. Curley told his young advisors and disciples: "**Every time you do a favor for a constituent, you make nine enemies and one ingrate.**"

James Michael Curley
Library of Congress

Only I Can Spread False Rumors: In 1965, after Hurricane Betsy flooded much of his city, New Orleans Mayor Victor Schiro told residents: "**Don't believe any false rumors, unless you hear them from me.**"

Victor Schiro
Official Portrait

Mayors

Shouldn't it be 'Puck' Players? After the Boston Bruins won the Stanley Cup Championship in 2011, Boston Mayor Tom Menino said at a press conference: **"Congratulations to the Boston Bruins for a great series bringing the Stanley Cup back to Boston . . . and great ballplayers on the ice and also great ballplayers off the ice."**

Tom Menino
Official Photograph

Gotta Love the Windy City: In 1931, Chicago Mayor William "Big Bill" Thompson derided his political opponent, Anton Cermak, for his ethnic heritage. Thompson proclaimed: **"I won't take a back seat to that Bohunk, Chairmock, Chermack or whatever his name is. Tony, Tony, where's your pushcart? Can you picture a World's Fair mayor with a name like that?"** Cermak replied: **"He doesn't like my name... it's true I didn't come over on the *Mayflower*, but I came over as soon as I could."** Cermak had the last laugh, unseating Thompson.

Anton Cermak
Library of Congress

It's Party Time Again: In his 1927 campaign for Mayor of Chicago, William "Big Bill" Thompson railed against incumbent Mayor William Emmett Dever for enforcing federal prohibition laws. Thompson told voters he would reopen businesses that had been shut down for serving alcohol under Dever's stewardship. Thompson proclaimed: **"I'm as wet as the Atlantic Ocean."** Thompson won the race and was the last Republican to serve as Mayor of Chicago.

William "Big Bill" Thompson
Library of Congress

The Politics of Kissing: In 1968, Norma B. Handloff, the Mayor of Newark, Delaware, told a luncheon gathering at a Temple University Club: **"Politicians are the greatest kissers in the world, and they don't kiss babies. Democrats kiss more than Republicans. They even kiss people they've met for the first time. Of course, I don't know what that proves."**

International Kissing Symbol

Mayors

Crime Report: Doing Great Outside the Murders: At a 1989 address to the National Press Club, Washington D.C. Mayor Marion Barry asserted: **"Outside of the killings, D.C. has one of the lowest crime rates in the nation."**

Marion Barry
Official Photograph

Just Don't Bury Me in New Jersey: In 2008, former New York City Mayor Ed Koch purchased a burial plot at the Trinity Church Cemetery in Manhattan. He told the *Associated Press* **"This is my home. The thought of having to go to New Jersey was so distressing to me."** In 2013, Koch was buried in this cemetery.

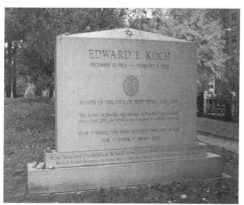

Ed Koch Tombstone
Photograph by Anthony22

It's Only A Game -- Take it Easy: While on a trip to Paris in 1996, San Francisco Mayor Willie Brown was asked on a conference call with San Francisco 49ers reporters jokingly, if the French would ever invest in a new stadium for the San Francisco 49ers. This was on the heels of a game where the team's backup quarterback Elvis Grbac had made too many turnovers, giving the game to the Dallas Cowboys. Brown responded: **"Well, I'm trying to get the French to invest in a new quarterback. This guy Grbac is an embarrassment to humankind."** A reporter asked if he thought his comments were harsh. Brown doubled-down, averring: **"After that interception and that bonehead intellectual breakdown in the last game against Dallas, and we lost it 20-17, he can't play in any stadium that I'm going to assist to be built."**

Willie Brown
Official Photograph

Mayors

Mayor Takes Neutral Position on Player Choking Coach: In 1997, Golden State Warrior Shooting Guard Latrell Sprewell received a one-year ban from the NBA for trying to choke his coach, P.J. Carlesimo. San Francisco Mayor Willie Brown told *The San Francisco Examiner*: **"Maybe the coach deserved choking. I'm not justifying what he did as right. But nobody is asking why he did it or what might have prompted him."**

Latrell Sprewell on the Cover of
Dime Magazine

Blame It on the Streets: Philadelphia Mayor Frank Rizzo (1982-1990), a former Police Commissioner, once observed: **"The streets are safe in Philadelphia. It's only the people who make them unsafe."**

Frank Rizzo
Official Photograph

Tammany Hall Stooge: John P. O'Brien was elected as Mayor of New York City in 1932. He was the handpicked candidate of Tammany Hall (The Democratic Political Machine). O'Brien was not his own man. The day following his inauguration as Mayor, a reporter asked him who he would appoint as the next Police Chief. Referring to the Tammany Hall bosses, O'Brien responded: **"I don't know, they haven't told me yet."**

John P. O' Brien
Official Photograph

The George Washington of Mayors: In 2005, Las Vegas Mayor Oscar Goodman took questions from fourth-graders at Joe Mackey Elementary School in Las Vegas. One student asked him if he had a hobby. Goodman responded: **"Drinking Bombay Sapphire Gin."** Some constituents were offended that he would say that to young children. Goodman responded: **"I'm the George Washington of mayors. I can't tell a lie. If they didn't want the answer, the kid shouldn't have asked the question."**

Oscar Goodman
Official Photograph

259

Chapter XIV

Celebrities Commenting on Politics

Celebrities Commenting on Politics

Baseball Birther: At the 2010 Baseball Winter meetings, Baltimore Orioles First Baseman Luke Scott met with reporters and expressed dissatisfaction with President Barcak Obama. David Brown of Yahoo Sports said to Scott: **"You don't think Barack Obama wasn't born in the United States do you?"** Scott answered: **"He was not born here. I was born here. If someone accuses me of not being born here, I can go – within 10 minutes – to my filing cabinet and I can pick up my real birth certificate and I can go, 'See? Look! Here it is. Here it is.' The man has dodged everything. He dodges questions, he doesn't answer anything. And why? Because he's hiding something."** The Baltimore Orioles issued a statement saying: **"Luke Scott's comments do not reflect the opinion of the Baltimore Orioles organization. The fact is that Barack Obama is our President, duly elected by the people of the United States. End of story."**

Luke Scott
Photograph by Keith Allison
From Owning Mills, USA

The Saga of a President and a Gangsta Rapper: George W. Bush and Gangsta rapper Curtis Jackson, a.k.a. "50 Cent," share the same birthday. Bush was born on July 6, 1946. Cent was born on July 6, 1975. In 2005, Cent told *Gentleman's Quarterly*: **"The President is incredible . . . a Gangsta. I wanna meet George [W.] Bush, just shake his hand and tell him how much of *me* I see in him."** However, in 2007 the rapper reversed course, telling *New York Magazine* that Bush: **"has less compassion than the average human."**

50 Cent
Photograph by Alex Const

Nothing but Dirt: Actress Tallulah Bankhead was a partisan Democrat and no fan of Richard M. Nixon. In 1958 she told a Democratic fundraiser at the Mayflower Hotel in Washington D.C., that: **"Dirt is too clean a word for him."**

Tallulah Bankhead
Library of Congress

Celebrities Commenting on Politics

Snooki Makes Belated Endorsement: Nicole Polizzi, a.k.a., Snooki of the Reality TV Show *Jersey Shore*, told Jo Piazza of the *Huffington Post* that she supported Donald Trump for President. She made this statement after Trump announced he would not run: **"I thought Trump was gonna run, but he's not, right? I would endorse him and vote for him."**

Snooki
Photograph by Jeff Lewis Chicago

Will Smith For President: In a 2007 interview with the newspaper *The Mail,* Actor Will Smith exclaimed: **"I'm going to be President of the United States. I always wanted to be the first black president but** [Democratic Presidential candidate] **Barack Obama stole my idea. That's ok with me. Barack can go first, then I'll have my turn."**

Will Smith
Photograph by Walmart Stores

The Real Power: In 1995, Dallas Cowboys owner Jerry Jones, a native Arkansan, said: **"Fifteen to 20 years ago, I was wandering around Arkansas, Bill Clinton was wandering around Arkansas. Who would have thought that one would go on to power and prestige and fame and the other end up the President of the United States."**

Jerry Jones
Official Photograph

He Likes Them Both: In his 2012 re-election bid, President Barack Obama picked up the coveted endorsement of Adult Film Star Ron Jeremy. Jeremy, however also had some kind words for Obama's Republican opponent, Mitt Romney. He told *The Boston Herald* that he thinks Mitt Romney: **"is a good man."**

Ron Jeremy
Photograph by Ron Francis

Celebrities Commenting on Politics

Jed Clampett Disses Jane Hathaway: In 1984, Nancy Kulp, who played secretary Jane Hathaway in the 1960's Television series *The Beverly Hillbillies,* became the Democratic nominee for a Congressional seat in the central Pennsylvania-based Ninth Congressional District. Buddy Ebsen, who in the same sitcom portrayed hillbilly turned millionaire Jed Clampett, endorsed Kulp's opponent, U.S. Representative Bud Shuster (R-PA). Ebsen's voice appeared in a radio commercial asserting that he had dropped Kulp a note that read: **"Hey Nancy, I love you dearly but you're too liberal for me - I've got to go with Bud Shuster."** Ebsen was not a resident of the district. Shuster won the race, mustering 67% of the vote.

Nancy Kulp
Publicity Photograph

Retired Porn Star Picks Romney: Mitt Romney picked up an unlikely endorsement in former Adult Film Star Jenna Jameson. Jameson, who enjoys a net worth of over $30 million, stated: **"When you're rich, you want a Republican in Office."**

Jenna Jameson
Photograph by Glen Francis

Rage Against Paul Ryan: In 2012, after Republican Presidential nominee Mitt Romney selected Paul Ryan as his Vice Presidential running mate, it was publicized that Ryan's favorite band was the rap metal band *"Rage Against the Machine."* The band's guitarist Tom Morello did not requite the love and blasted Ryan, exclaiming: **"Paul Ryan is the embodiment of the machine that our music has been raging against for two decades."**

Paul Ryan
Official Photograph

Celebrities Commenting on Politics

Lindsay Lohan Takes to Economics: Like many Americans, actress Lindsay Lohan is concerned about the Federal Reserve's policy of quantitative easing. She took to twitter to lament: **"Have you seen gas and food prices lately? U.S. money will soon be worthless if the Fed keeps printing money."** She provided a hyperlink to the National Inflation Center's website.

Lindsey Lohan
Photograph by Rafael Amando Deras

Tax Hike Stuns Jersey Shore: Among the provisions in the Patient Protection and Affordability Act signed by President Barack Obama in 2010 is a 10% surcharge on all customers who use tanning beds. This inflamed Nicole Polizzi (a.k.a. Snooki of the *MTV* series *Jersey Shore*). She said she no longer tans, and said of Obama: **"I feel like he did that intentionally for us."**

Nicole Polizzi (a.k.a. Snooki)
Photograph Taken by Amy Nicole Waltney

No Supporter of the Plight of the American Indians: In a 1981 interview with *Playboy Magazine,* Actor John Wayne discussed the taking of land of Native Americans by White settlers. Wayne exclaimed: **"I don't feel we did wrong in taking this great country away from them. There were great numbers of people who needed new land, and the Indians were selfishly trying to keep it for themselves."**

John Wayne
1965 Publicity Portrait

The Spears Doctrine: During a 2003 interview with CNN'S Tucker Carlson, he asked Pop Star Britney Spears for her opinion on U.S. involvement in the Iraq War. Spears' response was: **"Honestly, I think we should just trust our President in every decision he makes and should just be faithful in what happens."**

Britney Spears
U.S. Navy Photograph by Chief Warrant Officer Steve Rossman

Celebrities Commenting on Politics

Not the Most Artful Endorsement: Snoop Lion, formerly known as Snoop Dog, said at a Toronto Press Conference that he supported Barack Obama for President: **"I mean, Bush f##ked up for eight years, so you gotta at least give [Obama] eight years. He cleaned half the s##t up in four years, realistically. It isn't like y'all gave him a clean house. Y'all gave him a house where the TV didn't work, the toilet was stuffed up -- everything was wrong with the house."**

Snoop Lion
Photograph by Adulis "Chedo" Mokanan
of The Come up Show

Manichean Characterization: In 2000, actress Julia Roberts observed: **"Republican comes in the Dictionary just after 'reptile' and above 'repugnant.' I looked up Democrat. It's of the people, by the people, for the people."**

Julia Roberts
Photograph by David Shankbone

He Must be Undecided: In a 2014 interview with *Guns.com*, rock star Ted Nugent (who campaigned against Barack Obama's re-election in 2012), Nugent said: **"I have obviously failed to galvanize and prod, if not shame enough Americans to be ever vigilant not to let a Chicago communist-raised, communist-educated, communist-nurtured subhuman mongrel like the ACORN community organizer gangster Barack Hussein Obama to weasel his way into the top office of authority in the United States of America."**

Ted Nugent
Photograph by Larry Philpot of
www.soundstagephotography.com

Like an Informed Endorsement: In 2008, Kim Kardashian, star of the reality Television series *Keeping Up with the Kardashians,* announced her endorsement of Barack Obama for President at a launch party for *Girls Gone Wild Magazine.* She told the crowd: **"He just seemed very firm about the change, and that's like, his motto."**

Kim Kardashian
Photograph by Toglenn

267

Chapter XV

Miscellaneous Quotations

Miscellaneous Quotations

Take That, Tsongas: In 1995, when former U.S. Senator Paul Tsongas (D-MA) chided President Bill Clinton for not focusing on balancing the federal budget, former Clinton campaign advisor Paul Begala stated: **"The notion that he [Paul Tsongas] is questioning the President's moral authority is like getting lectures from [Conservative Talk Show Host] Rush Limbaugh."**

Paul Begala
Photograph by Gage Skidmore

The Establishment is not Stagnant: Knowing that no politician wants to be associated with the establishment, humorist Art Buchwald commented: **"If you attack the establishment long enough and hard enough, they will make you a member of it."**

Art Buchwald
MDC Archives

The People Have Spoken: The Bastards: In 1966, Democratic strategist Dick Tuck tried his hand at electoral politics. He lost a Democratic Primary to serve in the California State Senate. His campaign slogan was: **"The Job needs a tuck and Tuck needs a job."** Upon conceding the race, Tuck told supporters: **"The people have spoken: The Bastards."**

Dick Tuck Campaign Poster from 1966

What's a Junk Bond? During a 1990 debate for the Office of Treasurer and Receiver General of the Commonwealth of Massachusetts, Democrat William Galvin, trying to show that his Republican opponent, Joe Malone, was ignorant of economic issues, asked Malone the question: **"What's a junk bond?"** Without hesitation, Malone responded: **"That's what we'll have if you're elected."** Malone won the election.

Joe Malone
Official Photograph

Miscellaneous Quotations

Starr Does Not Shine Bright for James Carville: During Special Prosecutor Kenneth Starr's investigation of President Bill Clinton's involvement in the Whitewater affair, James Carville, a former campaign advisor to Clinton, lashed out at Starr, stating: **"As with mosquitoes, horseflies, and most bloodsucking parasites, Kenneth Starr was spawned in stagnant water."**

Kenneth Starr
Official Photograph

Franklin Prefers Turkey to Eagle: In 1784, U.S Minister to France Benjamin Franklin lobbied for the turkey to become the national symbol on the Presidential seal, not the American bald eagle. Franklin explained: **"The bald eagle is . . . a bird of bad moral character; like those among men who live by sharping and robbing, he is generally poor and often very lousy."**

Benjamin Franklin
Library of Congress

Neatness Isn't Everything: In 1974, State Representative Barney Frank, known for his disordered appearance, ran for re-election with the campaign slogan: **"Neatness Isn't Everything."**

Barney Frank Campaign Poster

Atheists and Agnostics Need Not Apply: Article 6, section 8 of the *North Carolina State Constitution* disallows any individual who does not believe in God from holding elective office. The Document states: **"The following persons shall be disqualified for office: First, any person who shall deny the being of Almighty God."**

American Atheist Symbol

272

Miscellaneous Quotations

Milk Cow Disease: In 2010, Ashley B. Carson, the Executive Director of The Older Women's League (OWL) wrote a column in *The Huffington Post* challenging former U.S. Senator Allan Simpson (R-WY), who was serving as the Co-Chairman of the Simpson-Bowles Commission on the Debt and Deficit. Carson challenged Simpson's assertion that Social Security is adding to the Federal Deficit. Simpson sent Carson an email in response stating: **"I've made plenty of smart cracks about people on Social Security who milk it to the last degree. You know 'em too...We've reached a point now where it's like a milk cow with 310 million tits!"** Simpson later apologized for making the comment.

Allen Simpson
Official Photograph

Congressional Idiocy: American Author Mark Twain averred in a 1891 draft manuscript: **"Suppose you were an idiot and suppose you were a member of Congress. But I repeat myself."**

Mark Twain
Photograph by Mathew Brady

He Built the House he was Born in: Robert Strauss, a long-time political operative who once chaired the Democratic National Committee, summed up the American politician's quest to appear to have come from humble roots when he said: **"Every politician wants you to believe he was born in a log cabin he built himself."**

Robert Strauss
U.S. Department of State

Former First Lady Pitches Margarine: In 1959, former First Lady Eleanor Roosevelt starred in a commercial for "Good Luck Margarine." In the commercial, Roosevelt asserts: **"Years ago, most people never dreamed of eating margarine, but times have changed. Nowadays, you can get margarine like the new Good Luck, which really tastes delicious. That's what I've spread on my toast, Good Luck. I thoroughly enjoy it."** Eleanor Roosevelt donated the Money earned from her appearance to UNICEF.

Eleanor Roosevelt
Franklin D. Roosevelt Presidential Library and Museum

273

Miscellaneous Quotations

Politician Does Not Think Too Highly of his Constituents: In 1871, *Harper's Weekly* ran articles exposing the corruption of New York State Senator William "Boss" Tweed and his political machine. Tweed commented to a reporter: **"I don't care a straw for your newspaper articles, my constituents don't know how to read, but they can't help seeing them damned pictures."**

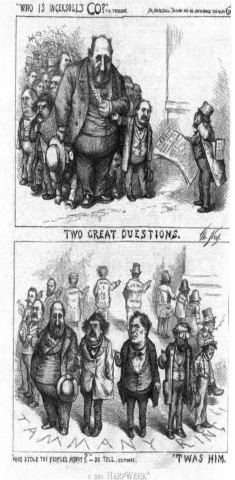

Political Cartoon by Thomas Nast of *Harpers Weekly*, depicting a corrupt Tweed Machine

Impish Dirty Trick: In 1970, 19-year old Republican operative Karl Rove, using a false identity, broke into the campaign office of Allan J. Dixon, the Democratic nominee for State Treasurer of Illinois, and purloined Dixon campaign stationary. Knowing when Dixon had scheduled a rally, Rove proceeded to advertise: **"Free beer, free food, girls, and a good time for nothing."** He distributed the homemade flyers at rock concerts and homeless shelters, inviting these people to the rally. Rove later become Deputy Chief of Staff under the administration of George W. Bush. Dixon later became a U.S. Senator from Illinois. Rove later apologized for his actions.

Karl Rove
Official Photograph

A Faith Healer? Speaking to a group of handicapped Texans sitting in wheelchairs, Texas House Speaker Gib Lewis said: **"And now will y'all stand and be recognized."**

Gib Lewis
Photograph by Bill Malone for the
Texas State Archives

274

Miscellaneous Quotations

Hitting is what Matters: Before the 1960 World Series, Yankees Catcher Yogi Berra drew a thunderous applause. The next day his manager Joe Garagiola said to him: **"You amaze me, Yogi. You've now become such a world figure that you drew more applause than either** [Indian] Prime Minister [Jawaharlal] **Nehru or** [Former President] **Herbert Hoover. Can you explain it?** Berra answered: **"Certainly I'm a better hitter."**

Yogi Berra
Baseball Digest

Taking on the Harvard Faculty: During an appearance in 1965 on *Meet The Press*, William F. Buckley, the publisher of the conservative *National Review* magazine and a critic of the liberal leanings Ivy League schools, observed: **"I am obliged to confess I should sooner live in a society governed by the first two thousand names in the Boston telephone directory than in a society governed by the two thousand faculty members of Harvard University."**

William F. Buckley
Photograph by Bert Goulait, U.S. Military

Somehow I Won. Now What Do I Do? In 1948, there was a wave of enmity directed toward the Massachusetts Republican Party, in part because of the party's support for a hike in the Massachusetts Transit Authority rates (the rates to use public transportation). 1948 effectuated a Democrat wave in the state, as Democrats took over the Massachusetts House of Representatives for the first time in history. One of the Republican casualties was Secretary of the Commonwealth Fred Cook, who had been in office for 28 years. Edward J. Cronin, an unemployed WWII Veteran who had only one campaign aide, his mother, defeated Cook in a stunning upset victory. The next day a reporter asked what he would do as Secretary of State. An astonished Cronin honestly replied: **"Plans? Haven't a one. It hit me so sudden I haven't thought of anything yet."** Cronin proved popular, serving as Secretary of the Commonwealth until his death in 1958. In his last campaign, he won re-election with 62.38% of the vote.

Edward J. Cronin
Official Photograph

275

Miscellaneous Quotations

Honest Graft? Political boss George Washington Plunkitt, a member of the New York State Senate in the late 1800's, coined the term **"honest graft,"** to provide a label for what happens when a politician uses the power of the political machine to benefit a political party, a constituent, or a personal interest. Plunkitt coined this word to distinguish the practice from **"dishonest graft,"** where one uses the power of personal gain strictly for self-aggrandizement. In defining the actions of his formidable political machine, Plunkitt said: **"I seen my opportunities and I took em."**

George Washington Plunkitt
Library of Congress

Excellent Observation: The American etymologist, poet, and translator John Ciardi observed: **"The [U.S.] Constitution gives every American the inalienable right to make a damn fool out of himself."**

John Ciardi translation of *Dante The Inferno*

Monkey Business: In 1922, Henry Fairfield Osborn Sr., the President of the American Museum of Natural History, identified a tooth discovered in Nebraska to be an "anthropoid ape." Osborn used this finding to make fun of former Democratic Presidential nominee, William Jennings Bryan. Bryan was a creationist who in his post-political life lobbied for state statutes disallowing the teaching of evolution. He represented the World Christian Fundamentals Association at the famous 1925 Scopes Trial. Osborne joked: **"I believe this is a case in which a scientist made a man out of a pig, and the pig made a monkey out of the scientist."**

Henry Fairfield Osborn Sr.
Library of Congress

Bad Dog: Texas President Sam Houston (before Texas became a State) said of Thomas Jefferson Green, a member of the Texas Republic Legislature: **"He has all the characteristics of a dog except loyalty."**

Sam Houston
Photograph by Mathew Brady

276

Miscellaneous Quotations

White House Chef is Not a Man: The picture below of White House chef Martha Mulvey appeared in *The Evening Independent* of St. Petersburg, Florida in 1923. The caption oddly reads: **"The White House Chef is Not a Man!"**

CHEF OF WHITE HOUSE

The White House chef is not a man. Mrs. Martha Mulvey came to the White House during President Taft's administration. She not only prepares the daily meals for the chief executive and his family, but she also plans all the state dinners.

Martha Mulvey
Photograph printed in *The St. Petersburg Times*, Copyright Harris & Ewing

Scary Thought: In his book *The Prince and the Pauper*, Author and historian Gore Vidal observes: **"Half of the American people have never read a newspaper. Half never voted for President. One hopes it is the same half."**

Gore Vidal
Photograph by David Shankbone

Fattman For State Representative: In 2010, Massachusetts State Representative candidate Ryan Fattman had many signs stolen. It is believed to be because of his last name. Fattman told WBZ-TV: **"Growing up with the last name Fattman prepares you very well for politics. They say it takes a fat man to find pork in the state budget."** Fattman won the race.

Ryan Fattman
Official Photograph

Miscellaneous Quotations

Using the Holy Bible to Explain Tax Deductions and Fertilizer: In the 1982 case of *Schenk v. Commissioner of Internal Revenue,* Fifth Circuit Judge Irving Loeb Goldberg wrote: **"To every thing there is a season, and a time to every purpose under the heaven: A time to be born, and a time to die; a time to plant, and a time to pluck up that which is planted, a time to purchase fertilizer, and a time to take a deduction for that which is purchased."**

Irving Loeb Goldberg
Texas Law Library, The University of Texas at Austin

The Ignorance of Youth: In 2011, after a proposed law ending Same-Day Voter Registration failed in New Hampshire, the state's House Speaker, Republican William O'Brien, told a Tea Party rally that: **"allowing people to register and vote on Election Day led to the kids coming out of the schools and basically doing what I did when I was a kid, which is voting as a liberal. That's what kids do — they don't have life experience, and they just vote their feelings."**

William O'Brien
Official Photograph

The Evils of Feminism: In 1992, televangelist and 1988 Republican Presidential aspirant Pat Robertson wrote a fundraising letter in opposition to a proposed Equal Rights Amendment to the Iowa Constitution. In the letter, Robert wrote: **"Feminism is a socialist, anti-family, political movement that encourages women to leave their husbands, kill their children, practice witchcraft, destroy capitalism and become lesbians."**

Pat Robertson on the Cover of
Time Magazine

Don't Run in Baltimore: In 1989, Democrat Thomas V. Miller, the President of the Maryland State Senate, took a call from a reporter about why he was holding a fundraiser in Baltimore, outside of his suburban Washington, D.C., District. Miller responded: **"It helps educate my constituents as to why Baltimore needs the economic help. Baltimore is a goddamn ghetto. It's worse than Washington. It's Shit."** Miller was considered a possible contender for Governor of Maryland in 1990, prior to making that inappropriate comment.

Thomas V. Miller
Official Photograph

Miscellaneous Quotations

James Baker's Visit to The People's Republic of Massachusetts: In 1984, while accompanying President Ronald Reagan on a visit to Guam, a reporter asked White House Chief of Staff James Baker if he had visited a Communist country prior to 1980 when he visited China. Baker responded: **"I've been to Massachusetts."** The Chairman of the Massachusetts Republican State Committee, Andrew Natsios, told *UPI:* **"given the voting habits of some parts of this state, I can understand his statement. "The People's Republic of China is more conservative than parts of Cambridge."** However, Democratic Governor Michael Dukakis was not amused, exclaiming Baker's comments were: **"an outrageous failure at humor which is a grievous insult to the citizens of a Commonwealth who were the first to lay down their lives against tyranny in the defense of freedom."**

James Baker
Official Photograph

Espionage: Allan Dulles, the first civilian director of the CIA, often called his agency **"The State Department for unfriendly countries."**

Allan Dulles
Official Photograph

Irish Joke: In 1905, New York State Senator William W. Armstrong met State Senator James H. McCabe, a stalwart Democrat. Armstrong mentioned to McCabe that he was Irish. McCabe asked Armstrong which part of Ireland he hailed from. Armstrong replied: **"From County Cavan. I am afraid you will think me rather a bad combination. I am an Irishman, a Protestant, and a Republican."** McCabe responded; **"Well, that is bad. In fact, I never knew of but one Irishman who could boast of a worse. He was a fellow that lived in my district. He was an Irishman, a Protestant, a Republican, and a homeopath."**

James H. McCabe
Official Photograph

The Deep South in Pennsylvania: Democratic Political Consultant James Carville described the political landscape of Pennsylvania as **"Philadelphia and Pittsburg with Alabama in between."**

James Carville
The Office of James Carville

Miscellaneous Quotations

I'm the Only Sane One in the Family: The Book: *Redneck Power: The Wit and Wisdom of Billy Carter,* by Jeremy Rifin and Ted Howard is about President Jimmy Carter's brother, who owns a gas station in Plains, Georgia. In 1976 Billy exclaimed: **"I got a mama who joined the Peace Corps when she was 68. I got one sister who's a Holy Roller preacher. Another wears a helmet and drives a motorcycle. And my brother thinks he's going to be President, so that makes me the only sane one in the family."**

Redneck Power:
The Wit and Wisdom of Billy Carter
By James Rifkin and Ted Howard

Who Would Want to be a Patriot Under this Definition? Nationally Syndicated Columnist William E. Vaughan observed: **"A real patriot is the fellow who gets a parking ticket and rejoices that the system works."**

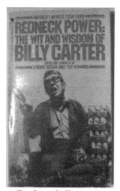

William E. Vaughan
Official Photograph

One-Armed Midgets: In 2009, Michael Steel, the recently elected Chairman of The Republican National Committee spoke of his vision for expanding his party's base. He told *The Washington Times:* **"We need to uptick our image with everyone, including one-armed midgets."**

Michael Steele
Steele for Chairman

God and the Tennessee General Assembly: In 1996, Democratic Tennessee State Senator Steve Cohen voted against a resolution encouraging businesses, homes and schools to post the Ten Commandments on their walls. He told *Newsweek*: **"God handed his word to Moses. He didn't need the Tennessee General Assembly's help."**

Steve Cohen
Official Photograph

Miscellaneous Quotations

Biblical Support For Marijuana Use: In support of marijuana legalization in her state, Oklahoma State Senator Constance Johnson told reporters her support is rooted in Genesis 1:29 which reads: **"Then God said, 'I give you every seed-bearing plant on the face of the whole earth and every tree that has fruit with seed in it. They will be yours for food.'"**

Constance Johnson
Official Photograph

The Wit of William F. Buckley: In 1965, William F. Buckley was the Conservative Party nominee for Mayor of New York City. When asked by a reporter what he would do if he were to get elected, he responded: **"Demand a recount."** Buckley lost the race to Republican John Lindsey.

William F. Buckley
Library of Congress

Texas Talk: Nationally Syndicated Columnist Molly Ivins would often muse: **"As they say around the Texas Legislature, if you can't drink their whiskey, screw their women, take their money, and vote against 'em anyway, you don't belong in office."**

Molly Ivins
Promotional Photograph

Spoken Like a True Autocrat: When a Republican member of the Georgia House of Representatives asked State House Speaker Tom Murphy (D-GA 1973-2002) a question about House Rules, Murphy responded: **"I'm not sure about the rules of the House, but this is how we do things here."**

Thomas Murphy
Photograph by Sethlywood1993

Miscellaneous Quotations

Santa Transcends the Cold War: In 1961, eight-year-old Michelle Rochon of Marine City, Michigan became concerned that the Russians were testing nuclear weapons at the North Pole. She had overheard her parents talking about the issues. She worried about how this would affect Santa Clause in his effort to make deliveries on Christmas Eve. Accordingly, she authored the following letter to President John F. Kennedy:

Dear Mr. Kennedy,

Please stop the Russians from bombing the North Pole because they will kill Santa Claus. I am 8 years old. I am in the third grade at Holy Cross School.

Yours truly,

Michelle Rochon.

To Michelle's surprise, the President actually wrote her back:

Dear Michelle,

I was glad to get your letter about trying to stop the Russians from bombing the North Pole and risking the life of Santa Claus.

I share your concern about the atmospheric testing of the Soviet Union, not only for the North Pole but for countries throughout the world; not only for Santa Claus but for people throughout the world.

However, you must not worry about Santa Claus. I talked with him yesterday and he is fine. He will be making his rounds again this Christmas.

Sincerely,

John Kennedy

John F. Kennedy
White House Press Office

Glossary of Political Terminology

Glossary of Political Terminology

Actual Malice: A precedent established in the Supreme Court case of *New York Times Co. v. Sullivan,* The court ruled that to establish libel against a public official, knowing falsity or reckless disregard for the truth must be proven.

Advisory Referendum: A measure that appears on the ballot which in non-binding. It is mostly used to engage popular opinion.

American Exceptionalism: Belief that America is superior to all other nations.

Anarchy: Absence of any governing authority.

Appellate Jurisdiction: The power of a Court to review lower Court decisions, and accept, modify or even overturn the decision of a lower level court.

Arkansas Project: An effort funded by newspaper publisher Richard Mellon Scaife to find damaging information on Bill Clinton.

Articles of Confederation and Perpetual Union: Written by the Continental Congress. This was the Constitution of the first thirteen colonies. This governing authority was written in 1776. Because of criticism from Federalists believing that the federal government lacked necessary power, it was eventually supplanted with the *U.S. Constitution.*

Australian Ballot: System employed in the United States in which all ballots are marked in secret.

Authoritarianism: System of government in which the state has much power over the individual.

Bicameralism: Two separate legislative chambers. At the federal level, the Congress is divided into the Senate and House of Representatives. The legislative branch in every state except Nebraska is also comprised of two chambers.

Bill of Attainder: The punishment of an individual without a trial. Article 1 Section 9 of the *U.S. Constitution* disallows this practice at the state and federal levels.

Blanket Primary: Primary in which the electorate can vote for members of different parties for different offices. For example, a voter could select a Republican candidate for Governor and a Democrat for State Senator. The leading vote-getter for each party goes on to compete in the general election.

Black Budget: Appropriations earmarked "secret" (usually military projects). They are kept hidden for national security purposes.

Blowback: A term coined by the CIA referring to the future negative unintended consequences of U.S. foreign policy, including covert operations. Many point to the Iran Hostage Crises in 1979 as being blowback by the Iranians for the U.S. support of the overthrow of Prime Minister Mohammad Mosaddeq in 1953.

Blue Dog Democrat: The modern term for a Conservative Democrat. Most come from more conservative parts of the country, including the South and the West, where the national Democratic Party is often looked upon as too liberal. The term was coined by U.S. Representative Peter Geren (D-TX 1989-1997) who said that Conservative Democrats were being choked blue by extreme Democrats and Republicans. Most Blue Dog Democrats are particularly interested in balancing the federal budget.

Boll weevils: A term referring to Conservative Democrats from the mid to late twentieth-century. A pre-curser to what is now known as a "Blue Dog Democrat."

285

Glossary of Political Terminology

Boondoggle: A project funded by the government with little redeeming value.

Budget Deficit: When annual government expenditures exceed annual government receipts.

Budget Surplus: When government receipts exceed government expenditures.

Bullet Vote: A voter has the option to select multiple candidates for an office, but chooses just one.

Bureaucracy: Commonly refers to the structure and regulation needed in a large organization such as a corporation or government entity to accomplish tasks.

Bush Doctrine: The U.S. will not distinguish between terrorists themselves and those who harbor the terrorists and will use force if necessary to "take out" regimes which represent a potential threat to the U.S.

Carter Doctrine: Offered in response to the Soviet Union's invasion of Afghanistan in 1980. President Jimmy Carter asserted that the U.S. would intervene militarily if necessary anywhere in the Persian Gulf to defend U.S. national interests.

Ceteris Paribus: Other things being equal.

Checks and Balances: A system in which different branches of government have oversight over the others, so none becomes omnipotent.

Clerk of the U.S. House of Representatives: The House's chief record-keeper. The Clerk is elected every two years.

Clinton Doctrine: The U.S. will intervene abroad to defend its values, including human rights.

Closed Primary: Primary election in which only members of one party are afforded the right to participate.

Cloture: Ending a filibuster. It needs the approval of 60 U.S. Senators.

CNN Effect: The belief that the images Americans see on their TV sets has a direct affect on how they view the foreign policies of their government. The term originates from the Somalia Crisis in the early-mid 1990's, when viewers saw the malnourished Somalis on TV. They then pressured their government to send troops to stop the suffering. Later, when they saw Somali's dragging a dead U.S. soldier through the streets, they demanded withdrawal.

Coattail Effect: The ability of a popular politician at the top of the ballot, such as a Governor or Senator, to bring voters to the polls who will also vote for other candidates of his/her political party further down the ballot. These other candidates could include members of the U.S. Congress, state legislators, and municipal officials.

Command Economy: System where the government rather than market forces centrally plans economic activity.

Commander-in-Chief Clause: Article 2, Section 2, Clause 1 of the *U.S. Constitution* says the President shall be: "Commander in Chief of the Army and Navy of the United States and the militia of the several states."

Common Law: The governing system based upon judicial precedence.

Common Victualler License: A license granted by a public entity allowing one to serve alcoholic beverages.

Glossary of Political Terminology

Communism: a system of government in which the entire population owns most property, and private property is extremely limited. Ex: North Korea, Vietnam, and Cuba.

Concurrent Resolution: A measure passed by both houses of the U.S. Congress that does not have the power of law and does not need the signature of the president.

Confederation: An alliance of groups.

Congress of the Confederation or the United States in Congress Assembled: The precursor to the United State Congress. It was the governing body of the United States from March 1, 1781 to March 4, 1789.

Congressional Delegate: A non-voting representative to the U.S. House of Representatives from American Samoa, Commonwealth of the Northern Mariana Islands, Guam, the United States Virgin Islands and the District of Columbia. They are elected to two-year terms. A Congressional Delegate has all privileges afforded other members, such as speaking privileges, drafting legislation, and committee voting. However, the Delegates are not afforded the right to vote on legislation.

Congressionalist: One who believes the U.S. Congress should have wide-ranging power.

Constitutional Republic: A system of government where the citizenry elect officials who must govern in a way that comports with a governing Constitution. The United States of America is an example.

Continuing Resolution: A Joint Resolution passed by Congress providing funding for government agencies at existing levels. This is a temporary measure to provide funding prior to the Congress and President working out an agreement for the full funding for the fiscal year.

Dean of the U.S. House of Representatives: Longest serving member of the House in consecutive terms. The Dean's only official duty is to swear in the Speaker of the House.

Declaration of Independence: Manuscript written by Thomas Jefferson in 1776 proclaiming independence of the U.S. from Great Britain.

Democratic Leadership Council (DLC): A now defunct non-profit corporation founded in 1985 to moderate the Democratic Party and expand its voter-base to include moderate voters. Former Chairman Bill Clinton used many of the themes of the DLC in his presidential campaign in 1992. Other former chairmen include then U.S. Senator Evan Bayh (D-IN), then U.S. Senator John Breaux (D-LA), and then U.S. Senator Sam Nunn (D-GA).

Democratic Peace Theory: Belief that liberal democracies do not go to war with each other because the majority of the population will never vote to go to war or elect people who would. Accordingly, if all nations were liberal democracies, there would be no war. Many Neo-Conservatives have adopted this premise.

De-politicized Citizenry: A system where the population is not actively engaged in the political decisions of their times.

Deputy President pro tempore: Any former President or Vice President who returns to serve in the U.S. Senate is entitled to this position, which includes an increase in salary.

DINO: Democrat-In-Name-Only

Direct Democracy: System where citizens participate in drafting and voting on laws. An example is a New England style town meeting.

Glossary of Political Terminology

Down Ballot: Candidates for offices, such as U.S. Congress, the state legislature, and municipal positions, whose office is not at the top of the ballot. The top might include candidates for President, Governor, Mayor, etc.

Dual Federalism: Doctrine espoused by U.S. Supreme Court Justice Roger Taney (1777-1864) which maintained that the state and federal governments should have separate but equal powers.

Earmark: Congressionally directed spending geared toward funding specific projects or programs such as constructing a new wing at a college, building a bicycle path, or preserving an historic landmark.

Electioneering: Actively working for a political candidate or ballot initiative.

Enumerated powers: Eighteen specific powers delegated to the United States Congress from Article 1 Section 8 of the *United States Constitution.*

Executive Agreement: An accord between the President and a foreign head of government that needs a simple up or down vote by both houses of Congress to win approval.

Ex post facto Law: A law passed "after the fact." Under the *U.S. Constitution*, no American can be penalized for violating a law before it becomes the law of the land.

Fascism: Authoritarian/nationalistic political ideology. Sometimes this is the amalgamation of religious and corporate interests.

Federalism: The delineation of powers between the federal and state governments.

Federalist Papers: Eighty-five articles written by John Jay, Alexander Hamilton, and James Madison and published in *The Independent Journal* and *The New York Packet.* They advocated for the ratification of the *U.S. Constitution.*

Filibuster: In the U.S. Senate, members are permitted to speak indefinitely on a subject to avoid a vote. Only with 60 votes can the Senate vote to invoke cloture, thus ending debate on voting. Then U.S. Senator Strom Thurmond (D-SC) holds the record for the longest filibuster. He spent 24 hours and 18 minutes filibustering the Civil Rights Act of 1957. There are also non-verbal tactical procedures within filibustering to delay a vote.

Free Rider: One who receives the benefits of government policy without incurring the costs.

Free Trade: Free flow of goods and services not subject to tariffs.

Functionary: A Government Official

Gerrymandering: The manipulation of the redistricting process at the state level to benefit the majority party and/or all incumbents. The term originated to describe Massachusetts Governor Elbridge Gerry's (1810-1812) successful attempt to maximize the numerical political advantage for his Democratic-Republican Party.

Great Society: An all-encompassing term for the social programs proposed by President Lyndon B. Johnson. Legislation was enacted in areas such as Health Care, Civil Rights, and Education Reform.

Gross Domestic Product: The market value of all goods and services produced in a country, usually annually.

Gross National Product: Measures of national income and output used to estimate the welfare of an economy through totaling the value of goods and services produced in an economy.

Glossary of Political Terminology

Half-Breeds: Moderate Republicans in the latter half of the nineteenth century who favored civil service reform.

Ideologue: A person with a certain grand design or philosophical mindset of how the world should be.

Impeachment: Article Two Section 4 of the *U.S. Constitution* states that "The President, Vice President, and all other civil Officers of the United States shall be removed from Office on Impeachment for, and Conviction of, Treason, Bribery, or other High Crimes and Misdemeanors." If a majority votes in the U.S. House of Representatives for impeachment, then the articles are sent to the Senate, where a two-thirds majority is required for conviction.

Imperialism: Encroachment of an empire on territory outside its borders.

Impoundment: The refusal of a sitting president to spend funds for something that the legislature has appropriated funds for.

Incrementalism: Achieving legislative goals step-by-step by passing a series of small legislation.

Incumbent: A current holder of an office.

Inflation: The rising prices of goods and services.

Infotainment: The amalgamation of news with entertainment.

Initiative: A vehicle for the citizens to propose legislation or constitutional amendments to be placed on the ballot for an up or down vote by the electorate. Accordingly, the usual legislative process is circumvented. Twenty-four states currently have some form of the initiative option.

Injunction: A Court order requiring a person or entity to do something or to refrain from doing a certain act or behavior.

Instant Runoff Voting: A voting system where voters rank all candidates. The candidate with the fewest first place votes is dropped and the voter's second choice replaces the first choice of those who placed him/her first. This process is repeated until two candidates remain.

Invisible Hand: A term coined by the Scottish Economist Adam Smith to describe his belief that there is a natural regulator in a free-market-system.

Isolationism: Belief that a country should be averse to all relations with other nations, including commercial, cultural, and military isolation.

Joint Resolution: A measure requiring approval of both chambers of Congress before going to the president for his/her subsequent approval or disapproval.

Judicial Review: Power of the Judicial branch of government to scrutinize for constitutional permissibility, actions by the Executive and Legislative branch. If the Justices rule the actions to be unconstitutional, they become null and void.

Jungle Primary: A primary election where candidates run for office on the same ballot. If no candidate musters a majority of the vote, there is a run-off between the two top finishers. This system is used in Louisiana.

Laissez-faire: A French word translated: "to allow to do, to leave alone." The term is used to mean that the government should not regulate the economy.

Lame duck: An incumbent elected official who has lost much of his/her influence because the official's term is nearing an end and they are not seeking re-election.

Glossary of Political Terminology

Layer-Cake Federalism: A system where the federal and state governments have clearly delineated and specific functions.

LBJ Rule: In 1959, the Texas legislature approved legislation allowing a politician to run for two political offices simultaneously. This benefited Lyndon B. Johnson in 1960 as he sought both re-election to the U.S. Senate and the Presidency. After failing to secure the Democratic presidential nomination, he ran for Vice President that year. He subsequently won both the Vice Presidency and re-election to the U.S. Senate. Other Texas officials, including U.S. Senators Lloyd Benson and Phil Gramm, and U.S. Representative Ron Paul, have used the law to seek higher office while running for re-election.

Legislative Referendum: The legislature refers a measure to the voters for their up or down vote.

Letters of Marque and Reprisal: Article 1, Section 8, Clause 11 of the *U.S. Constitution* gives the President the power to "grant Letters of Marque and Reprisal, and make rules concerning captures on land and water." It allows the president to search, seize, or destroy specified assets or personal belongings of a foreign party that has committed some offense under the laws of nations.

Libertarianism: A belief that government should be a limited-purpose entity devoted to protect a person's life, liberty, and property.

Line-Item Veto: Power of the executive to reject provisions in a piece of legislation without vetoing the legislation outright. At the federal level, the Line-Item Veto Act of 1996 was nullified in *Clinton v. City of New York*, 524 U.S. 417 (1998). The U.S. Supreme Court ruled that the Act violated the Presentment Clause of the *U.S. Constitution* because it impermissibly gave the President of the United States the power to unilaterally amend or repeal parts of statutes that had been duly passed by the United States Congress. At the state level, Forty-three state Governors have this privilege.

Lobbyist: Individual, representing a cause or organization, who tries to persuade government officials to support their point of view on issues.

Local Aid: Transfer of revenue from state to municipal governments to pay for local services.

Logrolling: When two members of a legislative body agree to support each other's legislation on separate issues.

Majority and Minority Leader: In both the U.S. House of Representatives and the U.S. Senate, these elected members serve as floor leader for their respective parties. When they are not there, a designee is selected. In the House, the Majority leader is second-in-command to the Speaker of the House.

Manifest Destiny: Originally referred to the belief that the U.S. was destined to expand from the Atlantic to the Pacific Ocean. Today it has come to mean that the U.S. must increase its territory.

Mayflower Compact: A document signed by 41 Mayflower voyagers on November 11, 1620 establishing the government structure of Plymouth Colony. The signers agreed to follow the contract and: "mutually in the presence of God and one of another, Covenant and Combine ourselves together into a Civil Body Politic, for our better ordering and preservation."

Micro Governing: Governing by focusing on specific small-bore issues.

Mixed Economy: An economic system that combines forces from multiple economic structures.

Moonbat: Term of derision for a liberal.

National Debt: The accumulative amount of annual deficits.

Glossary of Political Terminology

Nanny State: A pejorative phrase for a paternalistic government.

Neo-Conservatism: Former Cold War Liberal Democrats who became disillusioned with what they viewed as the Democratic Party's dovish foreign policy. Many supported then U.S. Senator Henry "Scoop" Jackson's (D-WA) bids for the Democratic Party's nomination in 1972 and 1976. After his loss, many gradually migrated to the Republican fold and supported President Ronald Reagan. Today, they are steadfast supporters of an activist foreign policy that promotes Democracy abroad. American intellectual Irving Kristol (1920-2009) is considered by many to be the Patron Saint of this ideology.

New Democrat: A Democrat who generally strives to bring the Democratic Party to the center of the political spectrum. The term New Democrat was popularized in 1992 when the Democratic Presidential Ticket of Bill Clinton and Al Gore came from this wing of the party. Most New Democrats are business oriented and favor fiscal austerity and free trade as a vehicle for economic expansion, rather than the more liberal view that government should redistribute the nation's wealth.

Nixon Doctrine: The U.S. will provide arms to allies, but will not do the actual fighting for them.

Nomination Papers: Papers that are required to be completed when an individual wants to run for public office.

Non-Interventionism: The doctrine that dictates that a country should avoid foreign entanglements with other nations while maintaining commercial and cultural intercourse. Thomas Jefferson said the U.S. should practice: "Peace, Commerce, and honest relations with all nations, entangled alliances with none."

Nonpartisan election: An election where candidates do not run as a member of a political party. Most municipal elections fall into this category.

Off-year election: Election held in the middle of a presidential term.

Oligarchy: Rule by the wealthy few.

Open Primary: Primary election in which members of all political parties are invited to participate.

Original Jurisdiction: Power of a court to hear a case for the first time.

Paleo-Conservative: Ideological descendants of a prominent philosophy in the Republican Party between WWI and WWII. They share a non-interventionist foreign policy, support for federalism, and oppose most government intervention in the economy. Many paleo-conservatives share a populist streak, opposing what they view as attempts by power elites and multi-national corporations to exert influence. In addition, many adherents to this ideology take a hard-line stance against affirmative action and illegal immigration. Examples include President Warren G. Harding (1921-1923), U.S. Senator Robert A. Taft (R-OH 1939-1953), and political commentator Patrick J. Buchanan.

Paleo-Liberal: An ideology that couples support for muscular foreign policy, including high defense spending, with an activist domestic policy, including a munificent social safety net. This belief was conventional liberal thinking during the first half of the Cold War. U.S. Senator Henry "Scoop" Jackson (D-WA 1953-1983) was a steadfast exponent of this ideology.

Partisan Election: Election in which candidates declare party affiliation.

Partisan: One who is a steadfast advocate of the interests of his/her political party or cause.

Glossary of Political Terminology

Patron: One who finances a political cause or politician.

Phone Mark: When a legislator does not get his/her earmark placed in legislation, a call is made to a government agency demanding funding. This is kept secret from the public, and is illegal in the U.S.

Plurality: Receiving more votes than any other candidate but not a majority.

Political Football: A topic which politicians debate, but without resolution. Politicians use the issue for their political advantage.

Political Parlance: Jargon related to politics.

Politicized Citizenry: A system where the population is actively engaged in the political decisions of their times.

Popular Referendum: A measure that appears on the ballot as a result of a voter petition drive. It affords the electorate an up or down vote on legislation passed by a legislative body.

Pork barrel spending: Government funding designed to benefit a special interest rather than benefit the public interest. It is often intended to benefit a constituent, a private company, or a campaign contributor of a politician.

POTUS: President of the United States.

President of the United States: The chief executive officer of the government who is both head of state and head of government. Presidential powers are derived from Article II of *The U.S. Constitution*.

President pro tempore *emeritus*: An honorific office awarded to any former President pro tempore of the U.S. Senate. While the office has no extra powers, its holder is awarded an increase in staff and salary.

President pro tempore of the Senate: Generally the most senior member of the majority party in the Senate holds this position. This person is the second-highest-ranking official of the United States Senate and is officially the presiding officer. Usually though, he or she delegates this duty to other members. Third in line of presidential succession, the office's powers are derived from Article I, Section 3 of the *U.S. Constitution*.

President-Elect: A winner of a presidential election who has yet to assume the office.

Presidentialist: An advocate of a strong federal executive branch.

Protectionism: The restriction of goods and services from abroad in order to protect domestic industries.

Reagan Doctrine: The U.S. will provide aid to forces fighting against communism, with the grand design of rolling it back.

Reconciliation: This process allows the U.S. Senate to consider any budget legislation without a filibuster.

Republicrat: A political pejorative used to define the common interests of the Republican and Democratic parties by those who think they are two sides of the same coin and have little differences.

Resident Commissioner of Puerto Rico: Non-voting representative to the U.S, Congress from the Commonwealth of Puerto Rico. The only representative elected to a four-year term. He or she

Glossary of Political Terminology

has all privileges afforded other members, such as speaking privileges, drafting legislation, and committee voting, except voting on final approval of legislation.

Rider: A provision attached to unrelated legislation. Sometimes these are provisions that may be too controversial to pass on their own.

Rider's Choice: Belief that the decision to wear a motorcycle helmet while riding a motorcycle should be decided by the biker, not the government.

RINO: Republican-In-Name-Only.

Rockefeller Republican: A moderate-liberal block of Republicans who generally favor the policies of fiscal austerity and social liberalism championed by Nelson Rockefeller who served as New York Governor from 1959-1974 and as Vice President of the United States from 1974-1977.

Root-Canal-Economics: The concomitant raising of taxes and cutting government expenditures, usually to balance the budget.

Sedition: Attempts by citizens to topple their government.

Senatorial Courtesy: When the President nominates an individual to the position of Federal District Judge, Federal Marshall, or United States Attorney, it is customary for the President to consult first with the senior U.S. Senator of that state, but only if that senior Senator is a member of the President's political Party.

Separation of Powers: Division of powers among the three branches of government.

Shadow Senator: Voters in the District of Columbia elect two residents to serve in this position. They have no office in the U.S. Senate, and have no Senatorial authority. They do receive an office in the District of Columbia, courtesy of District taxpayers. The job of the Shadow Senator is to lobby members of the U.S. Government to support greater autonomy for the District, with the ultimate goal being outright statehood.

Shadow Representative: Voters in the District of Columbia elect one resident to serve in this position. The person elected to this position has no office or authority in the U.S. House of Representatives. Their job is to lobby members of the U.S. Government for autonomy for the District, with the ultimate goal being statehood for the District.

Social Conservative: One who believes the government should enforce a moral code for its population. Most are opposed to abortion rights, gay marriage, and most support school prayer.

Socialism: A social and economic structure where property and resources are owned by the government rather than by individuals or private companies.

Speaker of the House: Serves as Presiding officer of the U.S. House of Representatives. Under the Presidential Succession Act of 1947, he or she is second in line in presidential succession. Responsibilities include: Calling the House to order, Administering the oath of office to House Members, Presiding over debate, recognizing Members to speak on the floor, and preserving order; or delegating that power to another Member of Congress, setting the legislative agenda, and leading the appointment process for the chairs of the various committees and subcommittees in the House (including conference committees which negotiate final versions of legislation).

Speaker pro tempore: Presides over the U.S. House of Representatives in the absence of the Speaker of the House.

Special Election: An election held to fill a vacancy between elections.

Glossary of Political Terminology

Spending Gap: When all but essential government services are halted because the Federal Government cannot agree on a budget.

Spoils man: A politician who supports the appointment of public officials based on partisan political considerations.

Stalwart: Republicans in the latter half of the nineteenth century who opposed civil service reform. They supported the candidacy of Ulysses S. Grant for the Republican nomination in 1880 when he sought a third term for the presidency.

Standard-bearer: A Representative of a Political party or political movement.

Stare decisis: Latin for: "to stand by things decided." This term refers to the judicial theory that previous court decisions should be precedent and not changed.

State of Nature: The "natural condition of mankind" before governments are instituted. Seventeenth Century French philosopher Thomas Hobbes maintained that all human beings are in a state of war and their lives are: "solitary, poor, nasty, brutish, and short." English philosopher John Locke believed that reason which teaches "no one ought to harm another in his life, health, liberty or possessions" is the governor in this state.

Statute: A law usually written by a legislative branch of a government.

Supply-Side Economics: An economic doctrine popularized by President Ronald Reagan and his Economic Policy Advisor, Arthur Laffer. It asserts that when marginal tax rates are decreased, economic activity increases, resulting in an increase of government revenue.

Supreme Court of the United States: The highest court in the country. Its powers are derived from Article 3 of the *U.S. Constitution*. Members are nominated by the President and confirmed by the U.S. Senate. To receive confirmation they need a majority vote. The Court is composed of eight Associate Justices and one Chief Justice. The Court serves as arbiter of the *U.S. Constitution*.

Tariffs: Taxes on trade.

Third Party: A political party not associated with the two major ones. Examples include the Green Party, the Libertarian Party, and the Prohibition Party.

Ticket Splitting: When a voter chooses candidates of different parties for different offices. For example, the voter may choose a Democrat for President and a Republican for the U.S. Senate.

Timocracy: A system of government where government participation is limited to property owners. It can also refer to a government where rulers receive their position based on the place of honor they hold in a society.

Town Meeting: A form of direct democracy in which all registered voters in a municipality are invited to attend and vote on town laws and budgets.

Transaction Costs: The cost of doing business. An example would be the commission paid to a broker to purchase bonds.

Transfer Payment: Money from a government to an individual without the obligation of the individual to pay it back.

Unfunded Liability: A liability incurred this year that does not have to be paid until sometime in the future.

Unfunded Mandate: Regulations imposed on state and municipal governments without reimbursement from the federal government.

Glossary of Political Terminology

Unicameralism: A legislative branch composed of one chamber. Nebraska is the only state that has this system.

United States Congress: The legislative branch of the United States Government. Its powers are derived from Article 2 of the *U.S. Constitution*. It is composed of the U.S. House of Representatives and the U.S. Senate. House members represent a district of a state, while senators represent the entire state. Each state has two senators and at least one representative. The representatives are apportioned based on population of the state. The smallest state in population is Wyoming, which has only 1 representative. By contrast, California, the largest state, has fifty-three representatives.

Utopia: A perfect society. The term comes from the title of a book written by English Statesman Sir Thomas More.

Veto: This term is Latin for "I forbid." It is used to refer to the rejection of a proposal by the legislative branch by a Chief Executive.

Vice President of the United States: The occupant of this office is the President and presiding officer of the U.S. Senate. Most of the time this power is delegated to the President pro tempore and to other senators from the majority party. In addition, the Vice President has the power to cast the deciding vote should the Senate vote be tied. Finally, the Vice President certifies the official count of the Electoral College during Presidential elections.

***Virginia Declaration of Rights*:** Adopted unanimously by the Virginia Convention of Delegates on June 12, 1776, it was written by Virginia Statesman George Mason. The document affirms the Right to: "life, Liberty, and Property" and delineates restrictions on government power. Its influence is seen in the *Declaration of Independence* and in the *U.S. Constitution*.

War Powers Clause: Article 1, Section 8, Clause 11 of the *U.S. Constitution* grants Congress the power to: "Declare War."

Wedge Issue: An issue which divides supporters of a political cause, candidate, or political party. For example, both labor unions and environmentalists are traditionally part of the Democratic Party's base, yet they disagree over drilling for oil in the Arctic National Wildlife Refuge in Alaska.

Whip: A member of the congressional leadership. Both the majority and the minority party in the U.S. House of Representatives and in the U.S. Senate have one. Their paramount responsibility is to count the votes of members within their own caucus while trying to encourage members to toe the party line.

White Primary: System used in the South in the first half of the twentieth century in which non-white voters were excluded from participating in political primaries. This was ruled unconstitutional by the U.S. Supreme Court in 1944, in the case of *Smith v. Allwright*.

Wilmot Proviso: In 1846, President James K. Polk requested a $2 million appropriation to purchase land from Mexico. U.S. Representative David Wilmot (D-PA) proposed a rider to the legislation to prevent slavery in the new acquisition. It passed the U.S. House of Representatives but was tabled in the U.S. Senate. The rider finally passed in 1862. By that time, Wilmot was no longer in Congress.

Wingnut: Term of Derision for a conservative.

Winner-Take-All: The Candidate who garners the most votes wins the election.

Writ of *Certiorari*: Request of the court to review a case.

Glossary of Political Terminology

Writ of habeas corpus: Latin for "To present the body." This refers to the right of a defendant to appear before a judge and hear the charges against leveled against him/her.

Writ of *Mandamus*: A court order usually requiring a person or corporation to take some specific action.

Unitary State: A system where the Federal Government reigns supreme over the states, and where state power is only what is explicitly granted to them by the Federal Government.

***U.S. Constitution*:** The governing authority of the United States. The document was adopted on September 17, 1787 by the Constitutional Convention and Ratified on June 21, 1788. Thirty-nine Delegates signed it.

Yellow Dog Democrat: A loyal Democrat. Originally referred to an Alabama Democrat in 1928 who voted for the party's Presidential nominee Al Smith, despite their misgivings.

Yellow Journalism: When a news reporter writes his/her opinion and portrays it as a fact, without providing fair coverage of opposing points of view.

Appendix

Appendix

**Instances in U.S. Political History When
the Winner of The National Popular Vote
Lost the Presidential Election**

In four of the fifty-seven Presidential elections since 1789, the Presidential candidate who garnered the most votes lost the election:

1824:   Andrew Jackson defeated John Quincy Adams in the national popular vote 151,271 to 113,122, and also defeated Adams in the Electoral College 99 Electoral votes to 84 Electoral votes. However, because Jackson failed to receive a majority of the Elector votes (due to the fact that there were two other strong candidates running: William H. Crawford and Henry Clay), the election was thrown into the House of Representatives, where supposedly a "deal "was made by the speaker of the House (Henry Clay) who was also one of the Presidential candidates, and his House allies, to get Adams elected President and himself appointed Secretary of State. Thus Andrew Jackson, the winner of the popular vote and the winner of the most electoral votes, lost the 1824 Presidential election.

1876:   Samuel Tilden won the popular over his opponent Rutherford B. Hayes 4,284,020 votes to 4,036,572 votes, but lost in the Electoral College by just 1 vote: 185 to 184. Unfortunately for Samuel Tilden, 20 electoral votes that had been in dispute went over to Hayes in a deal between the Democrats and the Republicans, wherein the Democrats agreed to accept Hayes for President if the Republicans agreed to remove federal troops from the South.

1888:   Grover Cleveland won the popular vote over Benjamin Harrison 5,534,488 votes to 5,443,892 votes, but lost in the Electoral College to Harrison, 233 electoral votes to 168 electoral votes.

2000:   Al Gore won the popular vote over his opponent George W. Bush 50,999,897 votes to 50,456,002 votes, yet lost to Bush in the Electoral College 271 votes to 266 votes.

Appendix

Near Misses

The following Presidential elections represent situations wherein the winner of the Presidency won the popular vote but only narrowly defeated his opponent in the Electoral College. These are called "near misses:"

1880:   James Garfield defeated Democrat Winfield S. Hancock by just 7,368 popular votes (4,446,158 votes to 4,444,260 votes). However, in the Electoral College the margin was much wider, with Garfield garnering 214 votes and Hancock mustering just 155 votes.

1916:   Woodrow Wilson won the popular vote over Charles E. Hughes by almost 600,000 votes (9,126,868 to 8,584,728), but just squeaked by Hughes in the Electoral College (277 votes to 254 votes. If just 12 electoral votes had switched to Hughes, Hughes would have become President.

1961:   John F. Kennedy won the popular vote over Richard M. Nixon by a mere 112,827 votes (34,220,984 votes to 34,108,157 votes), yet defeated Nixon by a very comfortable margin within the Electoral College (303 votes to 219 votes).

1968:   Richard M. Nixon defeated Democrat Hubert H. Humphrey by less than one percentage point in the popular vote (31,783,783 votes to 31,271,839), yet in the Electoral College Nixon won by over 100 electoral votes 301 to 191).

2004:   George W. Bush won nationally over John Kerry by over three million popular votes (62,040,610 votes to 59,028,444 votes), yet if only about 60,000 votes had switched in Ohio, Democrat John Kerry would have assumed the Presidency in the Electoral College.

Appendix

Electoral Vote Results for 2012 Presidential Election
Sorted by Number of Electors in Each State

State	Electoral Votes	Obama Popular Vote	Romney Popular Vote	Obama Electoral Votes	Romney Electoral Votes
Alaska	3	41%	55%		3
Delaware	3	59%	40%	3	
District of Columbia	3	91%	7%	3	
Montana	3	42%	55%		3
North Dakota	3	39%	58%		3
South Dakota	3	40%	58%		3
Vermont	3	67%	31%	3	
Wyoming	3	28%	69%		3
Hawaii	4	71%	28%	4	
Idaho	4	33%	65%		4
Maine	4	56%	41%	4	
New Hampshire	4	52%	46%	4	
Rhode Island	4	63%	35%	4	
Nebraska	5	38%	60%		5
New Mexico	5	53%	43%	5	
West Virginia	5	36%	62%		5
Arkansas	6	37%	61%		6
Iowa	6	52%	46%	6	
Kansas	6	38%	60%		6
Mississippi	6	44%	55%		6
Nevada	6	52%	46%	6	
Utah	6	25%	73%		6
Connecticut	7	58%	41%	7	
Oklahoma	7	33%	67%		7
Oregon	7	54%	42%	7	
Kentucky	8	38%	60%		8
Louisiana	8	41%	58%		8
Alabama	9	38%	61%		9
Colorado	9	51%	46%	9	
South Carolina	9	44%	55%		9
Maryland	10	62%	36%	10	
Minnesota	10	53%	45%	10	
Missouri	10	44%	54%		10
Wisconsi	10	53%	46%	10	
Arizona	11	44%	53%		11
Indiana	11	44%	54%		11
Massachusetts	11	61%	38%	11	
Tennessee	11	39%	59%		11
Washington	12	56%	41%	12	
Virginia	13	51%	47%	13	
New Jersey	14	58%	41%	14	
North Carolina	15	48%	50%		15
Georgia	16	45%	53%		16
Michigan	16	54%	45%	16	
Ohio	18	51%	48%	18	
Illinois	20	58%	41%	20	
Pennsylvania	20	52%	47%	20	
Florida	29	50%	49%	29	
New York	29	62%	36%	29	
Texas	38	41%	57%		38
California	55	60%	37%	55	
U.S. Total	**538**	**51%**	**47%**	**332**	**206**

Index

Index

A

A Youth's History of Kentucky for School and General Reading, 176
Abramski v. United States, 227
Abzug, Bella, 150
Acheson, Dean, 62, 125
ACORN, 267
Adams, John Quincy, 5, 299
Adams, John, 3, 31, 44
Agnew, Spiro, 45, 47, 48
Agribusiness Club of Washington, 159
Air Force One, 20, 71
Al Qaeda, 157
Albright, Madeline, 63
Alexander, Lamar, 123
Alito, Samuel, 227
Allen, Gary, 159
Allison Keith, 263
Ambassador to the Court of St. James (England), 197
American Atheist Magazine, 125
Americans for Tax Reform, 144
Amnesty, Acid, and Abortion, 91
Anderson, John, 123
Angle, Sharron, 216, 218
Aristotle, 34
Armey, Dick, 35, 115, 151, 152, 164
Armstrong, William W., 279
Arthur, Chester A., 9, 18, 22
Artic National Wildlife Refuge, 295
Articles of Confederation and Perpetual Union, 285
Askew, Reubin, 246
Auburn University, 242

B

Bacall, Lauren, 2
Bachmann Michele, 69, 80, 138, 147, 154
Baker, Howard, 37
Baker, James, 279
Ball, George W., 32
Baltimore Orioles, 263
Bankhead, John, 221
Bankhead, Tallulah, 263
Barker Odell, Benjamin Jr., 74
Barkley, Alben, 43, 44, 45, 50, 96, 201, 203, 222
Baruch, Bernard, 39
Baseball, 36, 59, 87
Baucus, Max, 239
Bauer, Gary, 236
Bayh, Evan, 287

Beaumont High School Yearbook, 59
Beck, Glenn, 143
Begin, Menahem, 248
Bellotti, Francis X., 250
Benjamin, Franklin, 272
Bentsen, Lloyd, 74
Berlandi, Angelo, 248
Berra, Yogi, 275
Berry, Marian, (Former Mayor of Washington D.C.), 141, 220, 255, 258
Berry, Marion, (Former U.S. Representative From Arkansas), 141
Bess Truman, 28, 34
Biaggi, Mario, 161
Biden, Joe, 78, 95, 96, 117, 128, 132, 204, 209
Black Hugo, 221, 226
Blackbourn, Lisle, 196
Blagojevich, Rob, 234
Blaine, James G., 19, 22, 79, 124, 158
Blease, Colman Livingston, 237
Bloomberg, Michael, 81
Blumenthal, Susan, 209
Boehner, John, 155, 167
Bono, Sonny, 154
Borah, William, 191
Boston Bruins, 257
Boston Red Sox, 217
Boxer, Barbara, 161, 211
Brady, Mathew, 12, 29, 138, 273
Braun, Carol Mosley, 138
Braun, Cecil Scott, 71
Breux, John, 287
Bricker, Thomas W., 205
Bristow, Joseph, 44
Britney Spears, 266
Brokaw, Tom, 89
Brooks, Jack, 144
Brown v. Board of Education, 228
Brown, David, 263
Brown, Joseph, 32
Brown, Scot,t 210, 211
Brownlow, Walter P., 152
Bruce Babbitt, 72, 97, 242
Bryan, William Jennings, 61, 84, 86, 89, 118, 122, 123, 276
Brynes, Jimmy, 126
Buchanan, Pat, 82, 99, 111, 291
Buchwald, Art, 271
Buck v. Bell, 226
Buck, Ken, 216
Buckley, William F., 275
Budget Reconciliation Act of 1993, 78
Buffalo Bills, 252
Bulloc, Steve, 239

Index

Bumpers, Dale, 184, 239
Bunning Jim, 220
Burchard, Samuel, 79
Burns, Douglas, 121
Bush George H.W., 16, 17, 26, 29, 63, 68, 70, 75, 77, 90, 100, 103, 114, 118, 125, 127, 128, 182, 217, 238
Bush, Barbara Pierce, 83
Bush, Barbara, 29, 83
Bush, Earl, 255
Bush, George W., 9, 17, 21, 23, 27, 29, 30, 34, 40, 63, 71, 73, 84, 85, 87, 91, 98, 108, 113, 119, 125, 132, 137, 153, 185, 187, 189, 246, 263, 274, 299, 300
Bush, Millie, 29
Butz, Earl, 56
Byrd, Robert C., 201, 212
Byrne, Jane, 162

C

Calhoun, John C., 101
Califano, Joseph, 57, 123
Calloway, Howard Hollis "Bo," 247
Camp David, 37, 71, 248
Cannon, Joeseph, 131, 169, 171, 172
Cape Wind Project, 193
Caraway, Hattie, 214
Cardoso, Fernando Henrique 40
Carney David, 84
Carol, Charles, 56
Carrow, , Edith, 33
Carson, Ashley, B., 273
Carswell, Harold, 194
Carter, Amy, 122
Carter, Billy, 36, 280
Carter, Jimmy, 16, 18, 36, 57, 60, 67, 69, 71, 79, 86, 89, 90, 92, 95, 121, 122, 127, 133, 134, 147, 148, 190, 248, 280, 286
Carter, Lillian, 67
Carter, Rosalynn, 134
Cartwright, Peter, 176
Carville, James, 279
Castle, Mike, 217
CBS News, 35, 192
Cedar Island Lodge, 6
Cermak, Anton, 257
Chaffee, Lincoln 251
Chamberlain, Neville, 168
Cheney, Dick, 27, 46, 67, 85, 87, 115, 120, 149
Chestnut, Tim, 213
Chisholm, Shirley, 149
Chlamydia, 146
chlorofluoro-carbon abatement, 126

Christ, Jesus, 12, 39, 142
Christie, Chris, 110, 237
Christopher, Ruddy, S., 15
Church, Frank, 191
Ciardi, John, 276
Civil Rights Act of 1957, 288
Claflin, William, 33
Clampett, Jed, 265
Clarke, Champ, 167
Clay, Henry, 59, 86, 138, 189, 299
Clay, Lucretia, 59
Clements, Bill, 240
Cleveland, Francis Folsome, 14
Cleveland, Grover, 14, 16, 28, 36, 79, 111, 124, 191, 299
Clinton , Hillary, 58, 59, 132, 136, 218
Clinton v. City of New York, 290
Clinton, Bill, 7, 8, 11, 15, 19, 23, 26, 33, 35, 48, 51, 71, 78, 87, 90, 99, 107, 112, 127, 129, 134, 146, 148, 150, 152, 154, 164, 184, 185, 190, 198, 210, 238, 241, 252, 264, 271, 272, 285, 287, 291
Clymer, Adam, 85
CNN, 235, 266, 286
Coakley, Martha, 211, 217
Coca-Cola, 237
Cochran, Thad, 130, 217, 222
Code of Federal Regulations, 51
Coffman, Mike, 157
Cohen, Steve, 280
Cold War, 291
Collector of Customs, 19, 22
Collins, John, 255
Colman, Debbie, 246
Common Sense, 31
Congress of the Confederation, 287
Congressional Quarterly, 157
Conkling, Roscoe, 19, 22, 76
Conlan, John Bertrand, 219
Constitution Hall, 37
Constitutional Convention, 296
Continental Congress, 285
Cook, Fred, 275
Coolidge, Calvin, 1, 4, 6, 10, 13, 17, 20, 22, 23, 31, 38, 40, 43, 45, 51, 76
Cornell University, 57
Cornyn, John, 221
Council of Economic Advisors, 19
Cousins, Norman, 37
Cox, Channing, 10
Crawford, William H., 299
Crist, Charlie, 252
Crocket, Davy, 175
Crockett, David "Davy" 8, 162

Index

Cronin Edward J., 275
Cruz, Ted, 185
Cummings, Edward Estlin, 4
Curley, James M., 256
Curley, James Michael, 177
Curtis, Charles, 181

D

D'Amato, Alfonse, 190
D'Amore, Tom, 79
Dada, Victoria, 77
Dahmer, Jeffrey, 161
Daley, Richard J., 75, 105, 255, 256
Dallas Cowboys, 258
Darwin, Charles, 176
Davis, Grey, 246
Davis, Joeff, 222
Dawes, Charles G. 45, 51
de Gaulle, Charles, 2, 61
Declaration of Independence, 15, 287, 295
Del Sol High School, 187
Delay, Tom, 119
DeMint, Jim, 218
Democratic National Convention, 71, 94, 105
Dempsey, Jack, 27
Denver Broncos, 77
Detroit Lions, 2
Deukmejian, George, 231
Dever, William Emmett, 257
Dewey, George, 5, 88
Dewey, Thomas E., 73, 89, 94, 103, 123, 129,
    132, 135
Diamond Museum, 19
DiFava, John, 234
Diggs, Charles, 146
Dime Magazine, 259
Dirksen, Everett, 188, 191
Dixon, Allan J., 274
Dole, Bob, 19, 80, 82, 85, 89, 90, 98, 113, 116,
    117, 121, 128, 169, 190, 192, 193
Dolph Briscoe Center for American History, 47,
    170
Dornan, Robert K., 146
Downtown Phoenix Kiwanis Club, 232
Dukakis, Michael, 70, 72, 114, 118, 128, 241,
    246, 248, 249, 279
Duke, David, 99
Dulles, Allan, 279
Dulles, John Foster, 58, 63, 129

E

Eagleton, Thomas, 91

Early, Joseph, 153
Eastland, James, 88, 199
Eastwood, Clint, 35
Ebsen, Buddy, 265
Edwards, Chet, 132, 160
Edwards, John, 120
Edwin Edwards, 240, 245
Ehrhard, Ludgwig, 12
Eisenhower, Dwight D., 10, 21, 37, 38, 39, 69,
    85, 127, 136, 205
Eisenhower, Dwight David II, 37
Electoral College, 295
Emanuel, Rahm, 177
Engler, John, 100
Enzi, Mike, 185
Ernst, Joni, 216
Executive Mansion, 21

F

Faircloth, Lauch, 220
Fala, 109
Fall, Albert, 3
Falwell Jerry, 194
Farley, James, 82
Fattman, Ryan, 277
Federalist Society, 225
Feeney, Tom, 160
Ferguson, James, 252
Ferraro, Geraldine, 78, 83
Fillmore, Millard, 13
Fingerhut, Eric,164
Finklestien, Mark, 77
Fleming, John, 164
Folsom, Frances, 16
Folsom, Oscar, 16
Ford, Betty, 133
Ford, Gerald R., 2, 11, 19, 25, 30, 36, 48, 69, 79,
    80, 83, 90, 95, 102, 109, 121, 133, 147, 150,
    190
Fordice, Kirk, 240
Foster, Vincent, 15
FOX Business Network, 49
Fox News, 138, 148, 175
Fox, Virginia 149
Frank, Barney, 34, 152, 156, 241, 272
Frankel, Max, 95
Franklin Butler, Benjamin, 240
Franklin D. Roosevelt Memorial, 109
Friedman, Kinky, 250
Frost, David, 9, 20

Index

G

Galvin, William, 271
Garagiola, Joe, 275
Gardner John W., 57
Garfield, James, 19, 22, 28, 300
Garner, John Nance, 47, 49, 68, 170
Gary, Hart, 122
Gephardt, Richard, 93, 122, 145, 155
Gerald "Pat" Brown Sr., Edmund, 247
Geren, Peter, 285
Gerry, Elbridge, 46, 288
Gifford, Frank, 39
Gillett, Frederick 171
Gingrich, Newt, 84, 91, 114, 168, 169
Ginsberg, Ruth Bader, 228
Girls Gone Wild Magazine, 267
Giuliani, Rudy, 108
Glenn, John, 76
God, 4, 24, 74, 105, 107, 125, 151, 161, 162,
    176, 211, 212, 222, 225, 228, 233, 239, 240,
    272, 280, 281, 290
Gohmert, Louis, 143
Goldberg, Irving Loeb, 278
Goldwater Barry, 49, 68, 72, 96, 103, 104, 109,
    131, 189, 194
Gonzalez, Alberto, 63
Good Luck Margarine, 273
Goodman, Oscar, 259
Gore, Albert, Sr., 209
Gore, Al, 35, 45, 46, 48, 50, 51, 87, 90, 93, 115,
    121, 126, 182, 291, 299
Gore, Thomas, 200
Gowdy, Trey, 149, 160
Graham, Lindsey, 111
Gramm, Phil, 110, 182, 290
Grand Canyon, 182
Grant, Ulysses S., 10, 13, 19, 22, 32, 33, 43, 134,
    294
Gravel, Mike, 68
Grayson, Allan, 143
Green Bay Packers, 2, 196
Gridiron Dinner, 58
Griffin, Jean, 234
Grimm, Michael, 155
Gutenberg Bible, 40

H

H. Elliot, Thomas, 177
Hagel, Chuck, 191
Haig, Al, 93
Haig, Alexander, 63
Haldeman, H.R., 60

Hale, Edward Everett, 189
Hall, Ralph, 175, 177
Halliburton, 46, 87
Halpin, Maria Crofts, 111
Hamilton, Alexander, 288
Handloff, Norma B., 257
Hanis & Andy, 59
Hannigan, Robert, 126
Hannity, Sean, 249
Harding, Warren G., 2, 4, 14, 17, 31, 55, 101,
    136, 291
Harke, Van, 233
Harkin, Tom 103, 128, 181
Harper's Weekly, 274
Harriman, Averill, 133
Harris, Fred, 73, 94, 186
Harrison, Benjamin, 7, 21, 104, 113, 299
Harrison, William Henry, 32, 101
Harvard University, 5, 27, 196, 226, 275
Hastert, Dennis, 172
Hatch, Orrin, 187
Hathaway, Jane, 265
Hayakawa, Samuel Ichlye, 212
Hayes, Rutherford B., 6, 76, 299
Hayes, Wayne, 156
Healey, Kerry, 249
Helms, Jesse, 184
Helsinki Accords, 95
Henderson, David B., 170
Henry Fairfield Osborn Sr., 276
Herman Miller Corporation, 127
Hickel, Walter, 237, 238
Hightower, Jim, 240
Hitler, Adolf, 156, 168
Hobbes, Thomas, 294
Hoke, Martin R. 164
Holder, Eric, 157
Hollings, Ernest "Fritz," 71, 76, 185, 188, 198,
    209
Holmes, Oliver Wendell, 226
Hoover J. Edgar, 5
Hoover, Herbert, 4, 12, 23, 31, 34, 38, 39, 80, 86,
    88, 128, 275
Hoover, Lou, 34
Houston, David Franklin, 61
Houston, Sam, 276
Huckabee, Mike, 75, 81, 87, 97, 106, 109, 236
Huey, Dewey, and Louie, 146
Hughes, Charles Evans, 225
Hughes, Harry, 248
Hughes, Rupert, 38
Humphrey, Hubert "Skip" III, 50
Humphrey, Hubert, 8, 47, 49, 50, 70, 71, 75, 96,
    103, 112, 133, 190

Index

Hurd, Peter, 19
Hussein, Saddam, 187, 220
Hutchinson, Asa, 252
Hutchinson, Tim, 252

I

Ickies, Harold, 62, 89, 137
Ida McKinley, 122
Ifell, Gwenn, 189
Ingles, Bob, I, 147
Introduction to the Rockefeller Files, 159
Ivins, Molly, 281

J

Jackson, Curtis, a.k.a. "50 Cent," 263
Jackson ,Henry "Scoop", 291
Jackson Lee, Shelia, 163
Jackson, Andrew 1, 5, 26, 32, 50, 197, 299
Jackson, Jesse, 84, 99
Jackson, Michael, 45
Jackson, Robert, 225
Jackzo, Gregory B., 160
Jacobellis v. Ohio, 225
Jamaican Bobsled Team, 93
James, Donavan, 57
Jameson, Jenna, 265
Jaworski, Leon, 127
Jay, John, 228, 288
Jefferson, Thomas, 3, 7, 15, 25, 46, 48, 56, 84,
    276, 287, 291
Jeremy, Ron, 264
Jerry Brown, 235, 238
Jerry Jones, 264
Jersey Shore, 264, 266
Jesse Ventura, 236
Jindal, Bobby, 231
Johnson, Andrew, 11, 44
Johnson, Constance, 281
Johnson, Gary, 124
Johnson, Hank, 158
Johnson, Hiram, 76
Johnson, J. Neely, 237
Johnson, Lyndon B., 3, 5, 11, 12, 15, 18, 19, 20,
    21, 24, 30, 34, 40, 47, 57, 61, 70, 96, 99, 103,
    134, 150, 170, 171, 191, 195, 196, 199, 226,
    288, 290
Jones, Lord Anthony-Armstrong, 40
Jordan, Michael, 45
Judicial Review, 289

K

Kagan, Elena, 227
Kanjorski, Paul, 143
Kardashian, Kim, 267
Kariotis, George, 249
Keel, Pauline, 77
Keeping Up with the Kardashians, 267
Kefauver, Estes, 127
Kemp, Jack, 90, 126
Kennedy Robert F., 58, 73, 209, 215
Kennedy Sr., Joseph, 27
Kennedy, John F., 7, 8, 25, 27, 31, 32, 58, 68, 70,
    73, 74, 80, 94, 98, 99, 102, 130, 131, 171,
    175, 196, 210, 215, 216, 221, 282, 300
Kennedy, Joseph P. Sr., 70
Kennedy, Ted, 7, 58, 86, 193, 196, 216, 221,
    222, 231
Kenneth Keating, 214
Kerry, Bob, 93, 102
Kerry, John, 58, 67, 71, 73, 106, 108, 113, 119,
    120, 125, 128, 137, 220, 232, 300
Kevin White, 255
Keyes, Allan, 213
Kilby, Thomas E., 221
King, Ed, 240, 246
King, Steve, 161
Kirk, Claude Jr., 246
Kissinger, Henry, 56
Koch, Ed, 250, 258
Kristol, Irving, 291
Ku Klux Klan, 92, 181, 245
Kucinich, Dennis, 82, 117, 148
Kulp, Nancy, 265

L

La Guardia, Fiorello, 136
Laffer, Arthur, 294
Landon Alfred, 82, 116, 135
Laughlin, Tom, 128
Lawless, Joe, 234
Lawrence, Eric, 170
Lazio, Rick, 218
Leahy, Patrick, 46, 183
Lebanese-Mack, Jim, 176
Lee, Mike, 192
Lemay, Curtis, 81, 88
Lew, Jack, 60
Lewis, Gib, 274
Lewis, John F., 49
Licht, Frank, 70
Lieberman, Joe 87, 91, 120, 196, 203
Limbaugh, Rush, 149, 271

Index

Lincoln, Abraham, 10, 16, 23, 24, 27, 30, 44, 62, 176, 212, 213, 220
Lincoln, Mary Todd, 24
Lindsey, John, 281
Lion, Snoop, 267
Lippman, Walter, 191
Little, Edward J., 161
Locke, John, 294
Lockhart, Joe, 7
Lodge Jr., Henry Cabot, 210, 215
Lodge, Sr., Henry Cabot, 196
Lohan, Lindsay, 266
Long, Huey, 62, 181, 201, 202, 214, 235
Lord Armstrong Jones of Snowden, 40

M

MacLaine, Shirley, 97
Macmillan, Harold, 31
Maddox, Lester, 232
Madison, James, 25, 288
Madonna, 81
Magnuson, Warren G., 186
Malone, Joe, 271
Maltzman, Forest 170
Manning, Peyton, 77
Marcy, William, 197
Marshall, George, 58, 198
Marshall, Thomas Riley, 43, 44, 51
Marshall, Thurgood, 226
Martin, Joe, 168, 169
Marx, Groucho, 22, 130
Marx, Karl, 130
Mason, George, 295
Massa, Eric, 143
Massachusetts Transit Authority, 275
Massachusetts, 10, 22, 105, 168, 288
Mathew Stanley Quay, 104
Mathews, Chris, 126
Maverick, Maury, 145
Maxwell House Coffee, 26
Mayflower Hotel, 263
Mayflower, 257
McAdoo, William Gibbs, 55
McCabe, James H., 279
McCain, John, 72, 81, 95, 96, 98, 106, 110, 130, 137, 177, 198, 211
McCarthy Eugene, 119, 192, 197
McCarthy, Joseph, 210
McCaskill, Claire, 210
McConnell, Mitch, 186, 221
McCormick, John, 216
McDaniel Chris, 217
McDonald, Larry, 159

McDougal, James, 241
McGovern, George, 23, 70, 88, 91, 97, 100, 105, 120, 134, 135
McGroarty Steven, 164
McHenry, Patrick, 151
McKellar, Kenneth, 194, 209
Mckelvey, Tara, 75
McKenzie, Richard D., 62
McKinley, William, 5, 6, 74, 89, 117, 122
McNary, Charles L., 104
McNutt, Paul V., 104
Mecham, Evan, 242
Meet the Press, 210, 275
Melih Esenbel, 56
Mencken, H.L., 24, 184
Menino, Tom, 257
Metropolitan Opera, 28
Miami Dolphins, 77
Michaud, Greg, 97, 126
Mihos, Chrity, 249
Miller, Thomas V., 278
Miller, William E., 96
Miller, Zell, 125
Mills, Wilber, 49
Mineta, Norman, 155
Mississippi Society of Washington D.C., 192
Mitchell, George, 183
Model Cities Program, 30
Modern Language Association, 77
Moe, Roger, 50
Mondale, Walter, 80, 92, 100, 118, 122
Montoya, Joseph, 184
Moore, Diane "Rasheeda", 255
Moore, Larry D., 250
Moran Jim, 141
Morgenthau Henry Jr., 33
Morning Joe, 97, 233
Morse, Wayne, 184
Mr. Ed, 97
MSNBC, 126, 164
Mulvey, Martha, 277
Murkowski, Frank, 193, 217
Murkowski, Lisa, 193
Murphy, Tom, 281
Murtha, John, 128
Muskie, Edmund, 107

N

Nader, Ralph, 127
NASA, 37, 45
Nash Thomas, V., 126
Nast, Thomas, 274
National Automobile Dealers Association, 26

Index

National Debt, 290
National Inflation Center, 266
National Meat Association v. Harris, 227
National Restaurant Association, 79
National Review, 28, 275
National Rifle Association, 108, 182
NATO, 61
Nelson, Jack, 81
New England Patriots, 252
New York Jets, 77
New York Times Co. v. Sullivan, 285
Newmax Media, 15
Newsbusters.org, 77
Newsweek, 280
Nixon, Richard M., 2, 9, 20, 22, 23, 35, 37, 39, 60,
 69, 80, 91, 98, 100, 103, 105, 109, 112, 115,
 125, 130, 134, 190, 194, 247, 263, 300
North, Oliver, 215
Norvell, John, 3
Novak, Robert, 91
Nunes, Devin 162
Nunn, Sam, 287
Nussle, Jim, 159
NY1, 149

O

O. Douglas, William, 63
O'Connor, Sandra Day, 194
O'Brien, Conan, 106
O'Brien, William, 278
O'Connell, William, 131
O'Donnell, Christine, 215
O'Neill, Tip, 48, 167, 168, 169, 171
Obama, Barack, 49, 60, 82, 84, 95, 102, 106,
 107, 110, 120, 128, 129, 132, 136, 155, 156,
 157, 164, 185, 186, 213, 216, 219, 234, 251,
 263, 264, 266, 267
Office of Treasurer and Receiver General of the
 Commonwealth of Massachusetts, 271
Old State House Museum, 238
On the Record, 60
Original Jurisdiction, 291

P

Pacifica Radio, 238
Pageant of Peace Ceremony, 8
Paine, Thomas, 31
Palin, Sarah, 124
Parade Magazine, 78
Parker, Dorothy, 4
Pastore, John O., 241
Paterson, David, 231

Patient Protection and Affordability Act, 266
Patrick, Deval, 234
Paul, Rand, 185
Paul, Ron, 93, 290
PBS, 242
Peabody, Endicott "Chub," 250
Peanut One, 69
Pell, Claiborne, 195
Pelosi, Nancy, 159, 172
Penrose, Boise 101
Pepper, Claude, 159, 212
Pepsi-Cola, 237
Perot, H. Ross 74, 126
Perry, Rick, 71, 78, 92, 107, 114, 250
Phillips Exeter Academy, 68
Philpot, Larry, 267
Pierce, Franklin, 14, 67
Pierce, Samuel, 55
Pitman, Benjamin, 22
Platt, Thomas, 21
Playboy Magazine, 49, 96, 235, 236, 250, 266
Plunkitt, George Washington, 276
Politico, 81
Polizzi, Nicole, a.k.a., Snooki, 264, 266
Polk, James K., 29, 138, 295
Pope Paul VI, 56
Post, Robert, 131
Potomac River, 3, 111
POTUS, 292
Presentment Clause of the U.S. Constitution,
 290
Princess Margaret Rose of Great Britain, 40
Princeton University Tigers, 61
Professional Golf Association (PGA), 186
Public Enemy, 141
Putin, Vladimir, 29
Putnam, Adam, 141

Q

Quayle, Dan, 51, 119, 145

R

Rabaut, Louis, C., 151
Rae, Dan, 217
Raese, Paul, 221
Rage Against the Machine, 265
Rainbow PUSH Coalition, 99
Ralph Yarborough, 213
Ramirez, Manny, 21
Randy "Duke" Cunningham, 91, 150, 151, 152,
 163

Index

Rangel, Charles, 149, 163, 252
Rarick, John, 146
Ratcliffe, John, 177
Rather, Dan, 35
Rayburn, Sam, 168, 170, 172
Reagan, Nancy, 27
Reagan, Ronald, 15, 16, 23, 24, 25, 27, 28, 29, 35, 36, 55, 63, 69, 72, 89, 98, 102, 109, 118, 162, 168, 171, 192, 194, 215, 238, 239, 250, 251, 279, 291, 294
Rebekah Baines Johnson, 20
Reciprocity Club, 14
Reed, Thomas Bracket, 167
Reid, Harry, 187, 219, 239
Reilly, John, 143
Resident Commissioner of Puerto Rico, 292
Richards Ann, 68, 116, 246
Richards, Keith, 236
Richardson, Bill, 136
Rizzo, Frank, 259
Robb, Chuck, 215
Roberts, John, 227
Roberts, Julia, 267
Roberts, Pat, 182
Robertson, Pat, 278
Robertson, William H., 19, 22
Robinson, Tommy, 245
Rochon, Michelle, 282
Rockefeller, Nelson, 38, 43, 293
Rogers, Will, 76, 92, 217
Rogovin, Mitchell, 123
Roman Hruska, 194
Romney, Mitt, 72, 77, 81, 97, 106, 108, 111, 222, 231, 232, 249, 252, 264, 265
Roosevelt Jr., Theodore, 40
Roosevelt, Eleanor, 1, 273
Roosevelt, Franklin D., 1, 8, 11, 24, 25, 28, 33, 39, 47, 49, 62, 75, 82, 86, 88, 90, 104, 108, 109, 126, 128, 130, 131, 135, 136, 273
Roosevelt, James I, 28
Roosevelt, Mark, 245, 247
Roosevelt, Theodore, 6, 7, 9, 10, 16, 26, 32, 33, 38, 40, 74, 123, 129, 131, 137, 169, 205, 227, 247
Root, Elihu, 55
Ross Jim Buck, 78
Ross, Grace, 249
Ross, Mike, 252
Rostenkowski, Dan, 162
Rove, Karl, 187
Rowan and Martin Laugh Inn, 103
Rubio, Marco, 187
Rudolph, Louis, 24
Rum, Romanticism, and Rebellion, 79

Rumsfeld ,Donald, 56, 60
Rusk, Dean, 61
Russert, Tim, 252
Ryan, Paul. 265

S

Sadat, Anwar, 248
Saint Anslem College, 78
San Francisco 49ers, 258
Sanders, Bernie, 163
Santa Claus, 282
Sargent, Claire, 214
Scalia, Antonin, 225, 226, 227
Schaefer, William Donald, 239
Schenk v. Commissioner of Internal Revenue, 278
Schilling, Curt, 217
Schiro, Victor, 256
Schlesinger, James, 60
Schrank, John, 129
Schroeder, Patricia, 36, 163
Schumer, Charles, 193
Schweitzer, Brian, 233, 235
Scott, Luke, 263
Sea Wolf Nuclear Submarine Program, 112
Sears Roebuck, 250
Senate Bill No. 93, 241
Sesno, Frank, 235
Shankbone, David, 231, 267
Sharpton, Al, 99
Shays, Christopher, 177
Sheppard, Morris, 190
Sherman, Brad, 153
Sherman, John, 12, 55
Sherman, Rob, 125
Short, Dewey, 144
Shultz, George P., 61
Shultz, Helena, 61
Shuster, Bud, 265
Silber, John 245, 251
Simon Cameron, 62
Simon, Paul ,105
Simpson-Bowles Commission, 273
Simpson, Allan, 273
Sir Cecil Spring-Rice, 33
Smathers, George, 212
Smith, Adam, 289
Smith, Al, 75, 90, 107, 296
Smith, Henry H., 170
Smith, Margaret Chase, 182
Smith, Will, 264
Snowden, Edward, 161
Sock it to Me, 103
Sparkman, John, 127

Index

Specter, Arlen, 189
Spiller, Clifford, 26
Spitzer, Elliot, 231
Spoils System, 197
Sprewell, Letrell, 259
Stalwart, 294
Stark, Peter, 144
Starr, Kenneth, 272
Statute of Virginia for Religious Freedom, 15
Steel, Michael, 280
Steiger Steve, 160
Steiger, Sam, 154
Stein, Herbert, 19
Stein, Jeff, 157
Stephen Douglas, 212, 213, 220
Stevens, Ted, 190
Stevens, Thaddeus, 62
Stevenson, Adlai, 83, 85, 105, 114, 115, 127, 241
Stewart, Potter, 225
Stimson, Henry, 57
Stockdale, James, 100
Stockman, Steve, 146, 175
Stovall, Dwayne, 221
Strauss, Bob 16
Strauss, Lewis, 186
Stump, Bob, 164
Sununu, John H., 77
Swift, Jane, 234
Symington, Stuart, 94

T

Taft, Robert A., 103, 291
Taft, William Howard, 12, 32, 38, 55, 110, 118, 171
Taliban, 141
Talk Back Live, 146
Tammany Hall, 259
Taney, Roger, 288
Taylor, Gene, 144
Ted Strickland, 106
Texas Monthly, 249
Thayer John T., 147
the Affordable Care Act, 162
The Alfred Whital Stern Collection of Lincolnian, 10
The Associated Pres, 252
The Associated Press, 160, 252
The Beverly Hillbillies, 265
The Blade-Citizen, 150
The Boston Globe, 130, 222
The Boston Globe, 240
The Carroll Daily Times Herald, 121

The Charlie Rose Show, 242
The Chicago Tribune, 132
The College of the Holy Cross, 225
The Columbia Free Times, 218
The Communist Manifesto, 130
The Daily Telegraph, 37
The Evening Independent, 277
The Five O' Clock Club, 161
The Jay Treaty, 228
The *Loan Ranger*, 70
The Los Angeles Times, 81, 148
The Midland Reporter Telegram, 17
The National Association of Counties, 172
The National Energy Act, 60
The New York Herald Tribune, 11
The New York Times, 59, 83, 85, 95, 124, 131, 144, 196, 203, 232, 233
The New Yorker Magazine, 77
The NewsHour, 189
The Older Women's League (OWL, 273
The Peoples Park, 239
The Pittsburg Post-Gazette, 128
The Rolling Stones, 236
The San Francisco Examiner, 259
The Saturday Evening Post, 167
The Sopranos, 71
The Three Stooges, 168
The Today Show, 29, 116
The Washington Post, 37, 119
The Washington Times, 46, 280
This Week, 81
Thomas, Bill, 156
Thomas, Clarence, 225
Thompson William "Big Bill", 257
Thompson, Fred, 181
Thompson, Ed Porter, 176
Thurmond, Strom, 204, 219, 234, 288
Time Magazine, 50, 60, 61, 68, 82, 103, 112, 128, 195, 212, 249, 255, 278
Tinkham, George, 163
Tonto, 70
Tower, John, 59
Traficant, James, 152, 155
Treen, David, 247
Truman, Harry S., 2, 10, 14, 21, 25, 28, 34, 37, 39, 43, 49, 58, 62, 67, 73, 94, 96, 98, 100, 102, 114, 123, 125, 126, 127, 129, 132, 134, 135, 169, 198, 202, 205, 211, 222
Truman, Margaret, 28, 37
Trump, Donald, 124
Tsongas, Paul, 92, 112, 183, 271
Tuck, Dick, 271
Tucker, Jim Guy, 241

Index

TV Guide, 20
Twain, Mark, 273
Twitter, 92

U

U.S. Chamber of Commerce, 59, 156
U.S. Conference of Mayors, 55
U.S. Constitution, 146, 285, 286, 288, 289, 290, 292, 294, 295, 296
U.S. Court of Appeals for the 7th Circuit, 225
U.S. House of Representatives, 168, 286, 287, 289, 290, 293, 295
U.S. Navy, 6, 23, 69, 88, 100, 222, 266
U.S. Postal Service, 213
Udall, Morris, 72, 83, 130, 141, 145
Udall, Tom, 183
UNICEF, 273
United Nations, 24, 121
United Negro College Fund (UNCF), 51
United States Smaller War Plants Corporation, 145
United, v, Federal Elections Commission, 218
University of California at Berkeley, 239
University of California at Davis, 72
University of Illinois, 138
University of Miami's Faculty Club, 127
University of Michigan, 2, 11
University of Virginia Law School, 221
University of Virginia, 15
Urban Development Action Grant, 162
USA Today, 36

V

Vagina Monologues, 256
Van Buren, Martin, 1, 8, 197
Van Susteran, Greta, 60
Vandiver, William Duncan, 161
Vanik, Charles, 154
Vardaman, James K., 214
Vaughan, William E., 280
Vidal, Gore, 277
Vietnam War, 57, 72, 111, 119, 151, 167, 191
Vinson, Fred M., 228
Volpe, Frank, 250

W

Walberg, Tim, 145
Walker, Robert, 168
Wallace, George, 72, 81, 88, 93, 111, 242
Walmart, 175
Walsh, John, 239

Warner Brothers, 69
Warner, John, 210, 219
Warner, Mark, 219
Warren , Earl, 228
Warren, Elizabeth, 211
Washington Hilton Hotel, 27
Washington Monument, 38, 190
Washington National Geographic Society, 19
Watergate, 9, 22, 35, 37, 105, 127, 201
Watson, James E., 101
Watts, James, 59
WBZ-Radio, 217
Weld, Bill, 220, 232, 245, 247
Welliver, Judson, 2
Wheeler, William, 76
Whitman, Ann, 38
Wieker, Lowell, 79
Willard, Robert F., 158
Williams, Clayton, 249
Williams, John, 192
Williams, Talcott, 101
Willie Brown, 258
Willkie, Wendell, 89, 101, 104, 108, 109, 131, 135, 136, 137, 144
Wilmot, David, 295
Wilson Rick, 252
Wilson Woodrow, 3, 6, 10, 18, 30, 31, 55, 61, 137, 196, 214, 300
Wilson, Henry, 43
Wilson, Joe, 157
Wilson, Theodore A., 62
Winfield S. Hancock, 300
Winston Churchill, 58
World Food Conference, 56
WPR-Radio, 251
WXXV-TV, 217
WZLX-Radio, 211

X

Xena, the Warrior Princess, 63

Y

Yahoo Sports, 263
Yale Law School, 2
Yale University, 13
Yankee Doodle, 13
Young, Don, 153
Young, Stephen M., 186

Z

Zirkel, Kenneth C., 246

16091857R00184

Made in the USA
Middletown, DE
04 December 2014